PETER WRIGHT walked the Watershed 64 days to cover the whole 1,200km, how much of the route went through wild land. He started to write this book as a journal of his journey, but soon began to research and find wider evidence for his observations of the wildness. He has long been interested in Scotland's natural environment and history, having volunteered with both the John Muir Trust, and the National Trust for Scotland. He has worked for some 20 years developing the Duke of Edinburgh Award in the Edinburgh area, for which he received the MBE. The National Trust for Scotland presented him with the George Waterston Memorial Award for outstanding voluntary commitment. Peter was instrumental in establishing The Green Team, and is now its honorary Patron.

Ribbon of Wildness

Discovering the Watershed of Scotland

PETER WRIGHT

Luath Press Limited
EDINBURGH
www.luath.co.uk

First published 2010

ISBN: 978-1-906817-45-9

The paper used in this book is recyclable. It is elemental chlorine free (ECF) and manufactured from sustainable wood pulp forests. This paper and its manufacture are approved by the National Association of Paper Merchants (NAPM), working towards a more sustainable future.

Printed and bound by
Thomson Litho, East Kilbride

Maps by Jim Lewis

Typeset in 10.5 point Sabon by
3btype.com

The author's right to be identified as author of this book under the Copyright, Designs and Patents Act 1988 has been asserted.

© Peter Wright 2010

As we approach 2014, the centenary of the death of John Muir, this book is dedicated to his memory and the inspirational legacy he has left for us to enjoy.

Contents

Map		8
Foreword	Robin Harper MSP	9
Acknowledgements		11
CHAPTER ONE	Introduction	13
CHAPTER TWO	The Reiver March	47
CHAPTER THREE	The Laich March	84
CHAPTER FOUR	The Heartland March	125
CHAPTER FIVE	The Moine March	160
CHAPTER SIX	The Northland March	208
CHAPTER SEVEN	Conclusion	238

APPENDICES

ONE	Munros and Corbetts on the Watershed	251
TWO	Key Areas with Conservation and Biodiversity Objectives	255
THREE	Agencies and Organisations with an Active Conservation or Biodiversity Role	259
FOUR	Land Classification and Capability for Agriculture on the Watershed	264
Bibliography		265
Index		267

Map of Scotland showing the Watershed, North Sea and Atlantic Ocean

Foreword

IT IS WITH THE GREATEST of pleasure that I sat down to write a few words by way of introduction to this highly original work. Peter has dedicated most of his working life to encouraging young people to get into the outdoors, not least through his huge contribution to the development of the Duke of Edinburgh's Award in Scotland, his creation of The Green Team, and his part in the development of the John Muir Award. Ever since Rev A.E. Robertson climbed all of the 238 then known mountains in Scotland over 3,000 feet, we have been more than mildly obsessed with seeing the hills as simply a challenge in themselves – an environment to be conquered.

Peter's approach is more leisurely and thoughtful, and provides a very distinctive view of a Scotland whose history, politics, geography and landscapes have been subtly shaped on either side of the windy ridges which sweep northwards all the way from the Lowlands to Caithness.

To the west, the Gaels, Norsemen and the Earls of Orkney, to the east the Picts and the Britons, and to the south the Romans, Angles and Saxons; these ridges kept cultures apart and slowed the rate of assimilation in such a way that the spirit, the cultural song of these diverse interests, survives in so many ways that add to the present richness and value of our heritage.

You can stride with Peter on this journey, on your own ribbon of wildness and appreciate the full richness of the landscapes that fall away on either side of it. You can experience the beauty and the contrasts between the wetter west with its lochs, woods and rocky shorelines, and the softer straths of the east, and reflect on how these landscapes shaped our history, psyche, and our cultures down the centuries. You will be moved; it will undoubtedly raise your spirits.

Thank you Peter for a gentle view, your perception of our landscapes shaped by a journey, a thoughtful stroll rather than just a physical challenge; an engagement with what lies beside and behind us, as well as that which lies ahead, a truly original and three-dimensional view.

Robin Harper MSP, 2010

Acknowledgements

THE GENESIS OF *Ribbon of Wildness* lay in a long and largely solo walk, but many people – both friends and strangers – helped along the way and the whole experience was undoubtedly enriched by their generous interest and support. The process of research for the book was similarly helped in no small measure by advice that was freely given, and the enthusiasm of the many people that I consulted. The list of all those who have helped would be a lengthy one, and might well run the risk of appearing as a litany of names and interests. And there would be the danger of causing offence by inadvertently omitting some who had in good faith been unstinting with their contribution. So the prudent, but no less sincere course, is to record an all-embracing 'thank-you', with my genuine gratitude to each and every one who played a part in shaping what appears here in this book; your help is warmly appreciated.

I make one exception, though. My family has been very understanding, and shown a lot of patience, as I have become somewhat engrossed in this great interest. So I want them to know that their support is not received lightly; I am immensely grateful.

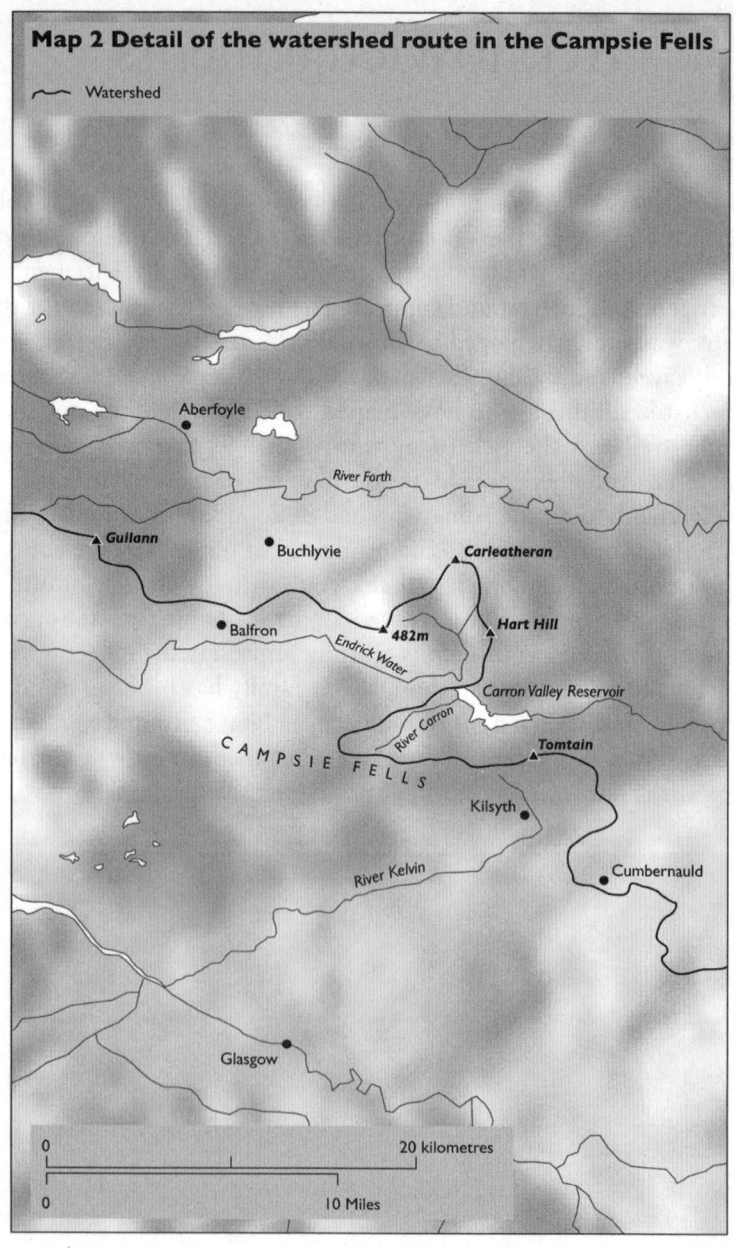

CHAPTER ONE

Introduction

THE GREAT ENVIRONMENTALIST John Muir (1838–1914), in summing up his introduction to nature wrote, 'When I was a boy in Scotland, I was fond of everything that was wild, and all my life I've been growing fonder and fonder of wild places and wild creatures'. This pithy observation will have struck a clear chord with countless people in Scotland and beyond, as it echoes down the years to the present day. For many of us it is the wild places, and their spirit of wildness, which give the defining inspirational experiences; we are at one with the immense quality and diversity of our surrounding landscapes. With Muir, we grow ever fonder of Nature and her wildness.

And there is delight for us in the detail as well as the grandeur – moments of pleasure to be had in coming upon a single wild flower, or the enchanting sound of the skylark on the moor, every bit as much as the bigger landscape and wide mountain vistas. We are in its thrall.

Perhaps it was simply the desire to tackle a really challenging journey that prompted my interest in this venture, for having done a number of coast-to-coasts, and other such walks, I developed an appetite for more. Some of the books about long walks that I had read had prompted me to think of something ambitious of my own, and a wider passion for Scottish landscape, combined to pose a quest for the largely unknown. It was somewhere amongst this jumble of tantalising imaginings, that I conceived that Scotland must have a watershed. One of the few subjects that I had any great interest in at school was geography, and that interest had lingered down the years, so the idea of a watershed (which I will expand on shortly), seemed appealing. Thus, I got the necessary research underway, and started planning for what would be a logistical challenge in itself.

So, what started as a mental exercise, turned into a physical epic, and has become my great passion – for reasons that will most surely become evident. Writing a book about it, or more precisely, about what I discovered over 64 days of walking and my subsequent research, has all taken me down a track that I never envisaged. I had thought that simply walking it would be enough, but something even bigger, every bit as compelling and immensely enriching has grown from my challenge.

It is my great privilege to share some of this experience with those who care to read *Ribbon of Wildness*, and to discover why I have chosen this title. They may well see Scotland, her landscapes, our interaction with them, in an entirely new light. They may just see the possibility of a new challenge, and all the delights that this could bring.

To start with, we must look briefly at some of the forces and timescales that created the Scotland we know and value today. Here we find that this landform evolved like a vast three dimensional jigsaw puzzle, with a number of the pieces coming together having variously drifted half way across the face of the planet. Scotland is the sum of its parts, and took a great many millions of years to develop. The oldest rocks here are amongst some of the most ancient on earth, at over 4,000 million years. They, along with their younger neighbours, were at times submerged under the oceans, or drifted as the sands of the hot deserts, or lay as the floor of vast swamps. They were then either thrust upwards by forces that are almost beyond comprehension, or were subjected to great heat or severe cold. They were compressed by the immense weight of overlying layers of rock, or the ice cap that lay on top, and was a mile or more deep. In places volcanic action further mixed the chronology of the different strata that make up the layers. Younger rock poured out on top of much older, with almost cataclysmic compression. The force of colliding tectonic plates caused further distortion and twisting, and in time great cracks appeared and sliced across the crust. The land on either side of these fault lines experienced further change, with the two sides moving sideways and very slowly in opposite directions. In some locations the immense pressures involved in this distortion of the earth's crust caused one side of the fault to over-ride the other, forcing the lower level down into the earth's mantle, and thus creating a geological conundrum. Fire, water, movement, time, fracture and eruption are just some of the direct causes of what lies beneath, but are fundamental to the landscape of Scotland we see today.

That is not all, for a number of Ice-Ages, the most recent ending only 11,000 years ago, left their mark. Having ground down and removed the surface rocks, they eroded ever deeper into the crust. Thousands of metres of rock were removed in the process and then as the ice finally melted sea levels rose; as with a great sigh of relief parts of the land rose too, when the great weight of the ice, which had borne down upon it, finally disappeared. Two thirds of what became Scotland almost separated from the rest and would have

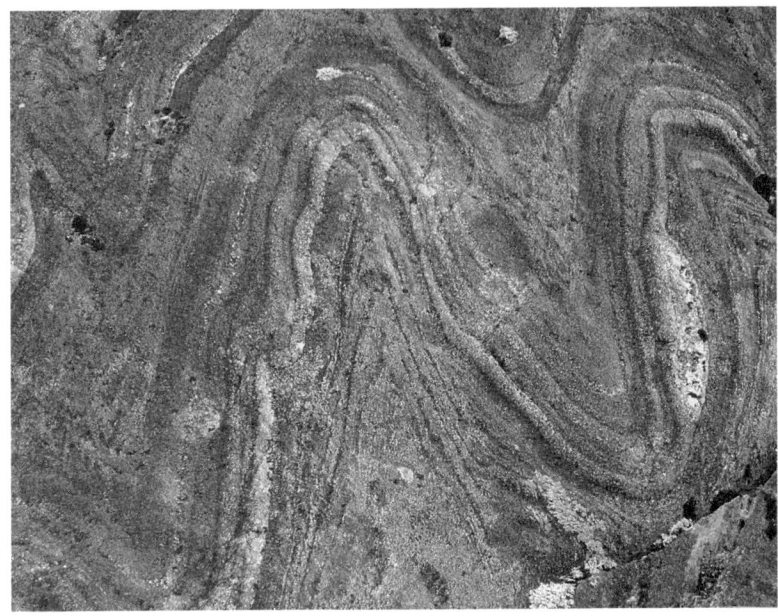

Stone saga

become another island, but the tide turned, and the shape of the land that we know and love was established.

Gradually the land was colonised by plants, birds and animals which migrated northwards across the land bridge that then linked us to mainland Europe. Gradually too our landscape took on a fertile living mantle, and the round of the seasons established a perceptible pattern from year to year. But climate change – yes, there is nothing new about that – heralded colder and wetter conditions, which had a lasting impact. We can still see evidence of this today, in the large areas of peat that started to form during this period. And finally, the actions of man over the last ten or more millennia, have left their mark as we have used and abused the resources of nature at our disposal. So what we have today in our landscapes is the product of a multi-dimensional geological process, with the impact of climate changes and the lasting affects of our own efforts. James Hutton (1726–97), the founding father of much of our geological understanding, in describing geological processes saw '... no sign of a beginning, and no sign of an end.' A contemporary of his wrote '... we grew giddy as we gazed into the abyss of time.' This helps to put our own relative insignificance on the face of the earth into some perspective, but as we shall see our actions have probably had a greater effect than our brief tenure might otherwise justify.

How do we make sense of this rich tapestry – our landscape? Well, the best way to start is simple and practical, with a visit to the higher ground; for it is from some elevated vantage point that the patterns and variety of the countryside becomes clear. From the higher ground we can see the valleys, lochs, hills, moors, fields, distant coast and islands unfold into wide panoramas which expand outwards to the horizon. The Watershed is on the higher ground, it is the continuous spine of Scotland, and it is from this elevation that our great country can be viewed and appreciated, in a novel and immensely revealing way. This book invites you to make a journey of discovery of much that this geographic feature has to offer. It has been obscure until recently, but certainly now merits wider appreciation; it is a sleeping giant that begs to be woken by popular interest and involvement. And the word giant is apt, for the Watershed is on a grand scale at some 1,200 kilometres from end to end, and an average elevation of around 450 metres above sea level. It is consistently on the higher ground.

It will be argued that it is a unique linear geographic feature, that its distinctive quality is that it is relatively wild, or wilder throughout – that there can be no other single entity in the physical geography of Scotland that largely maintains this character on such an epic scale. The Watershed truly is an artery of nature, which flows all the way from Peel Fell on the border with England, to distant Duncansby Head, overlooking the waters of the Pentland Firth, with the Orkney Islands beyond.

The description of what the Watershed is that establishes its linear location is not complicated: any map of Scotland shows that its landform faces in two distinct directions: east towards the North Sea on the one hand, and west to the Atlantic Ocean on the other.

Now imagine that you are a raindrop about to descend on Scotland: whether you end up in that ocean or that sea will clearly be determined by where you land, and the Watershed is the defining line. And although it is a rather rambling line, it is none the less definitive. If, as that raindrop, you land to the east of the line, then by bog, burn and river, you are bound for the North Sea, and should you land on the other side of that line, then you are westward and Atlantic bound.

This simple definition does require further examination; some explanation is called for.

As recently as 6,000 years ago, before sea levels rose to their current levels, what we now call mainland Britain was physically part of Europe, with a large area of land called Doggerland filling the English Channel and the southern part of the North Sea. At the northern end of the UK, what later became the Orkney Islands formed a peninsula at the upper extremity of this very different looking landmass. But then, as now, there was a distinct body of water to the east, which was to become recognised as the North Sea, and all of the water to the west of this was the Atlantic Ocean, or connected directly to it. Thus what we now call Scotland has, since at least the end of the last Ice-Age, had a clear east-west divide, and that line of demarcation has since extended northwards through Orkney and beyond, to the Shetland Islands. This has been critical in helping to determine the northern terminus of the Watershed on the mainland of Scotland.

Each major part of the Watershed has a distinctive geological and physical character, and the main fault-lines form the points of transition from one to the other. It is largely from this that each section derives its' particular landscape type and special qualities.

There have been a small number of people who have walked versions of the Watershed, most notably Dave Hewitt. His excellent book on his trek entitled *Walking the Watershed,* set the northern end at Cape Wrath – the top left hand corner. Whilst his account of his journey makes an excellent read, and has a compelling narrative about what can only be described as a very demanding continuous walk, I differ on the significance of where the Watershed ends in the north. He was, I believe, enticed by the promise of including Foinaven in his journey, and hence heading towards the wilds of Cape Wrath. However, I would argue that there is only one geographically correct Watershed, and the North Sea-Atlantic Ocean divide is the simple key to it. This very clearly brings both of the island groups of Orkney and Shetland into the picture. The body of water off the short north coast of Scotland is most certainly part of the Atlantic Ocean. Were you to stand on the western shores of either Orkney or Shetland, and remark to yourself and your companions 'next stop America', your gaze would be across the Atlantic swell. Finally, the rocks from which both Caithness and Orkney are formed show geological continuity; these areas are part of the same structure. From all of this, it can be seen that the northern terminus of the geographic Watershed on the mainland is firmly anchored to Duncansby Head.

So, whilst the definition of the watershed is fairly simple, and plotting it on a map is relatively straightforward, it begs the question as to what and where are the existing geographical or cartographic references to it? The answer would appear to be that there are none; there are no maps showing the Watershed in its entirety – I could find nothing definitive. Having been unable to unearth any precise references to it, I decided to do something about this gap in our available material, and this book is the result.

Having defined what I meant by 'the watershed', and clarified its geographic credentials, I started with arguably the two most significant geographic organisations: The Royal Geographic Society and The Royal Scottish Geographical Society, and I drew a blank with both. Neither organisation could provide any reference to what I was looking for. I then wrote to a number of seemingly appropriate academics on the subject, and again drew similar blanks. I dug deep into the very comprehensive and contemporary publication *Scotland – Encyclopaedia of Places and Landscapes* (2005), but still the Watershed remained elusive. I visited the National Library of Scotland Map Library at Causewayside; still nothing! A good friend who is both a geographer and climber pointed me in the direction of Francis Groome's *Ordnance Gazetteer of Scotland* (1884), and this set the quest rolling. Here I did find an unequivocal definition of the northern end – Duncansby Head.

This quest had intrigued me, not least because in this day and age, when it would seem as if everything has already been weighed, measured and counted, it was strange to find something as seemingly simple as the Watershed unaccounted for. And this became even more tantalising as the watersheds of other countries and continents are both defined and well known. In the Americas, the watersheds of both North and South are almost celebrated, and closer to home Nicholas Crane's wonderful book *Clear Waters Rising*, which is about his 10,000 kilometre journey along the watershed of mainland Europe, from Cape Finisterre to Istanbul, is popularly acclaimed. These watersheds are very much on their respective maps.

It is perhaps useful at this stage to consider at what point in the development of the mapping of Scotland that the Watershed could have been plotted with any accuracy. When was it that maps had reached a sufficient degree of sophistication, with enough key information, to allow for a reasonably placed line to be drawn?

In the second century AD, Ptolemy produced a map of the British Isles for the benefit of the Roman administration, and given that much of Scotland was beyond the accepted limit of both the Roman Empire and its occupation or incursion, the map was somewhat vague as to what lay beyond their frontiers. Scotland is depicted as being orientated west to east, thus lying at right angles to England. The original of this map has been lost, but a 12th or 13th century copy survives. From this and other related references, a version was printed in the late 15th century. There are a number of recognisable features on this map including some of the major firths and rivers, but the layout and information is wholly insufficient to draw any watershed. Similarly, the Gough map of about 1360, whilst pointing Scotland correctly on its north-south axis, and showing some features that we would recognise, offers a confusing correlation of other features; it lacks a convincing overall shape. By 1546, Lilly had drawn a map which was getting much closer to the Scotland we know, but certain key features were either missing or still misplaced.

Just twenty years later, in about 1566, two maps appeared which did offer a much clearer picture in terms of shape, key features and their correlation to each other. An anonymous Italian map almost provides the necessary detail and in the right place, but it put the Great Glen crossing at the wrong end of Loch Lochy, and so fails the test. Lawrence Newell's map, on the other hand, offers a convincing route around and between all of the key features for plotting the Watershed. Critically, it locates the Orkney Islands in exactly the right place off the far north east coast. Thus, 1566 or thereabouts is the essential date for determining the point at which map making, and the surveying techniques to go along with it, had advanced sufficiently to show most of the major rivers flowing in the correct direction, and their correlation one with the other. In ... refore, the Watershed could have been plotted almost ... go.

While there are a number of other maps from this period which would also serve to show that mapmaking had become much more sophisticated, it took another 100 years for an atlas to appear, which would be the defining publication. Joan Blaeu's *Atlas* of 1665 provides a series of maps which not only show clearly the upper reaches and profiles of all of the river catchments, but also some very useful information about the general locus of the Watershed. The maps would appear to have been surveyed and hence drawn from the perspective of the lower ground; the more populated areas of the river valleys. From there, they project an image of the headwater areas as sparsely populated, with very few settlements. These areas are shown in a vague manner, with the county or geographic area boundaries sweeping through a seemingly unknown terrain; through landscapes with apparently few defining features – areas of little significance. Perhaps this says more about how these areas fitted into the warp and weft of community life than anything else. At that time there were very few roads, and wherever possible, water and sea travel was still very much the norm. The higher, remoter areas were undoubtedly less well known, and indeed of lesser importance. Their relative emptiness was real; they offered few resources that could be exploited, they were more exposed and much less fertile.

The first six-inch to the mile Ordnance Survey maps do show a watershed in a number of places, notably in the far north. These are drawn in a series of generally straight lines linking specific identifiable points, and therefore have what may be described as a rather mechanistic approach to something which in reality should be shown as an organic flowing line; for the Watershed is just that. Those areas in which a watershed is shown are far from comprehensive, and a number of lesser watersheds between river valleys are shown. So it is fair to conclude that the intention was not to delineate and show the Watershed as a whole, but rather to include a watershed when this seemed appropriate.

Part of the image of the border between Scotland and England is its troubled but colourful history. It is an area filled with the romance of stories of war and pillage, of great families constantly struggling to assert their power and control. For not only was much of this strife about the meeting of two nations frequently in dispute, but local feuds played a major part too. It is this legacy, in the form of the Border Ballads and tales that have been handed down as a celebration of great deeds, loves lost and won, truth, loyalty and despair.

Indeed, the line of the border itself took a long time to become recognised and accepted, especially at the eastern end around Berwick-upon-Tweed. But the border line as we know it today was established in 1249 with the Laws of the Marches and further ratified in 1328 at the end of the 30-year Wars of Independence – with some subsequent minor adjustments, and not a little continuing political assertion, even to the present day. The word march is given to mean a *boundary* or *frontier*; and we will hear a lot more of this. In the context of the border it is used to describe three divisions or sections, along with the hinterland on either side of this border. Each of the three marches had its own wardens, legal and organisational arrangements; each had its own distinctive mechanisms for resolving, or attempting to resolve peaceably, disputes and offensive deeds. The three marches were the Eastern, Middle and Western.

What is it then that determines the start or southern end of the Watershed of Scotland?

Firstly, a look at the English side to discover what forms the northern end of the watershed of England. The eastern side is straightforward, with the basin of the River Tyne which drains into the North Sea below Newcastle-upon-Tyne and which comes westwards as far as Haltwhistle on Hadrian's Wall. But the west is less clear, as on the Western March, the border follows the Kershope Burn and the River Esk, and then jumps west to pick up the River Sark just north of Carlisle. Much of the Esk above Canonbie is in Scotland forming Eskdale, which of course rises on Eskdalemuir.

South of Kershope Forest, three rivers form the northern tributaries of the River Eden catchment which flows through Carlisle, and thence into the Solway Firth. The Rivers Lyne, King Water and Irthing respectively form the upper reaches of the western side of the watershed of England. Put simply, the River Eden and its catchment flow into the Solway Firth in the west, and the River Tyne and its catchment drains east into the North Sea. From this, the critical point is to discover where the divide appears on the border itself.

The Middle March of the border extends some 50km south west from the Cheviot to the Kershope Burn, 5km south of Newcastleton. On the English side, the Watershed comes from the south west to Peel Fell from the Larriston Fells via Deadwater. And from Peel Fell it then runs north to Hartshorn Pike, with the Scaup Burn draining to the Kielder on the one hand, and the Peel Burn draining to the Liddel Water in Liddesdale on the other. The border is therefore not quite on a watershed line between the Kielder and the Tweed catchments in this area. But further to the north east, they merge again at Carter Bar.

The summit of Peel Fell is some 50 metres or so on the English side of the border and at 602 metres is the highest point in this area. Given the drainage patterns around it, it is the logical, if not the exact, starting point for the Watershed of Scotland. The word *peel* has a number of recognised meanings, and in this context is seen to refer to a *significant boundary* – which the border most certainly is. Thus the meaning of Peel Fell can be interpreted as the *boundary mountain*.

Throughout the last 1,000 years of history, much of the Watershed of Scotland has been a boundary in one form or another. But it is as if it had been drawn on a map with invisible ink and needs some magic formula to be brushed on to make the line appear fully, for there are many different layers of traditional boundaries waiting to be revealed. In addition to this great east – west demarcation, it has been throughout history, and indeed continues to be, a variety of different boundaries or marches. A journey back through the pages of history begins to reveal its significance. Some 220km of the Watershed currently forms the boundary between different Local Authority areas, and thus almost one fifth of its length has a contemporary legal status, with these boundaries having been established as recently as 1996. Prior to 1975, when the old County structure disappeared, as much as 35 per cent of the Watershed was drawn as County boundary. And, since the origin of many of the counties was the earlier sherriffdoms, we see these boundaries stretch well back into medieval times.

A study of Andy Wightman's *Who Owns Scotland* shows that as much as 70 per cent of the Watershed still forms a boundary between different estates or other land holdings. There is a fence, or the remains of a fence-line, along almost three quarters of its length, and a drystane dyke on a number of short stretches. As a boundary, it will appear on countless title deeds as a march to many a farm, forest or shooting estate. The shepherds, foresters and keepers will know it well, but it is very much the hinterland of the holdings that they patrol, and therefore the least utilised part of them. It is at the extremity – the wildest part.

Until comparatively recent times, the Parish played a major part in people's lives – including matters of church, education, some significant aspects of administration, and social organisation in societies and other local associations. Although there were changes over the years with a slow process of Parish divisions or amalgamations, and transfer from one presbytery to another, the picture remained largely stable for hundreds of years. And this Parish structure, which was at the heart of local life, dated back to Mediaeval times. It was, however, a casualty of the Local Government re-organisation of the mid-70s, and the Parish boundaries were removed from the popular Ordnance Survey map series at about the same time. The sense of local identity which this Parish structure had maintained was replaced by the new concept of *community*, and the establishment of Community Councils. With as much as 80 per cent of the Watershed having formerly been Parish boundary, its significance to people living on either side of it today continues. It now marks out the upper extent of their Community Council or school catchment area, and the area of benefit for other local associations. In some places, the advent of greater mobility, which the car has brought, will have had an impact on how local is indeed local, especially in the realms of economic activity, but the concept of *local* prevails none the less.

The significance of the Parish boundary was further reinforced in historical times when witches, villains and, tragically, suicides could not be buried in consecrated ground. In such cases, a kind of no-mans-land on the Parish boundary was often chosen. How many such unmarked graves are there on the Watershed itself? No one will ever know.

So, as the magic formula is painted onto the map, and the layers of demarcation, organisation and sense of place for local people do indeed begin to emerge, it is clear that all but a small proportion of the Watershed has significance as a boundary of one sort or another. And these boundaries continue to influence people's current thinking, identity and activity, to the present day.

When I finally set out to take a pencil and plot the Watershed on a map, the concept was relatively simple, for many of the factors I have described were fairly clear. The only real prerequisite was an ability to read and interpret a map, so the starting point was a paper exercise – no boots or walking poles required. The major river valleys and their tributaries were clearly marked, but there were a few areas which needed some more careful consideration, and these included:

Coulter to Biggar Common
Black Law wind farm to Kirk o' Shotts transmitter
Cumbernauld
Carron Reservoir in the Campsie Fells
The Great Glen crossing
West end of Loch Quoich
Rhidorroch in Wester Ross
The northern terminus

As these sections were finally clarified thanks to some very helpful advice from Walter Stephen, a clear line was completed on my large bundle of 24 different 1:25,000 OS sheets. It was a great revelation.

The Watershed has been described as lying on the higher ground, and with an average elevation of some 450m above sea level, it is indeed often in the clouds. The lowest point is at Laggan in the Great Glen: a mere 35m, whilst the highest point is Sgurr nan Ceathreamhnan in Kintail at 1,151m. It starts at 602m on Peel Fell, finishes at 60m above the waters of the Pentland Firth, and takes in a commendable 44 Munros (mountains over 3,000ft) along the way.

It is the elevation of the Watershed that is one of its supreme qualities and makes it special. It offers wide views to the traveller, with great panoramas across vast swathes of mainland Scotland and beyond. A journey on the Watershed presents an unfolding and evolving kaleidoscope of landscape and Nature; Scotland the Best, viewed consistently from an elevated position. And it is this which gives it a unique distinction – as a single geographic feature running the length of the land, which lays the headwaters of most of the major river catchments and systems at its feet. It is a linear vantage feature from which the eye is led outwards and down the river valleys and lochs towards the coast, thus providing a tangible geographic and visual link to many of our urban settlements and wider landscapes.

The elevation of the Watershed has had another significant effect, one that generally maintains its relative wildness throughout. As our distant ancestors gradually settled and made use of the available resources around them, they chose first the coasts, islands and the lower reaches of the river plains. The process of settlement then continued further upstream, and out into the wider countryside, which saw their impact on the landscape grow and expand. Forest clearings and the emergence of basic farming, building, burial and celebration all show now as markings or shadows in the earth. And this process continued with the Roman invasion in some areas, and the seemingly empty period that followed their departure. The Church made its mark with the growth of monastic settlement and economic exploitation over wide areas, and these were in turn carved-up during the Reformation to herald the new regime. Great estates, industrialisation and an increasing urban population with its needs, all contributed to an ever-changing landscape. A myriad of other land-altering influences have all come and gone and left their mark. But throughout much of history, the higher ground had little to offer or exploit; it was the least affected by man's efforts. Sheep and deer grazing may have had some impact on these elevated areas, but the general impression is of wilder and untamed terrain.

What then of the social and economic place of the Watershed today? In addition to its varied and only slightly diminished role as Local Government or estate boundary, the Watershed has been and continues to be a boundary in other ways. Because of the local identity which still prevails around villages and towns, the community and social organisation which this brings tends to turn its back on the higher ground; local people's orientation is towards their own side of the Watershed, facing downstream. Without being necessarily conscious of its particular status, people's communities of interest are demarcated in part by the Watershed. Communication plays a significant part in this, for even in this age of motor transport, there are nonetheless fewer roads and railways crossing the Watershed than there would be elsewhere further down in the river valleys. And there are no such lines of communication running along the Watershed – it is our empty quarter. If its place as a boundary of one sort or another can simply be seen as one of the major *causes*, then the *effect* is its wildness.

In the past, self-sufficiency in each community for its needs, including food, materials, manufacture and commerce, would have served to limit the need to transport across the Watershed; other more accessible sources and resources would have been used when the need arose. This is not to say that people did not cross the Watershed, as there is indeed plenty of evidence where path and track crossed, but there is no doubt that it was an inhibiting factor. Whilst the decline in local production for local use has been largely replaced by national and international markets, there remains the vestige of local influence in some of the services and the more recent drive to create local markets.

That the route of the Watershed is distinctively wilder in character throughout its long meander as the backbone of Scotland is hardly surprising. As a boundary, it is at the outer limit of community, Local Authority and estate, beyond the pace of everyday life and use. Its elevation puts much of it beyond, indeed well beyond, the commercial tree line. The terrain it crosses is therefore amongst the least cultivated and wildest land, but herein lies the paradox.

The temptation to regard hill, mountain and moor, especially the more scenic areas, as entirely natural and unaffected by the actions of man, is a mistake. Whilst the tourist literature and romantic song may wax lyrical about the 'bonnie purple heather', or even make bolder statements about 'last great wildernesses', they would be misguided. There are very few places anywhere in Scotland that have either not been affected by human action in the past, or have retained a truly natural state. For much of Scotland was originally covered in trees, and what was subsequently called the Forest of Caledon, with some form of woodland cover extending well into the mountainous areas, with the more elevated areas as patchy scrub, and only the higher summits clear of it. The start of felling to make way for early forms of farming and construction dated back to the times when we made that transition from hunter-gatherers to farmers; to the point at which we became more settled. The loss or removal of trees and the erosion of forest cover is one of the significant factors in altering the nature and appearance of the landscape and its biodiversity.

Climate change some 5,000 years ago wrought further change, as cooler and wetter conditions prevailed. This period heralded the start of the formation of peat and peat-bog on a major scale in most areas; many areas of the ancient forest succumbed to this hostile habitat, and the great tree stumps which we often see today, either sticking forlornly out of the side of a peat hag or standing skeletal in the heather, are often the legacy of that climate change. The impact of this, and the evidence it has left, can be seen in many locations on the Watershed and in the surrounding landscapes.

Fast forward a few millennia then, and into the agricultural and industrial revolutions of the 18th and 19th centuries, and huge swathes of fertile land were given over to productive use. Whilst the higher more remote areas largely escaped these dramatic forms of change, they did nonetheless experience slower, but often equally profound, alteration. Over several hundred years, sheep grazing, and an increasing deer population, and a number of natural processes have gradually eroded tree cover, including those areas which are so keenly regarded as being in their natural state. Overgrazing by both species set in a cycle of decline; young tree shoots were eaten, the woodland became singularly mature, old trees fell, and there was nothing to replace them. The inevitable outcome of this process which may have taken many hundreds of years to evolve is an arboreal desert. This in turn altered the entire ecosystem, and changed everything which grew in it or sought to live on it.

There are differing theories about the overall extent of woodland loss, at what rate, and in which periods in history; and other factors have played a part too. Great loss there has been, and this has undoubtedly changed both the character and appearance of much of our landscape. It has affected the true extent of its wildness.

The definition of the term 'wild land' and the concept of wildness have been given greater clarity in the Scottish Natural Heritage (SNH) policy statement on *Wildness in Scotland's Countryside*. This offers the useful distinction between *wildness as the quality enjoyed* and *wild-land or places where wildness is best expressed*. It expands on the importance of land use planning as the key to protecting wild land, giving Local Authorities the lead in ensuring that this is carried out effectively in their respective areas. It goes on to propose the six key attributes in the identification of wild land:

- Its perceived naturalness.
- Lack of constructions or other artefacts.
- Little evidence of contemporary land uses.
- Rugged or otherwise challenging terrain.
- Remoteness and inaccessibility.
- The extent of the area.

Having walked the whole Watershed, my direct experience is of frequent evidence of all six of these attributes, in varying degrees and combinations, and of the very largely continuous wildness as the *quality enjoyed*.

Clearly not all areas which might be accredited as being wild land would fully match all of these criteria, but this does offer an important yardstick in helping to pin down the principal characteristics. The report does acknowledge too that some wild land could be 'quite close to settlements' – the assumption that it is to be found in only the remoter uninhabited areas is misleading. This raises the issue of fences and dykes (or their remains which may be of Victorian vintage), ancient cairns, bothies, tracks, trig points, masts, pylons, and hydro-electric installations; many of these are to be found in the major wild areas. But the list of attributes of wild land provides a valuable mechanism for objectively identifying these areas.

The John Muir Trust (JMT) seeks to achieve its mission 'to conserve and protect wild areas of the UK in their natural condition, so as to leave them unimpaired for future enjoyment and study', through its care for wild land, wildlife, education and adventure. It has done much to establish that whilst people and wild land are inseparable, their awareness and actions are critical.

A further major milestone in promoting the care of the natural world and wild places in Scotland was reached in July 2005 when the concordat between SNH and the JMT was signed. This was informed by the earlier SNH policy on *Wildness in the Scottish Countryside* on the one hand, and the JMT's *Wild Land Policy* of 2004 on the other. It is a seminal agreement between the two key players in this field; one which will serve the interests of wild land appreciation and protection well into the future. It establishes the importance of the concept of wildness and its immense value to those who live, work and play in Scotland.

The classification of land for agricultural purposes offers the next very useful picture in relation to the Watershed, and its suitability or otherwise, for cultivation or grazing. There are seven broad categories of potential land use:

Class	Potential capability
1	Of producing a very wide range of crops
2	Of producing a wide range of crops
3	Of producing an average range of crops
4	Of producing a narrow range of crops
5	Is improved grassland
6	Is rough grazing
7	Has very limited agricultural value

Some 88 per cent of the line of the Watershed falls within either the Class 6 or 7 categories, and therefore has very limited or no agricultural value whatever. About 8 per cent would be deemed to fall within Class 5, and is thus uncultivated but capable of being used only for grazing purposes. The proportion of the Watershed which fits into Class 4 is limited to some 2.5 per cent, which could produce a narrow range of crops, whilst only 1.5 per cent at most would be within Class 3, and support even an average range of crops. There is no Class 2 or Class 1 land anywhere on the Watershed. This exercise shows that by far the majority of the line of the Watershed is across land which is non-arable and of limited or no use agriculturally.

In gradually building the picture of the underlying factors which either serve to contribute to, or indeed define, the wilder characteristic of the Watershed, so the argument for its distinctive contribution to the geography of Scotland is expanded too. And the notion of a *Ribbon of Wildness* moves on from being a rather subjective observation to a case that bears much wider scrutiny.

Although it is the hills and mountains that form the milestones along the Watershed, because they *are* the higher ground and establish the divide, it is the major rivers and their catchments that truly place the Watershed in its wider Scottish context. They describe the direction which water will take to ocean or sea; they are part of the bigger picture and provide the route for that watery journey. The author Neil Gunn, evocatively describes the life of a river:

Going from the mouth to the source, may well seem to be reversing the natural order, to be going from the death of the sea, where individuality is lost, back to the source of the stream, where individuality is born.

The major rivers and their tributaries to the east of the Watershed include the Tweed, Forth, Tay, Spey, Ness, Affric, Oykel and Shin; these are all bound for the North Sea, and their combined catchment areas constitute a sizeable proportion of central and eastern Scotland. The major river systems on the Atlantic side include the Liddel, Esk and Moffat, which flow into the Solway Firth in the south. These are followed by the Clyde, Orchy, and Etive, and then the various shorter waters which drain into Loch Linnhe, including the Coe, Leven, Spean, Lochy and Dessary. The next rivers all typify the character of this part of the northwest Highlands, where the Watershed is well towards the western sea-board. Indeed there are short stretches in which the line of the Watershed swings even further west than some of these sea lochs' eastward penetration. For example, Sgurr na Ciche and the remote section within the Rough Bounds, lies some 20km west of Loch Eil at Banavie, and is almost 5km west of Kinloch Hourn to the north. Much of the line of the Watershed in the northwest runs parallel or close to the line of the Moine Thrust, a geological feature created when two tectonic plates collided, with the one over-riding the other – thus pushing up a long ragged mountain formation. Moving further northwards, these short swift rivers include the Shiel, Ling, Carron, Ewe, Broom, Canaird, and Laxford, whilst the slower eastern run towards Duncansby Head includes the Strathmore, Naver, Halladale and Thurso.

From this it can be seen that the place of the Watershed and its related river systems within the wider Scottish landscape is vast. Only the relatively small area to the east in Aberdeenshire and Angus, bounded by a line from near Arbroath to Carn na Fhidhleir in the southern Cairngorms, and then running north to meet the Moray coast near Portsoy, is not part of this picture. The Watershed has a defining place in the geography of all but a small proportion of the entire Scottish mainland.

Land designation for wildlife, conservation, scientific or scenic purposes has seen some 25 per cent of Scotland given some form of protection in recent years. This serves to demonstrate the high quality of landscape and wildlife which we enjoy on our own doorstep, and as will be seen, adds weight to the argument concerning the wilder character of the Watershed. The key forms of designation which have a direct bearing on the line of the Watershed are:

Designation	Abbrev	Summary
Sites of Special Scientific Interest	SSSI	Areas protected for their geological, botanical or zoological importance – covering 11 per cent of Scotland.
National Nature Reserve	NNR	Now over 70 of these areas in Scotland, in additional to smaller Local Nature Reserves.
Special Areas of Conservation	SAC	Areas cover a range of valuable non-bird habitats.
Special Protection Areas	SPA	The conservation of wild birds is the main purpose in this form of protection, with over sites 70 throughout Scotland.
National Scenic Areas	NSA	An immense total, of over 1 million hectares of Scotland are thus protected, for their visual and aesthetic qualities.

Scottish Natural Heritage is the Government agency which has general oversight of the designation processes, and of monitoring and review. The Local Authorities have a number of responsibilities in relation to these sites too, including the production of Structure Plans and the preparation of Biodiversity Action Plans. All these plans and designations serve to place the Watershed into the wider context of the surrounding areas and landscape. For the one-fifth of its length that forms the boundary between different Local Authority areas, there is the need for collaboration and consultation. The relatively recent creation of the two National Parks for the Cairngorms and the Loch Lomond and Trossachs areas adds a further valuable dimension to how we care for the areas which have come under greatest pressure from the often conflicting interests of conservation, tourism, and the economic wellbeing of the communities within their bounds. The Watershed of Scotland forms a unique link by wildness between these two National Parks.

The total designated length of the Watershed is currently about 295 km or some 27 per cent. One of the questions which this book poses is the extent to which further protection can, or should, be obtained for a greater proportion of the Watershed, given its largely wilder character and unique contribution to the Scottish landscape.

The case builds.

A remarkable statistic about the Watershed is the small number of houses or other buildings that are located on, or immediately beside it; other than Cumbernauld's presence, it has a particularly uninhabited air. A few stretches in the central belt are over fields, but these are represented by the less intense form of agriculture – Classes 3 and 4. About three quarters of it is or has been a fence line, and the extent to which this is aesthetically intrusive is open to debate. In places, it undoubtedly is, but in others it has served to keep activity at bay, and in fact helps to protect some habitats. The following list of manmade structures on the Watershed, or which cross it, may at first seem to adversely affect its otherwise peaceful character, but when put into the context of a line which is well over one 1,000 kilometres in length, it is not overbearing:

Lighthouse	1	Ruined castle	1	Quarries	2
Former open cast	2	Airfield	1	Houses *	21
New Town	1	Reservoir	1	Masts	40
Wind farms (at 2009)	2	Hydro dams	1	Ancient cairns	20

'A' roads	24	'B' roads	39	'U' roads	8
Dual Carriageway	0	Motorway	2	Railways	10
Canals	2	Marked tracks	26	Marked footpaths	63

* excluding Cumbernauld

In many locations, however, habitation has receded from the Watershed, and reinforced its emptiness. The identifiable ruins or sites of around 20 houses on or adjacent to it provide the evidence for this.

In addition to the different forms of land designation for conservation or agricultural purposes, the Watershed can be seen in its wider context, as relating to a variety of other forms of land use. There are a number of areas of commercial forest, especially in the south of Scotland. The Watershed has been spared from in this otherwise dense dark-green cloak. It remains as an unplanted strip of land, of varying width, on either side of a fence line or the remains of one; it has survived as such largely by virtue of its place as a land ownership boundary.

A number of large areas are managed to provide a clean water supply for urban areas, and in this context, land use is strictly controlled, and in some locations sheep farming is now being reduced or removed altogether, to be replaced by extensive native forest. The vast water catchment areas which have been given over to hydro-electric power generation, whether for national grid or aluminium smelting, have been substantially altered in the process. New reservoirs have been created where none existed before, or natural lochs have been submerged under much larger sheets of water; these have wrought changing landscapes, some of which can be seen close to the Watershed. Whilst in a number of locations water is conveyed across the Watershed in tunnels and artificial channels to boost the supply to some distant turbine on the other side; the water pochle!

Three National Trust for Scotland (NTS) properties, a Royal Society for the Protection of Birds (RSPB) reserve, and one Geopark all add to the variety of important landscapes and habitats that the

Watershed traverses. The John Muir Trust is a key partner in the care and sensitive development of a number of sites. An impressive roll-call of all of the national environmental agencies completes the immense but hitherto disconnected conservation and increasing biodiversity of the Watershed – they share an expansive community of interest in this.

The hill and mountain names and their meanings give an evocative impression of how our ancestors viewed the world about them, and in particular how important these landmarks were to their lives and lore. Many of the names show close affinity with Nature, and in addition to simple colour, texture and shape, helped to establish popular description of these defining landmarks. These descriptions in turn became names which were used in charters and deeds as fixed points of reference. And with the evolution of maps, culminating in the establishment of the Ordnance Survey, these names then became official. The general prominence of the Watershed on the higher ground, and its place as a form of boundary or barrier, gave many of these hills and mountains an added significance. It is clear that our ancestors made remarkable sense of what lay around them, without the assistance of all that we can take for granted today, especially in the disciplines of land survey and cartography. It is evident that in some places prominent hills had two different names conferred on them by the communities on either side – they each saw the same eminence from their own perspectives, and claimed it as their own. Some hill names changed over time, with the relatively more recent Ordnance Survey designations becoming the permanent labels.

Rivers and burns were of particular importance, as they provided the best locations for early settlement: water supply was ready to hand, and cultivation areas nearby. This held true even at the more marginal headwaters in the hills, where we often find the uppermost settlement is called Waterhead, or more specifically with name that refers to the river itself, such as Kelvin Head, Core Head, or Avon Head. In a number of locations the water or a geographic feature gave its name to the hill on the horizon – the hill on the

INTRODUCTION

Watershed, for example, Donald's Cleuch Head, and Cauldcleuch Head.

The names that the hills and mountains acquired over time give an evocative picture of our ancestors' honest yet colourful approach to their surroundings. They didn't have time for leisure activity as we know it, but they clearly appreciated what they saw as the distinctive shapes and character of these high places. Some hills were associated with mythical tales and were thus established within the local lore and legends, whilst others were vested with religious significance, and had a cairn or other marker built on the summit to commemorate some long forgotten ceremony in community life. Whilst a perceived similarity to some part of the human body, both female and male, was not lost on the ancients either. A sample of these tops and their meanings gives a lively impression of what our forebears saw in the landscape around them:

Carlin Tooth	*witch's or old woman's tooth*
Tomtain	*hill of fire*
Stronend	*end of the nose*
Beinn Chabhair	*mountain of the antler or hawk*
Ben Lui	*mountain of the calf*
Meall a Bhuird	*hill of the roaring*
Sgurr Mhurlagain	*hill of the wool basket*
Sgurr na Ciche	*hill of the pap, or breast*
Beinn Tharsuin	*transverse hill*
Sgurr nan Chaorachann	*peak of the field of the berries*
Ben Hee	*fairy hill*
Ben Griam Beg	*small dark hill*

The ancient village of Cumbernauld grew up on the eastern side of the Watershed and, had it not been for the establishment in the 1960s of the New Town of that name, there would have been no urban settlement whatever on our *Ribbon of Wildness*. There it is, ever controversial, and people either love Cumbernauld or condemn it, probably in equal measure. One of the greatest redeeming features in the design and landscaping of Cumbernauld though was the decision to plant large numbers of trees, and to conserve some ancient native woodland on either side of the town. Viewed from a number of the nearby vantage points, it is the greenery which effectively softens the image, and almost achieves natural continuity. Other perspectives are less forgiving, and it has taken careful route planning to plot the course of the Watershed through this otherwise harder landscape.

Journeys with a purpose have long been part of particular religions and cultures, with pilgrimage being the most popular amongst them; the basic idea being that some form of sustained hardship and effort will bring the individual closer to God. Such a journey will give the pilgrim time to reflect on his or her life, and resolve to be a better person in the future; having done some form of penance on the move, a higher form of grace will be achieved. But there are a number of more eco-inspired journeys and individuals that perhaps put a journey on the Watershed into a more relevant context today. John Muir embarked on a series of wilderness journeys in which he set off with only the wild surroundings to guide him. *A Thousand Mile Walk to the Gulf*, and *Travels in Alaska* are the more notable of these, and he gives both a perceptive and inspirational account of these epic ventures that would be hard for most of us to emulate today. A number of artists have used journeys with nature to inspire their work, and created 'natural art' as markers along the way. Richard Long and Andy Goldsworthy are perhaps amongst the better known of these, and the inspiration that they drew from the experience of a journey with nature has given both pleasure and delight to many.

The scope for popular involvement has been greatly enhanced with the development of long distance routes throughout the UK and beyond, and for the thousands of people who tackle the likes of the West Highland Way each year, it is perhaps *the* single opportunity in which at least an element of self-reliance and significant effort in a semi-natural environment will be undertaken, so it becomes a memorable experience. The round of the Munros has taken off as the great popular challenge, and the overall number of

INTRODUCTION

completions grows inexorably each year. Whilst it could be perceived that getting to the top of the hill and then back down again is often the sum total of the experience with Nature for some, there is perhaps no knowing what the individual gets from their surroundings with each outing. Many books have been written, and documentaries produced, about demanding journeys in summer or winter conditions, continuous and unsupported, solo or accompanied, and by people of all ages and abilities. Each one has been a journey with a purpose, and the opportunity for a wider public to read about it and capture even a modicum of the challenge and excitement knows no bounds.

The new access rights to the countryside are to everyone's advantage and have done the improbable, which was to get some measure of consensus on entitlement and good practice. The Watershed could become the next popular *big walk with wildness*; a unique experience with Nature, which is within the capability of all who are reasonably fit and experienced. Although my initial thoughts had been that it would never catch on, and there may be a number of impracticalities, I can now see the possibilities, and will introduce these in due course. A note of caution here though: because there are a number of locations on the Watershed that are most definitely not for the novice or inexperienced, and there are a large number of fences and major bogs to be negotiated along the way! The apparent emptiness is deceptive: in reality, many people's livelihood depends on some activity or job taking place on or about the Watershed. So a significant level of sensitivity to their needs and rights is imperative.

The traditions of journeys with Nature, and the creative inspiration that this can bring, should not be underestimated.

For those who in principle stick rigidly to imperial measures, *Ribbon of Wildness* will, in part at least, be a betrayal, because I use the metric system. The insidious process of metrication started some time back, and was imposed upon our maps well over 30 years ago, so that now all our measurements on the hill start as metres and kilometres whether we like it or not. I have, however, opted to stick with that, simply in order to maintain consistency, and to ensure that the reader will be able to match this text with their own maps.

The significant length of the Watershed and the variety of terrain it passes through are just two of the factors that give this geographic feature such appeal. But they also present a challenge – how best to break it down into more manageable stretches? I have identified it in five sections which, though very different in length, have each got their particular character. They are in part determined by the geological structure of Scotland, and use some geological features as their parameters.

I have chosen to approach this description of the Watershed of Scotland from south to north, in part because that is the direction in which I walked and explored it, but also because its northern terminus at Duncansby Head points tantalisingly towards South Ronaldsay in the Orkney Islands, via the Pentland Skerries – unfinished business, but that is perhaps for the future. I have described in some detail the ways and extent to which the Watershed is a boundary, and therefore adopt the most fitting word for a boundary in Scottish lore and language – a *march*. Each of the five Marches of the Watershed has its own distinctive terrain and place in the geography of Scotland.

The Reiver March

The Border Reivers were primarily of the great landholding families that occupied that area, and much of their lawless reiving or cattle rustling epitomised the times that they lived in. The Armstrongs and Scotts, Livingstones and Elliots, and many others, whose deeds of theft, pillage, murder and retribution have been handed down to us in publications like Wilson's *Tales of the Borders*, in the writings of Sir Walter Scott and, most beautifully, in the Border Ballads.

Starting at Peel Fell on the border with England, this first 133km of the Watershed runs at an average elevation of some 550m above sea level. It sweeps through the higher ground in both Wauchope and Craik forests, on what are aptly described as 'the rolling border hills'. It then follows in a great S-shaped gesture round the headwaters of the Ettrick and then the Moffat Waters, and onto one of the higher tops in the area, Hart Fell. From there it runs across the head of the Devil's Beeftub and onto Clyde Law where the start of both the Tweed and Clyde Rivers are but a few kilometres apart. Thus far its journey has been largely westward, but here it swings sharply north along more of these 'rolling hills', by Gathersnow Hill and Culter Fell, and finishes at the dramatic Southern Upland Fault. On Gawky Hill the land falls away steeply to the northwest; it is almost like standing on a high shoreline looking across a broad expanse of rippling loch, in hues of brown and green.

The Laich March

Laich or *low* is a very Scottish word which aptly describes much of this, the second section, running for some 175km from the Southern Upland Fault line on Gawky Hill to the Highland Boundary Fault line on Guilan, to the east of Loch Lomond. The average elevation of the Laich March is 280m, which is about half that of the Reiver march. As the line meanders across this lower area, often referred to as the Central Belt, it appears to make a dash from hilltop to outcrop, almost avoiding the flatter and more fertile land on either side. It also seems to weave round and past nearly all of the settlements that are seemingly in the way. But of course the reality is the other way round, as the settlements generally developed off the highest ground. There is only the one exception to this: Cumbernauld.

From the evocatively named Gawky Hill, the line crosses to Shaw Hill, skirts Coulter, and rises to Biggar Common, Black Mount, and then touches the south Pentlands at Craigengar. Leven Seat and Black Law are followed by Kirk o' Shotts transmitter and the M8 crossing, with Black Loch and Limerigg moors coming before the urban expanse of Cumbernauld with all its trees. The Campsie Fells present another S shaped sweep as the Carron and Endrick Waters appear to push the Watershed west, east, and then back to the west again, where, at Stronend, which stands out like the bow of a great ship, it drops steeply to Balglair Muir. A final sweep past Balfron to Moor Park then brings it to a steep ascent of the fault line and onto Guilan.

The Heartland March

In the third march, the Watershed ventures into what is often regarded as the 'heartland of Scotland', with a great sweep eastwards into Badenoch. At an average elevation of 610m, it is the highest of the marches, and at 240km, it is the second longest.

It starts by heading north over Ben Lomond to Beinn a Chroin, past Crianlarich and on to Ben Lui. Dropping down past the old mines to pass Tyndrum and almost as far as Loch Lyon before ascending to Beinn Achaladair, it crosses the railway at the head of the Water of Tulla. A majestic circumnavigation of Rannoch Moor follows with the heights above it at Black Mount, before crossing to A Chruach. Swinging back across the railway at the snow tunnel between Rannoch and Corrour stations it progresses northeast via Ben Alder to Feagour near the head of Loch Laggan. Running westwards again, it crosses Carn Liath, and is briefly overshadowed by Creag Meagaidh before slipping between the sources of the River Spey on the one hand and the Roy on the other. And the final stretch looks down benignly on the Corrieyairack Pass before dropping steeply through the forest into the Great Glen at Laggan.

The Moine March

For mountaineers and those who love remoteness, this march has everything to offer. The 330km stretch reaches an average elevation of 595m, and much of it runs in close parallel to the line of the Moine Thrust. This is a geological feature, a fault line running close to much of the north-west coast, which has had a major impact upon the landscape of that part of Scotland.

The steep climb out of the great trench that the Great Glen Fault created is rewarded with fine views up Loch Ness, and down towards Ben Nevis. From Ben Tee the Watershed then makes a swoop westwards past Loch Arkaig and Glen Dessary into the area known as the Rough Bounds. On Sgurr na Ciche it turns northwards over a roll-call of the great peaks, including those on south Glenshiel ridge – Beinn Fhada, Stuc Mor, Sgurr Chaorachain and Moruisg, before dropping down close to Achnasheen. A circuitous route takes it to the Fannichs – by the loch first, and then to the fine group of mountains which are presided over by Sgurr Mor. Across the Dirrie More at Loch Droma, and north via Beinn Dearg, it leads on to Seana Bhraigh and into a vast emptiness of Rhidorroch Forest and the Cromalt Hills to head of Strath Oykel. The magnificent wildness of Inchnadamph Forest takes in Breabag, Conival and Beinn Leoid, with the steep drop through rough woodland to the pass between lochs More and Merkland. And, with a final flourish, it takes in a great horseshoe over Carn Dearg and onto Ben Hee.

The Northland March

The Vikings came this way and left their mark in the place names, the Clearances came too and left the glens largely empty of people, and the wealthy from elsewhere sought a tax-break in the alien forests they planted. Neil Gunn celebrated the landscape in his writing though, and told us of the wide skies and light which this northland boasts. Whilst not the shortest of the marches, at 180km, its average elevation of just 240m brings it down gently to the final headland, with its vistas across the Pentland Firth.

The descent from Ben Hee onto the moors at the start of the Flow Country is steep and ragged; a last rocky encounter. There are fewer landmark hills here, though the scattered peaks make a bold statement in an otherwise flatter landscape. Some large peat bogs dotted with lochans take the Watershed on a southward line past Loch Fiag to Crask and its lonely but hospitable inn. Eastwards from there, it trails through Ben Armine Forest, which like so many such forests is more for deer than trees, and round above Loch Choire, to Truderscraig, with its many archaeological sites. Ben Griam Beg looks down over a large area of the Flow Country which the RSPB has taken into its enlightened custody. The Knockfinn Heights follow, and then almost 30km of blanket bog with Ben Alisky barely rising above the heather before the A9 is reached just north of Latheron. A meander across the flat lands of Caithness by Spittal, Bower and Slickly follows, and the end is almost in sight, with the last 5km along the cliff tops leading to Duncansby Head itself.

Ribbon of Wildness is offered as an introductory guide to the Watershed of Scotland, the identification of its place in the landscape and in history, and its unbridled value to us today. It teases out some of its characteristics, both simple and subtle, and maps out the many ways in which its wilder nature contributes so much to the wider Scottish landscape and, potentially, our understanding of it. This book poses many questions too, some of which are addressed within these pages, and some will come out of the response to *Ribbon of Wildness*, whilst others will find resolution at a highly personal level for each reader who treads lightly. The potential spiritual dimension to every encounter with wildness is both individual and unmistakeable.

There is much in the way of both interest and incident to pull together and record for the first time; this book is a celebration of that diversity. In adding the whole of this major geographic feature and its highly distinctive character to the Gazetteer of Scotland, it will set out a process for popular involvement in building up a comprehensive body of knowledge about its largely continuous wildness; and the unique contribution it should make to the lives of the people of Scotland and our visitors.

The following chapters invite you to make a journey for yourself, one which will certainly be novel, hopefully will be filled with interest and enjoyment, will and resonate with the sights and sounds of all that is best in our remoter countryside.

The image of a man in his late 50s, with a well packed rucsac on his back, map in hand, and a great deal of enthusiasm in his heart,

INTRODUCTION

is an appealing one. And so I made my way across a border moor on a January morning, having been seen safely on my way by Charles and Sue, and Dawn and Gavin respectively. Just before the summit which is the start, I was enthralled by the appearance of a broken spectre round my own shadow, cast on the moor in front of me. A delightfully positive portent of many good things to come.

RIBBON OF WILDNESS

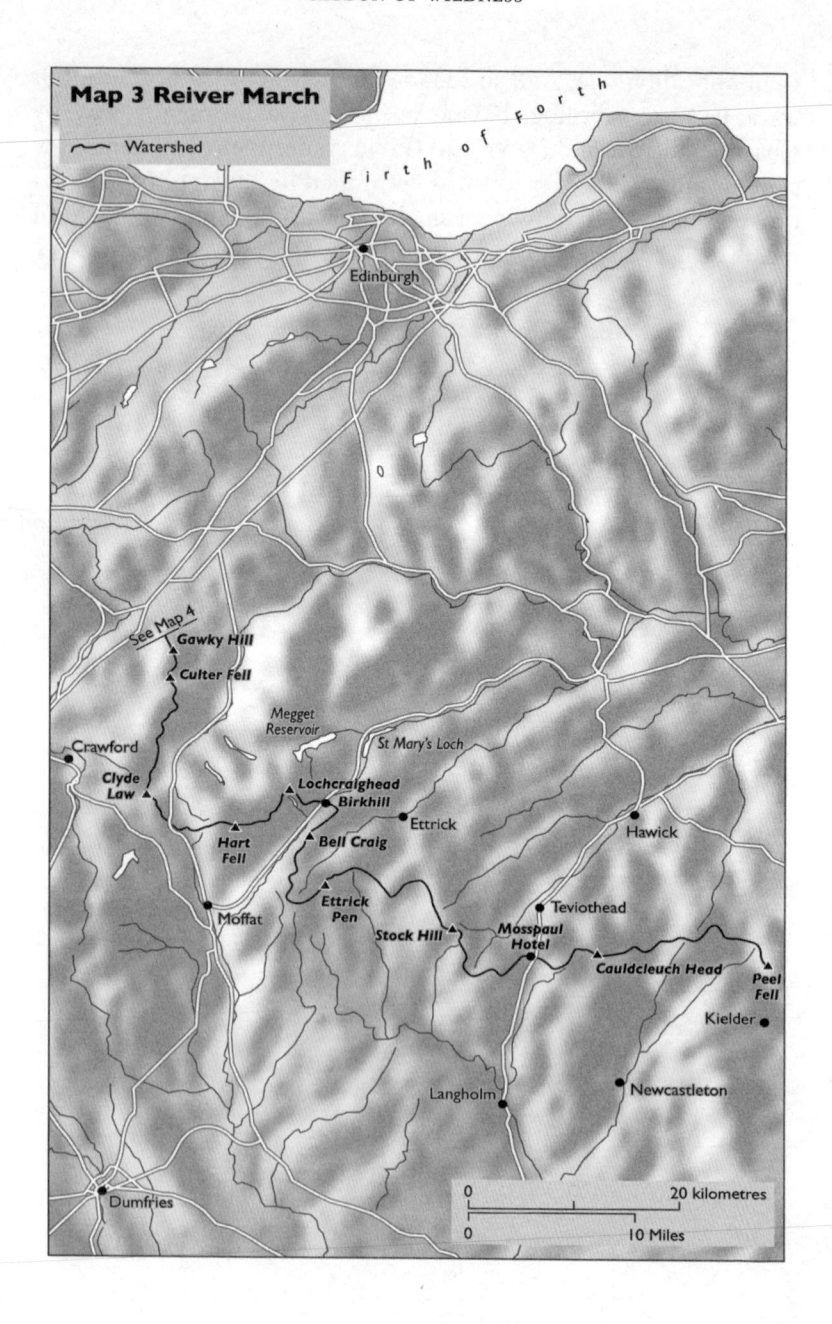

Map 3 Reiver March

CHAPTER TWO

The Reiver March

Rivers rise among these rocks and mosses,
Start their sea-wards course;
From wildness to wildness
In a round that spans time.

AS YOU CLIMB Peel Fell from the English side by Kielderhead, there is a great sense of anticipation, for this open moor is but the precursor to a remarkable journey of discovery that runs the length of Scotland. Nearing the summit of the Fell, the sweep of the horizon steadily widens to reveal the full circle. The cairn which had been the target of the ascent is now eclipsed by this expanded panorama, stretching out in every direction. The first inviting view of the Reiver march reaches ahead in many hues of green and brown, across rolling hills, moorland and forest. The curtain has been raised, and the stage is set for a unique experience in which the sleeping giant, the Watershed of Scotland, will be roused.

This is an excellent vantage point for the first scene in this epic drama, and it is well worth spending some time taking it in and appreciating where it all begins. To the south, morning light catches the surface of Kielder Water, in marked contrast to the surrounding dark green forest. Beyond, the tight and familiar profile of the Lakeland Fells stands out, with Skiddaw and Blencathra marking the highest points, as seen from this direction. Turn clockwise, and the Solway Firth comes into view as its waters widen towards the Irish Sea. The Isle of Man forms a vague shape in the horizon's haze; the southern shore of Galloway drifts off into uncertainty to the south-west. The rippling rolling hills through which the Watershed meanders take up the western vistas, and somewhere in their folds lie the upper reaches of the River Tweed. To the north, the great wide basin which forms the mid and lower Tweed valley is punctuated by the Eildon Hills, standing sentinel above those fertile lands, which the Romans, the Abbots, and the great estates tilled. The final feature in this scene-setting panorama is dominated to the east by The Cheviot, with its tail of smaller hills running off southwards.

The probable derivation for the name Peel Fell is of interest; with Peel in this case referring to the boundary or border, and Fell coming from the Viking word fjall, a mountain – hence, *boundary mountain*. At 602m it stands out amongst its smaller neighbours, and is on the edge of the Kielderhead and Emblehope Moors SSSI in Northumberland. Managed by the Forestry Commission as part of its Kielderhead Conservation Area, it has been part of the expansive Kielder Forest for well over 60 years. The upper tree line on both sides is about 460m, so the crown of the Fell above that is open and unplanted. A reduction in both grazing and burning since the 1960s has enabled good bog moss regeneration, whilst the predominant plant species include hare's tail cotton grass, heather, cloudberry and deer sedge. The animal life on these higher areas includes hare and feral or wild goats. This scattered herd of over 60 animals is descended from domestic stock of Mediaeval origin. They are about half the size of contemporary domestic goats, and their colours vary from white to black and brown. They are generally well adapted to this terrain, although they present a problem for forest owners as they can browse young trees. The current regime is benign, and from time to time, they are simply moved away from the forest areas. Golden plover and dunlin breed well on the higher areas.

That the Watershed should start on an area that is both a Site of Special Scientific Interest (SSSI), and a Special Area of Conservation (SAC) is very apt, for it is a diverse habitat, which is being managed in a way which will enhance its many qualities. And the image of a small group of wild goats munching contentedly in the morning sun, very much at home with their surroundings, is an abiding one. The views over both the immediate surrounding hills and moors, and beyond these towards the major landmarks of southern Scotland, have helped to place the Watershed in its wider context. The headwaters of the River Eden are left behind as the Reiver march moves off the northern flanks of Peel Fell towards Hartshorn Pike (545m). To the left, the Peel Burn, which flows into the Liddel Water, establishes a place in the Scottish river systems. Whilst to the right, there is a brief dalliance with the Scaup Burn which merges downstream with the Kielder.

Much of this area is covered with blanket bog and peat, so one of the early encounters is with an area of peat hag. The exposed banks of peat are up to two metres high, and these form a random barrier interspersed with the bog itself. This provides a first experience of bog-hopping on the Watershed; the first of many to come. And it is a lesson on the diversity of peat and peat bogs, for they are not confined to the hollows or just the lower ground, but have formed on the higher ground and even on the gentler slopes too. This should come as no surprise; as every walker knows only too well that Scotland's hills have more than their fair share of peat and bogs. In places on the Watershed, the water appears to have difficulty making up its mind, and so it gathers and provides an ideal environment for yet more peat to form; a living habitat.

The word hart has an ancient origin, meaning a deer, so Hartshorn refers to a deer's antler. The word pike is more commonly associated with the Lake District, but its origin is from the Norse word *pik*, meaning a peak. Hartshorn Pike therefore means the *peak of the deer's antler*. But, before getting to its summit, another natural feature presents a hazard to be treated with respect – shake holes. These are shallow hollows in the surface, where rock on, or below, the surface has either been eroded or collapsed, leaving a distinctive depression of about two meters in diameter, and up to one metre deep. The vegetation on the bottom of these shake holes is richer than on the surrounding hillside; it is more sheltered, has generally been less grazed, and the disturbed soil provides a more fertile habitat.

At Hartshorn Pike, the Watershed turns sharply to the left and the drainage to the north of here is the Raven Burn, which finds its way to the Jed Water before entering the River Teviot and then the

River Tweed above Kelso. From the slope of Hartshorn Pike, the wide green cloak of Wauchope Forest stretches west over hill and dale for over 15 kilometres. At first it looks like an impenetrable mass of dense coniferous cover, its planting structure following the glens and cleuchs which lead up to the higher ground, and seems to offer no way through. A fence-line, however, runs down towards the forest, and it appears to be more or less on the Watershed, and so acts as a guide. On getting closer to the forest edge, it is apparent that the fence runs into a narrow gap in the trees, a gap that becomes a ride. This unplanted strip of land, which is perhaps 15 metres in width, has the remains of a fence running up the middle of it, and appears to be going directly towards the next goal, Wheelrig Head (448m).

Another ride crosses at right angles to the Watershed just beyond Wheelrig Head. The Wheel Causeway is an ancient track or road, now overgrown but left unplanted. There are differing theories as to its origin, but Mediaeval is the most probable, and it provides a route between Jedburgh and Carlisle. It would seem to have been replaced by a route further west in the 17th century, and was then abandoned. A short distance to the south lay the settlement of Wheel, with its Wheel Kirk and cluster of houses. Edward 1 came this way and found shelter here in 1296 on his pilgrimage to Whithorn in Galloway. It was first mentioned in a charter of 1346 and is shown on a map of 1595. Wheel Kirk merged with Castleton in 1604, and it seems likely that it fell into disuse shortly thereafter. But it is recorded that it had a well of pure sweet water to refresh the traveller and pilgrim journeying across these hills. Nothing much remains now of either kirk or settlement; the heather has slowly overwhelmed them.

Back on the Watershed, the fence-line appears to miss the higher point of Needs Law (444m), by some 50 metres, where there is an ancient cairn and some large boulders known as Mag and the Bairns on the open hill top. The dictionary definition of this Scots word law is: a *rounded hill generally of somewhat conical shape, and frequently conspicuous among others*. Prior to the advent of the surrounding forest, it would most certainly have stood out in the otherwise rather featureless moorland.

Just beyond Rushy Rig (416m) comes the B6357 from Bonchester Bridge to Newcastleton, with its puzzling name of 'Note o' the Gate'. The only explanation for this that has come to light relates to the rather hectic journey that Mary Queen of Scots made in October 1566 from Jedburgh to visit the injured Bothwell at Hermitage Castle. The story goes that her horse stumbled, and someone tactfully advised her to 'tak note o' the gate', or watch the road. True or not, we will hear more of this royal journey in due course.

A short distance to the south lies Singdean Farm where, in the 1820s, the shepherd, one Walter Scott, chanced on an alleged herbal cure for cancer. He had met a doctor from Paris, who informed him that he could find all of the herbs he needed on the hills around, to make up what became known as the Singdean cancer plaster. The fame of Walter and his cure spread, and attracted the enthusiast and the sceptic in almost equal measure. The cause was helped by a few eminent people who had been sceptical, but were somehow converted, and who thereafter spoke with authority on the efficacy of the potion. It was applied as a kind of poultice as near as possible to the area of the body that had the cancer, and then it would miraculously cure the patient of this dreadful affliction. Two further generations of the Scott family were to practice the use of this cure before it finally lost favour. But it is worth considering that in our present day, when herbal remedies have found a new and rapidly growing market, and the multi-national drug companies are investing vast sums in researching the effects of traditional or native medicines, we may yet hear more of the Singdean cancer plaster.

The Watershed climbs from the road following the fence, which is the boundary to the Forestry Commission land on the right. The unplanted strip on either side of the fence-line, though grown tall and rank with ungrazed vegetation, is nonetheless negotiable. Wigg Knowe (491m), with its prominent communication mast, rises in an open area round much of the hilltop. The military seem to have taken over some of this area, with the creation of an incongruous

After the flurry. This would have been familiar territory to
'The Herd Laddie o' the Glen'. It captures one of those magical moments
– almost as transitory as the rainbow.

concrete slab, and a number of signs delineating both its purpose and the right to exclude the public if it is in use. Fanna Swire follows; the word swire meaning *a hollow or declivity between two hills*. Onwards towards Fanna Hill (514m), with its trig point, where the line of the forest to the left is well below the fence, giving an open feel to the area. This openness then expands to wide views back towards Peel Fell and its southern neighbour Deadwater Fell, with the clutter of masts and other communications equipment on top.

The *Herd Laddie o' the Glen* is the name of a book published recently to celebrate the life and work of Willie Scott, shepherd, songwriter, singer and crook-maker who died in 1989 at the grand old age of 92. His songs brought to life the hill farming and lore of the area for many an appreciative audience, and he wrote about both contemporary and historical events in a way that wove the language and music of the border hills into the story. He lived most of his life in the Saughtree area just off the Watershed, and with dog and crook he tramped these familiar hills.

Back into the forest, and Laidlehope Head and Crow Knowe are followed by Kiln Knowe (430m) with its trig point. Sitting just above Lime Kiln Edge this is an area of serious humps and hollows that, though softened now by vegetation, must have resembled a moonscape in the early 19th century, when limestone was quarried and then processed in the kilns to make lime mortar. A large number of native deciduous trees have been planted beside the B6399 Hawick to Newcastleton Road; these have taken the harshness from the forest edge, and added varied colour and texture where it had been lacking. Another gap in the forest beckons though, and leads up Whitrope Hass – hass, *a narrow place* – towards Sandy Edge.

The survival of the line of the Watershed has been a welcome discovery. It marks out a narrow strip of land that has been unploughed, undrained and unplanted, and retains a vestige of the original vegetation prior to the coming of the forest. Yes, it has grown rank, but in time it will be the seedbed for the expansion of the Watershed and its regeneration. This alley in the trees is a survivor that is to be nurtured and encouraged. The restocking design plans which the Forestry Commission has drawn up for the next generation of forest are a delight to see. The sharp edges and straight lines, which had an almost industrial appearance, will be replaced by gentle curves and flowing lines. Wider margins to the burnsides will replace the crowded planting. Areas of native deciduous trees will give a richer diversity, and the wildlife will return after an absence of perhaps 40 years in some places. Hill tops will be left clear, with the planting kept well back from the higher ground. And, in many places, the open line of the Watershed will be broadened to leave the high ground exposed.

The Forestry Commission is to be congratulated for the changes that are being wrought in these forests; changes that would have been inconceivable in the early days. Public access is being encouraged, and recreation provided for. Education now has its place in

A line in the forest. The watershed has miraculously survived the otherwise dense green cloak. This will be the seed-bed for regeneration in the future.

the forest, and the returning wildlife is giving good cause for celebration. In the lower reaches of Wauchope Forest, red squirrels have found rich pickings amongst the plentiful supply of pine cones. Roe deer are widespread and there is an expanding population of sika deer. Although badgers are scarce, there are foxes to be seen, or their paw-print trails spotted in the morning following an overnight snowfall. Information about the life of the forest is readily available, and new public uses are being found for these areas which hitherto had only one crop – timber (and much of it poor quality at that). It is to be hoped that the energy, enthusiasm and interaction which volunteers bring to conservation and the environment can be unleashed in the forests, and especially on the regeneration of the wider wilder Watershed.

Standing on Sandy Edge, it is hard to imagine the piece of industrial archaeology that lies some 70 metres beneath the surface.

But the Whitrope railway tunnel, all 1,208 yards of it, was hewn beneath this part of the Watershed in 1860. This is on what became known as the Waverley Line, which ran from Edinburgh to Carlisle, and was constructed between 1859 and 1862. The tunnel is the highest point on the line, at 1,006 feet above sea level. During the construction there were wild scenes amongst the navvies, who were working in hard and dangerous conditions. On more than one occasion the military was brought in to try to maintain order. The line closed in 1969 under the Beeching Cuts, and whilst it may be some time before the whole line reopens, if at all, the plans for the reinstatement of the northern section, from Edinburgh to Galashiels, are progressing well.

Railways and the age of steam hold a fascination for many people and, just beyond the southern end of the Whitrope tunnel, a group of enthusiasts has cleared almost 40 years of neglect, and re-laid a short stretch of track including a system of points. Rolling stock now sits on this new track, and in time the sounds of steam will echo again. What has been achieved here by volunteers is impressive and what will be achieved in the future will be remarkable. Such is the potency of voluntary effort.

Just before Leap Hill (472m) the Watershed emerges from the forest, with open moor to the left, only to plough back deeply into the greenery again, as the boundary is a few metres off the line on the right. But in time the restocking plans should put this right. Turning the corner at Black Rig, Scaw'd Law (503m) *dappled hill* comes into sight. Maiden Paps, which could be seen clearly projecting out of the forest from back at Sandy Edge, are distinctive, if rather unequal, in size. It is not uncommon for hills that resemble the female breast to be called paps – they are to be found on Jura, in Glencoe and elsewhere, or with the Gaelic names *ciche* and *cioch*, further north.

The 200m ascent onto Greatmoor Hill (599m) gives a hint that the terrain is changing from the gentler rolling hills towards those that are both steeper and higher. Wauchope Forest is receding, with the planting to the right keeping well back from the Watershed, and with wider views opening up in every direction. Ring ouzel, curlew, dunlin, redshank, hen harrier, buzzard, raven, merlin, peregrine falcon, and both black and red grouse are some of the notable bird species to be found in these higher areas – a rich and varied picking for the ornithologically inclined. And with the better drainage that the steeper slopes give; the going is generally firmer under foot. On the open hill to the south of the line there are trackmarks to follow beside the fence, where a shepherd has passed on his quad-bike; a modern aid to herding sheep and of benefit to the Watershed walker too.

Beside Swire Knowe (459m) a gate in the fence indicates a footpath crossing, with a ride running off at right angles down into the forest on the right. This is one of the ancient crossings; tracks which simply took the shortest route between two settlements through a gap in the Watershed ridge – though, at almost 450m, this is still a high point on the route through. The earlier reference to Mary Queen of Scots' journey from Jedburgh to Hermitage is picked up again here, for this is the more probable point where she crossed the Watershed. Just to the south is Queen's Mire, where tradition has it that her horse got bogged down. The day on which this journey was undertaken was one of continuous torrential rain, in which both the countryside and the Queen were thoroughly soaked. Crossing a bog on horseback on such a day was fraught with danger, so the tradition about her horse's difficulties may well be true. She paid a heavy price for this intrepid visit to Bothwell; as a result of being soaked for the whole October day, she caught a severe fever, and was gravely ill for some weeks thereafter.

Windy Edge leads onto Cauldcleuch Head (619m), the highest hill in Roxburghshire. The top is fairly flat and therefore poorly drained, making the going a bit soft and wet underfoot. It is also rather dominated by three converging fences. However, if these comments seem in any way negative, the hill is in every other respect a rewarding climb. The views north over Hawick and into the mid part of the Tweed valley are inviting. The Eildon Hills still stand sentinel, and the northern rim of this wide basin is marked

Queen's crossing. Mary, Queen of Scots passed this way
on her hectic day-trip from Jedburgh to Hermitage and back.

with the flowing lines of the Lammermuir Hills beyond, pointing tantalisingly towards the North Sea. Looking south, the Lake District fells maintain a familiar presence on the skyline. The view back over Wauchope Forest to the start of the journey leads to the familiar outlines on Deadwater Fell and the Larriston Fells, which mark the border with England. And, to the west, the clutch of steeply rounded hills on either side of the A7 at Mosspaul offers an inviting prospect.

These hills have names which, like so many in this area, resonate with interest. Footman Hass leads on towards Langtae Hill (544m), which in turn points to Millstone Edge (567m) – were millstones to grind the corn for our ancestors ever hewn from these rocks? Tudhope Hill (599m) is followed by the intriguing Carlin Tooth (511m), from a carlin, a *witch* or *old woman*, this hill does have a rough profile, especially from the south. It is preceded by one of the ancient footpath crossings, and Bye and Dod Hills complete the collection on the east side of the A7 crossing.

As noted earlier, the Watershed often acts as a County or Local Authority boundary, thus providing a logical upper barrier to community life, parish, land ownership and economic activity. Ancient land ownership patterns, or the need to locate a building firmly within one jurisdiction, have created a deviation from the Watershed. Mosspaul Inn is south of the line, but lies within the Scottish Borders area.

Reaching the Mosspaul Inn on the A7 is a strange experience; after so much isolation, this is the first habitation which is even close to the Watershed. It has an interesting history, having been established as a coaching inn in 1767 or earlier, with stabling for 43 horses, it provided the necessary change of horses for the mail coach. Its provenance is much older though, with the first reference to it appearing in the early 16th century, and the name is believed to derive from the name of a chapel dedicated to St Paul which stood on or near the site. The name is therefore from the *chapel of Paul by the moss*. Robert Gowenlock was the landlord for a total of 45 years, from 1816 to 1861, during which time it was the meeting place for the Wisp Club. This association of local farmers and businessmen met and dined annually on the first Friday after the Spring Horse Fair in Dumfries, to determine the local prices for wool, sheep and cattle. Whether this then operated as a cartel is unknown, but it first met in 1826 and ceased in about 1858. Dorothy and William Wordsworth stayed here for a night in 1803 on their return from a Scottish tour, and she later wrote of Mosspaul's isolation, bleakness and the romantic beauty of its setting. The coming of the railway further east in 1862 spelt the end of the coaching days here, with the last coach running in July of that year. The licence for the inn lapsed in 1865, and the building gradually fell into a derelict state.

However, a company was formed in 1899 with the purpose of building a new inn to cater for the large numbers of people who had taken to riding bicycles as a means of transport and recreation. At the opening ceremony, several thousand people, many of them cyclists, turned out to witness and share in the occasion. Mosspaul Inn had entered a new era. As the 20th century progressed, the advent of motor transport continued the revival of this hostelry, and at one time it also boasted a bowling green and filling station. A caravan site still occupies a small field to the side. The building has been altered and extended over the years, and has lost its Edwardian charm, but in season it still caters for travellers on this high pass.

The link with travel on horseback continues though, when each June the Mosspaul Ride-out takes place as part of the Hawick Common Riding. This involves as many as will take part, riding on an arduous 24-mile round trip over hill and moor. At the inn there is then due ceremony and refreshment before the return journey. Those who participate in this traditional event, which has run for over 100 years, become members of the Ancient Order of Mosstroopers, a reference to the much older days of reiving and marking-out the local territorial boundaries.

This clutch of hills continues with Comb Hill (513m), Wisp Hill (595m), with its trig point and ancient cairn, and Ewenshope Fell (493m). The strangely named Ewes Doors follows, which is perhaps a reference to a narrow gap in the hills that opens south to the Eweslees Burn. The Elliots and Scotts had a skirmish here in 1566, in which a number of the Scotts were killed. This incident brings the reiving and local strife of the period right onto the Watershed. An ancient mound on the shoulder which leads onto Pikethaw Hill (564m), and the widely-held belief that there was a pre-Reformation chapel in the area suggests a place which had greater significance in the past. Piket would appear to refer to *skinny* or *gaunt*, and it is indeed part of a pronounced and narrow ridge. Rashiegrain Height (507m), Corbie Shank, and Causeway Grain Head (490m) complete this section with its open steep sided hills. The close link between hill or place names and wildlife is one of the recurring themes on this journey, and this is evident in the name

Corbie Shank, with the word *corbie* being the Scottish name for raven or hooded crow.

The entire length of the River Tweed and most of its tributaries right up to their source at the Watershed are protected as SSSI – a very linear 2,597 hectares of designated water-course, river and burn bank. There are seven locations in which this SSSI comes to within a few metres of the Watershed, and in some of these the area of bog which feeds the upper reaches of the burn is also protected. There are two such areas here, near the head of the River Teviot, and these are located on either side of Corbie Shank. They appear on the SNH map as bulbous areas of protected land at the top of the Wrangway and Giddens Cleuch Burns.

Looking north-west from Causeway Grain Head, a rippling sea of dark green with random angular patches of brown, stretches for almost 20km through Craik and Eskdalemuir Forests. Planted predominantly in the 1960s and '70s they form a vast blanket on the landscape in which smaller features are lost, and even larger ones are hard to spot: Sitka spruce, larch and lodgepole pine are the main species. From this vantage point, the view seems to confirm all of the controversy surrounding this kind of forest, which was so ruthlessly imposed across large tracts of our countryside. The Forestry Commission led the way with almost military determination and manner, and this was followed by a succession of wealthy individuals who found this investment to be very tax efficient. Companies like Tilhill and David Goss came along and made the whole process easier for these investors, and Kronospan, the world's largest producer of timber board and laminate, soon got in on the act hereabouts. Two major losses occurred as a result of this. Firstly, almost the entire local farming population was cleared, thus breaking a continuous link with the land, which went back several hundred years. And secondly, a monoculture appeared that had very little place for native species of plant, bird and mammal. Much has been written about the impact of this on our landscape and its gloomy aspect.

It should be noted that the primary reason for planting so much commercial forest in the first place was to make the UK less dependent on foreign timber imports. Two world wars had greatly influenced successive governments, and served to generate policies, structures and organisations that would rapidly reverse the enormous loss of woodland throughout the country. Plenty of trees were planted, but not necessarily the right ones, or the best for some locations and purposes. But, thankfully, times change and research to improve tree stock offers the likelihood of much better returns in the future. The groundswell of popular opinion and action demands a more diverse approach, and one that would take wildlife, landscape and people's use of the forests into account. A new era has dawned in which our commercial forests can have a number of complementary uses simultaneously.

This area between White Hope Edge (477m) and Ewesdown Fell (449m) is rich in historical and literary association. The Teviot Stone marks the source of that river, and a plaque was attached to it by the Callants Club in 1931, reads: 'Does your memory, Teviot wake/To your birth by Teviot stane.' Sir Walter Scott wrote in the *Lay of the Last Minstrel*:

> The staghound weary with the chase,
> Lay stretched upon the rushy floor,
> And urged in dreams, the forest race
> From Teviot-stane to Eskdale moor.

And there can be few more delightful comments on a river than his:

> The waters o' the Teviot
> Are drumlie at Trowmill,
> But ootbye Rashiegrain
> Fresh sprung frae Teviotstane,
> The're clear as crystal rill.

A succession of hills, all around the 450m mark, lead along the line that is in places crowded between the serried ranks of Sitka, and in other places open onto a wider stretch, where the increased light plays benignly on this remnant of native moorland. Cat Rig, Eweslees Knowe, Stock Hill with its trig point, Ladshaw Fell and, via Craik Cross Hill, the site of the signal station on the Roman road is reached. From *Lay of the Last Minstrel* we hear:

> On my hills the moonbeams play
> From Craik-cross to Skelfill-Pen,
> By every rill and every glen.

The Craik Cross road would have been the Roman equivalent of a 'B' road, as their more significant routes northwards were either east of here on Dere Street, at Carter Bar, or just west of the Devil's Beef Tub. However, this crossing was of sufficient importance to merit the construction of a signal station, which is now marked as a grassy mound beside the Watershed crossing. And the remains of a Roman Fort at Eskdalemuir provide evidence of lasting use of the route over a significant part of the Roman occupation. The important sites at Trimontium near Melrose, Cramond, and the brief northern boundary of the Roman Empire at the Antonine Wall would have generated a lot of traffic in both directions for both soldiers and goods. On a quiet sunny day it is hard to imagine the Roman legions passing this way, with the calm being shattered by orders shouted, and the ribald military humour causing laughter and banter in the ranks.

To the right, the Forestry Commission is expanding the public use of the forest with extensive way-marked walks, a mountain bike trail, part of which runs along the Watershed westwards from Craik Cross, and by encouraging educational groups to use the forest for learning programmes. Craikhope Centre, just 2km to the north, provides an excellent base for groups to work from, and to enjoy the benefits of residential experience. As the first generation of trees is felled, the restocking plans for this forest will provide a gentler landscape, with more open areas, and more of the higher ground will be left unplanted. In time, native woodland and scrub will regenerate, and this in turn will encourage biodiversity; landscapes that will be much richer in wildlife, colour and texture. These areas will provide a magnificent opportunity for the involvement of volunteers in helping the regeneration process; their energy, interest and participation in the forest would add significant value.

Gleds Nest is marked a short distance beyond Cherry Lair (430m). The name gled usually refers to a kite, but can also relate to other birds of prey such as buzzards. Nearby is a burn, rather grimly named Corse Grain, giving some reference to a corpse, but who may have died up here we can only wonder. In earlier times almost every feature would have had a name which linked it with an incident, its character or appearance, or some other association; references to wildlife are very common and add to the image of wildness. Many of the links are now lost, and names have been corrupted, to further obscure an earlier connection. But the mapmakers have fixed these names at a particular point in time, so the process of change has been halted. Post Office Knowe poses a real puzzle though, as there never was a post office, settlement, or even a road here, so why the name? The local writer and historian David Hill sought to address this conundrum with the following *couthie* verse (which is part of his larger work entitled 'Chucks-Mei, A choice of Pleasures, People and Places' of 1957):

> Scotland Sheet Five is a square o' singing waters,
> And names that are sangs, gin ye've a lug to hear:-
> Coplaw, Gair, Langtae, Byehass, Ladder Law,
> Brunt Rigg, Lamblair, Cauld Face, Blaeberry,
> And ... Post Office Knowe ...
>
> Whae named yon hill-top 'Post Office Knowe',
> Fer frae the haunts o' men,
> Oootbye Craik Cross abune Borthwick-heid?
> I'd fairly like tae ken.
>
> And whae brings the letters to Post Office Knowe,
> Sae fer frae the haunts o' men?
> A whaup wheels roond the pillar-box cairn,
> Cryin, 'I dinna ken'.

Whae reads a' the cotton gress postcairds there,
Sae fer frae the haunts o' men?
A black-faced yowe looks up frae her bite,
Beh-in' ' I dinna ken'.

They've a tod for a telegraph-boy, nae doot,
Sae fer frae the haunts o' men,
And the grey hill-brock draws his pension there,
For ocht I ken.

The telephone linesman's a laverock there,
Fer frae the haunts o' men,
As he spiels up and doon the ledder o' sang,
Blithly, I ken.

But . . . whae's poastmaister on Post Office Knowe,
Sae fer frae the haunts o' men?
The wund gangs reeshlin' throw the bents,
Cryin' 'I dinna ken ... I dinna ken ...
Unless its ... Auld Nicky Ben'.

Archie Hill (443m) and Moodlaw Loch are then reached by a difficult stretch where the Watershed, the forest boundary, and the County boundary don't match up. This involves some meandering to pick up rides to find a way through. But this is an unusual problem, and the restocking plans will surely put it right in due course. A loch without any apparent inlet or outlet is a rare thing, but Moodlaw Loch shows neither. Sitting right on the Watershed, it was at one time the meeting of three counties: Dumfriesshire, Roxburghshire and Selkirkshire. Modern convenience now has the boundary between Dumfries and Galloway and the Scottish Borders taking a short horseshoe slightly to the north, but in earlier days it was a tradition that a rowing boat could be manoeuvred to the middle of the loch, with parts of it and its occupants then being in different counties. A succession of low lying hills including Black Knowe (451m), Quickningair Hill (488m), Aberlosk Hill (454m), Tima Head

(441m) and Muckle Knowe then bring the Watershed down a hundred metres or so to the B709 crossing.

This lonely road which links Eskdalemuir with Ettrick is not without interest though. A short distance to the south is a farm with the prosaic name of Foulbog, conjuring some unpleasant images, but this is perhaps redeemed by the names of the Hazel Linn and Gled Linn close by. The Tomleuchar Burn Flows south to meet the White Esk close to Eskdalemuir Seismological Station. Two other establishments further downstream have served to further put this area on the map, though for somewhat different reasons. The observatory that moved here from Kew in London 100 years ago continues to monitor solar radiation, atmospheric pollution, and geomagnetic fields, amongst other disciplines. A few kilometres further downstream lies the Samye-ling Tibetan Centre, founded in 1967 as monastery and international centre for Buddhist training. Back on the Watershed, the Tima Water flows north from here to meet the River Ettrick, and the striking architectural form of Over Dalgleish, which looks almost incongruous. This modern interpretation of a Scottish tower house, surrounded by its offices and formal parkland, is a bold statement of someone's status; perhaps in time its crispness will mellow.

The climb to Cross Hill (442m) *crossing hill* – of the watershed, is succeeded by Mid Rig (466m), then on to Blue Cairn Hill (523m) which follows the Watershed up out of the forest and onto the open hill tops around Bloodhope Head (535m). This ascent is another transition on the Reiver March; from the forests of Craik and Eskdalemuir, to what are often referred to as the Moffat Hills. A great sense of anticipation builds as the gap in the forest widens and the views expand to more distant landmarks. The forests have had much more of note than at first seemed likely and already the Reiver March has taken on a distinctive character, where different forms of wildness survive, or will develop as a new regime prevails. The distance travelled from Peel Fell is beginning to map out a new appreciation of this area, in which the changing countryside offers an unfolding picture of both interest and appeal.

The hills which lie ahead are well over 200 metres higher than many of those before, heralding a markedly different landscape. It includes the largest area of montane plateau in the south of Scotland, and this has provided an environment in which a range of Arctic-alpine plants either flourish or have a foothold. Large parts of the higher ground are well above the commercial tree-line, and it would seem to be an area in which there has been little change: but that appearance is deceptive. The Royal Forest of Ettrick covered much of the area that lies in a wide sweep to the north of Bloodhope Head. The views over the hills around upper Ettrick, Yarrow and Tweed take in much of what had been a royal hunting forest, which successive monarchs and their followers used throughout the 14th and 15th centuries. The tree cover on the higher, more exposed, ground would have been of patchy scrub, whilst the lower slopes and valley bottoms had denser cover, with clearings where limited farming was carried out. The trees were predominantly oak, birch, holly and hazel, but recent research has shown that as many as 17 different native species grew here. Change occurred in the 16th century, when James V decided to increase his revenues from the forest area and duly had 10,000 sheep turned out on the countryside. The cycle of decline then evolved, and by the end of the 19th century hardly a vestige or remnant of the ancient forest survived. It was also found though, that if an area were kept free of sheep for a few years, the forest would start to regenerate of its own accord.

The Cheviot breed of sheep is the most common in the area, but some farmers prefer the smaller, sturdier blackface. Whilst it is sheep that have denuded the woodland cover so thoroughly, there has nonetheless been almost 400 years of farming continuity in these parts, and this has a social, economic and environmental legacy which should not be disregarded. The life of the glens has a rich, if diminishing, cultural scene. Hill farming is in decline, for a variety of often complex reasons, and the notion that it could or should be entirely replaced by any other, perhaps equally singular, forms of land use does not represent good stewardship of the land.

On the Ettrick horseshoe. This magnificent dyke gives a decisive line to the Watershed.

The life of a hill shepherd is anchored to the annual calendar for the flock. The cycle begins with tupping in November, when the rams are put out to the ewes. Some feeding may be necessary during the winter months, and a heavy snowfall will undoubtedly mean checking and counting the sheep, and occasionally even digging them out of the snow drifts. April is lambing time, with long days spent on the hill, and all other aspects of family and social life put on hold for at least two months. This can be an anxious period of the year, as much of its success depends on the weather; a long cold winter or late spring means little early grass, and a lot of hungry sheep. The shepherd hopes for as many twin lambs as possible in the flock; this will largely determine the profitability of the season. The mortality rate, how well the ewe takes to her lambs, how much milk she produces, and all the variables in the weather, are just some of the factors that preoccupy. Although ewes have a wonderful ability to identify their own lambs, avoiding major disturbance to the flock is critical, especially where there is a large crop of twins. These may be on the low ground, which will have more grass earlier than the hill, but for walkers this is the very area that gives access to the hill. A major disturbance to a flock with twins, where mother and lambs get separated, may take hours to resolve itself, and in that time some of the lambs will perish.

A quieter time follows the lambing, though the flock will still need attention on a regular basis, but this at least gives the shepherd time to catch up on the rest of life, and do many other things around the farm which have been neglected. Depending on the farm, this may include hay, silage or other crops, repairs to fences and dykes, and a multitude of other tasks. Clipping follows in early July, and this involves gathering a confused and reluctant flock which may be widely scattered; ewes and lambs will get separated. Mechanisation and contract clipping has made this an easier and quicker part of the routine, and has the advantage that mother and lamb will be reunited as soon as possible. Wool prices from hill flocks have slumped in recent years, so the profit from selling the fleeces has all but gone. Dipping follows, with a repeat of the gathering, and then the very reluctant sheep are put through a dipper tank containing a chemical liquid that will eliminate parasite infection of the wool and skin. It's also a time to sort out the sheep, remove the barren, do some marking, and hopefully count a good crop of lambs. Sheep sales start in September, and it is here that the profitability of the whole exercise is made or lost, and reputations are established for good or ill. Getting a good flock of breeding ewes becomes the focus of time and effort, with the gimmers (young ewes) being kept separate from the rest. The tups then receive attention, the best will be kept, the old will be sold, and some new stock bought in. Building them up to top condition is the next priority for the herd, and they tend to be given the best grazing. And so comes November and the round continues.

The tools of the trade for a shepherd include a good dog or two, crook, bunnet, good boots and waterproofs, a quad-bike, and a small shoulder bag containing a collection of lotions and potions, bits of string and a well honed knife. This may not seem much for such a job, but the most important are the skills and knowledge obtained from experience, some formal training, and an inherited 'way with sheep'. The hill farming way of life revolves around a combination of the seasons and shepherd.

If the need to reduce timber imports to the UK, and to facilitate greater local production, led to the creation of a vast forestry industry, the same should be said of the need for indigenous food production. There are compelling economic and environmental arguments to support our own farming industry in most areas where animals and crops can grow. The upland areas are fast becoming a neglected asset. The view from the Watershed should be of a diversity of land use in which appropriate farming thrives alongside timber production, giving a varied texture to the tapestry of ground cover and wildlife.

Around Bloodhope Head, a succession of well built cairns on or near the Watershed looks odd at first, for they don't appear to mark the highest points, and in places there is a solid dyke on the horizon. The most likely explanation is that successive shepherds built and maintained these cairns as markers near the head of a hirsel area – the traditional name for a particular flock of sheep and the hill ground that they inhabit. If the weather closed in, these cairns ensured that the shepherd returned by a safe route home. Even experienced shepherds at times become disorientated in mist or a snowstorm, and find themselves, to their dismay, retracing their steps. A short stretch between forest plantations on Mitchell Hill and Phawhope Kipps takes the Watershed through a brief dark green alley, at the lowest point is a feature marked as Glendearg Steps. This is a series of large stones forming a causeway across an area of bog. It is a quiet spot now, but there is a sinister history, for nearby, in 1820, a peddler by the name of John Elliot was murdered; his resting-place is in Eskdalemuir kirkyard. The perpetrator of this dreadful act was subsequently traced to Aberdeen; he was duly brought back, tried and hanged.

Ettrick Pen (692m) is then reached, and time should be taken to appreciate the panorama offered by the summit. There are a few places on the route where two or more rivers appear to be competing to push the Watershed one way or the other. This creates big S-shaped double sweep, and the view to the north-west from here shows such a formation. Firstly, the head of the Ettrick takes the Watershed a further 3km to the west, then it swings 10km to the east at the head of the Moffat Water. The source of the Tweed then takes it back to the west for some 6km; a prime example of the meandering of the Watershed.

The word *pen* has an ancient pre-Gaelic origin, from the Brittonic or Old Welsh language; it means a *head* or *hilltop*. On Ettrick Pen the remains of a cairn suggest that it had some religious or ceremonial function in the distant past. This is a hill with not one, but two, names. When Joan Blaeu produced his *Atlas Maior* in 1665, he clearly marked this hill as 'Pen of Eskdalemuir'; the people on that side of the Watershed from whom he got his advice about the names of the surrounding hills clearly felt it was on their horizon – it was their hill. Yet in the 1840s, when the Ordnance Survey was carrying out its first survey of this part of the UK, and the hill became Ettrick Pen, suggesting that the surveyor had approached it from the other side, where the people of Ettrick claimed it as their own. It remains the latter today.

Hopetoun Craig (632m) and Wind Fell (665m) bring the Watershed down to Ettrick Head via the simply named Little Nick – no doubt when viewed from a distance the profile of these hills has a little nick appearing between them. At Ettrick Head, the Southern Upland Way crosses – there could be a sign here pointing to Portpatrick 203km on the one hand, and Cockburnspath 137km on the other. Just over 2km to the right lies Over Phawhope Bothy; with its open door and generous woodpile, it offers shelter and warmth to the traveller.

Capel Fell (678m), Smidhope Hill (644m), White Shank (622m) and Fauldside Hill (568m) maintain good height between them before the Watershed drops to just under 500m at the Bodesbeck path crossing. Some 4km of this section is marked by a superb and well maintained example of the drystane dykers' craft, giving an image that could be aptly be described as 'The Great Wall of Ettrick', as it curves and rises across successive hill-tops. A steep climb to Bodesbeck Law (665m) offers splendid views along the steep sided Moffat Water valley, and across to the Carrifran Burn to Raven Craig at its head.

There is a story told by James Hogg, the Ettrick Shepherd, which is associated with Bodesbeck Farm down in the valley below – the tale of the *Brownie of Bodesbeck*. Legend has it the brownies, or little people, had laboured hard to help make the farm the best in the area, but in their support for the farmer they were betrayed. One night, as usual, he left out food for them, but on this occasion it was just a mess of inedible bread and milk. They knew that they deserved better, and as they abandoned their task and fled, they called back in disgust:

Ca' brownie, ca'
A' the luck o' Bodesbeck
Awa to Leithenha.

Bodesbeck Law. Where the brownie put a curse on the ungrateful farmer.

By this stage in the venture, I felt that I was getting into my stride, and whilst back at the start, all I could say was that I would give it my best shot; with thorough planning, preparation, fitness, weather, enthusiasm, and all the rest, contributing to this goal. My daily routine was taking shape well, I had found good camping locations, my equipment was clearly proving fit for purpose, finding adequate sources of drinking water without loosing much height was working out well, and carrying a relatively heavy pack was becoming easier as the days ticked by. Out on these much more open hills, after the long forest section, was having a good effect too, as I felt that it was preparing me for the more rugged terrain that would lie much further ahead, beyond the Highland Boundary fault.

Some very cold weather on this section had proved challenging, so I amended my plans by stopping short of what I had intended, and picking up where I had left off a few weeks later. Although it

THE REIVER MARCH

was still early in the season, I was nonetheless surprised at how few people I was meeting each day – the emptiness of the Watershed was becoming very evident. There was a time when these hills were much busier, but I suspect that widespread use of cars, and the popular fashion that the Reverend Robertson inadvertently started, sees climbers and walkers head further north, to tick some boxes. So these hills, the rolling border hills, are the quieter for it, and those who venture here will be assured of solitude.

My daily routine involved rising at 7.00 and aiming to start walking at about 8.00. I would then travel for about two hours, and stop for a short brew-break. With the Jetboil stove I could do this easily, as it would boil water in just two minutes. Lunch would follow after another two hours of walking, and consisted of a Sainsbury's quick snack, black tea, a biscuit and perhaps an apple. Another two hours, and another brew-break, with tea and a Ma Baker giant bar (I got through quite a few of these). Then, after another two hours or so, I would start looking for a suitable place to camp. Dinner was either a Wayfarer or Mountain House meal, bit of cake, tea and biscuit. It had developed into a very personal routine. Although not everyone would either care for, or approve of the fare, it suited me well, and certainly got me to where I wanted to be.

The succession of tops along the ridge above the steep scree which forms the side of the upper Moffat Water valley gives a litany of fine names: Whiteyaud Head, *hill of the old white mare*, Nowtrig Head (608m), Mid Rig (616m), and Bell Craig (623m), where the Moffat Hills SSSI and National Nature Reserve (NNR) start. On the left, lies Mirk Side, so called because it rarely gets much sunshine. Following the fenceline, and with firm dry terrain underfoot, come Skawd Law and Andrewhinney Hill (677m), which is most likely named after a herd that tended his sheep hereabouts. Looking to the left there is a fine view of the Grey Mare's Tail waterfall, with Loch Skeen above it, and with Lochcraig Head beyond. Brockhope Head (647m), referring to a brock or badger, Mid Rig (644m), Trowgrain Middle, suggesting a trow or troll, and finally Herman

Law (614m) completes the fine procession. The hills which run right round the head of the upper Ettrick are often referred to as the Ettrick Horseshoe by hill walkers: a round of over 30km from Ramseycleuch, 20km of which is on the Watershed. With fine walking which maintains its height well, and offers firm ground much of the way, it is a good day out which presents grand views over the surrounding hills, valleys, and well beyond. The steep descent to the head of the Yarrow and Moffat Waters brings the Watershed down to the A708 at Birkhill.

This unassuming whitewashed cottage, which is only the second dwelling on or adjacent to the Watershed, was formerly a small inn. It was here that Charles Lapworth, who later became Professor of Geology at Birmingham University, stayed as he sought to unravel the geology of this area. At Dob's Linn just across the valley, he discovered that there were the remains of small sea creatures, called graptolites, in the black shale rocks. From this he concluded that these rocks had been formed as sediment at the bottom of a sea that was much warmer than those surrounding the Scottish shores. This was a groundbreaking discovery, as it reinforced the thesis that some rocks that make up Scotland had their origin elsewhere on the globe. Lapworth's contribution to our understanding of geological processes and timescales was of great significance, and much of this was discovered as he stayed here in 1878. The Birkie Cleuch that runs steeply up the hillside beside the cottage refers the birch trees, which still survive safe from the sheep in the steep sided gorge.

Watch Knowe (605m) is credited to have been used in the Covenanting times as a lookout point, and beside it the Causey refers to a *crown* or *prominent place*. Now, it is the haunt of another small herd of feral goats, the hills hereabouts being one of only a few locations in the south of Scotland where they have survived. Visitors to the Grey Mare's Tail and Loch Skeen above it are generally assured of a sighting, though the goats' camouflage is good, and the mottled brown, grey and white blend well into the surrounding heather. They appear content and assured in their surroundings and, unlike sheep, they generally don't panic at our approach; they can often be found grazing in some sunny hollow, and a photograph of them can be a rewarding moment.

With some 16km of the Watershed in this area stretching round the outer boundary of the Moffat Hills SSSI and Special Area of Conservation (SAC), this is a valued upland habitat for both geological and biological interest. The site extends to some 2,857 hectares, and encompasses almost all the upper Moffat Water valley.

The rough moorland on the Causey leads along the side of Loch Skeen to a steep ascent of Lochcraig Head (801m), from where the views towards the source of the Tweed become the new delight. Almost 15km away, the hills round Clyde Law offer a prospect of things to come. Gameshope Bothy, some 2km to the west towards the head of Fruid Reservoir, provides good high-level shelter for the night, but the supply of timber for the fire, which Over Phawhope guaranteed, is less likely from these moors. Talla Nick gives another link with Talla, one of the main reservoirs which provide Edinburgh with its water supply. Like Fruid and Megget nearby, these waters are hemmed in tightly between the hills on either side, and closely follow the turns of the valleys they now occupy. The loop round the head of Loch Skeen, one of the highest lochs in Scotland at 512m, is completed with Firthybrig Head (763m) and Donald's Cleuch Head (776m). This area is a property of the National Trust for Scotland (NTS), and the footpath from the Grey Mare's Tail car park in the valley below provides good access to these hills. Whilst most of the visitors are content with views of the famous waterfall, some do venture up to the outfall end of the loch, and a favourite outing for hill-walking fraternity is the round of the tops listed here. In Wilson's *Tales of the Borders*, there is a wonderful romantic description of this landscape, with its grandeur and terror, wild sounds and fearful weather: he paints a graphic word-picture which is very much of its time.

Firthope Rig (800m) provides the first view from the Watershed down into the Carrifran Glen Native Woodland, an initiative by the Borders Forest Trust with the John Muir Trust as active partner.

Lochcraig Head. The tranquil scene on this occasion belies its winter potential.

This started in the 1990s with the imaginative and ambitious plan to recreate a forest habitat as it would have appeared some 6,000 years ago. The whole valley was cleared of sheep, and a process of planting started. Core samples taken from the deep peat in Rotten Bottom up on the Watershed revealed which tree species had grown here all those millennia ago. The pollen samples which this provided pointed to the 17 different species which flourished there before the colder wetter conditions came, and the peat started to form. With this crucial information, the Trust set about finding local trees from as many of these species as possible, from which to take seed and grow the stock needed for planting. Almost 10 years on, over half a million trees have been planted, the valley is changing. With some of the first trees now over three metres tall, they are producing their own seeds for the first time; a new cycle has been born. Voluntary effort by young people involved in the Green Team and other organisations has played a big part in this innovative project, and it is to be hoped that this points the way for other similar projects elsewhere. Young people can have a worthwhile part to play in the conservation of the Watershed.

In 1990 a hill-walker was making his way across Rotten Bottom, and chanced upon an ancient bow sticking out of the side of a peat hag. This was duly excavated, and is now referred to as the Rotten Bottom Bow; one of the best such yew bows in the UK. It can now be seen in the Museum of Scotland in Edinburgh, and it provides a tangible link with the hunter-gatherers who lived in this area 6,000 years ago.

The Moffat Hills SSSI on the Watershed ends on the summit of Hart Fell, where a collection of fence-lines are confusing and walkers need some care in picking the right descent. The names Raven Craig (685m) and Hart Fell (808m) give yet another link with the wildlife of the area both then and now.

These hills are imbued with the legends of King Arthur and Merlin, who was variously a bard or sorcerer; one shoulder of Hart Fell is called Arthur's Seat. In his great study of these legends, Nikolai Tolstoi tells us that Merlin lived in the 6th century, and was a bard advisor to the Celtic King Gwenddolau. In the battle of Arderydd, in 573, the king was killed. In despair, Merlin fled into the vast forest area that surrounded Hart Fell, and he then lived out his life in a cave. The location was well chosen, as this is one of the highest hills in the area; it gives an excellent vantage over the surrounding landscape, with extensive views in every direction. And Hart Fell had religious significance for the local population; it was a special place and it is near to the source of the three great rivers – Tweed, Annan and Clyde. The Tweed was known to be of importance to the Druids, who believed in the power of nature and the mystic qualities of a wooded stream. Merlin's retreat to Hart Fell would have been a comfort to him, as his former world lay in ruins. There would have been succour for him in this holy place.

Over the next succession of tops, another transition takes place towards the slightly lower hills on the west side of the upper Tweed Valley. The top of the steep sided head of the River Annan catchment culminates in the Devil's Beef Tub, or the Marquis of Annandale's Beef-stand. This is a reference to where he is alleged to have hidden cattle that had been stolen on a reiving mission in the area, and it is not hard to see its strategic advantage for this activity. Barry Grain Rig, The Gyle, Whitehope Knowe (613m), Whitehope Heights (637m), Spout Craig, Chalk Edge Rig (500m), Great Hill (466m) and Annanhead Hill (478m) are a chain of hills which drop steeply for some 300m on the south side, but slope gently northwards towards Fruid and the strangely named Crown of Scotland, to the north. A lonely cottage called Earlshaugh would suggest a link with the Mediaeval hunting days.

In *Redgauntlet*, Sir Walter Scott paints a vivid picture of the Devils Beef Tub:

> It looks as if four hills were laying their head together,
> to shut out the daylight from the dark hollow space between them.
> A d—d deep, black-guard looking abyss of a hole it is.

The place also has a grim connection with the covenanting time, for on the 12 August 1685, one James Hunter was being pursued by dragoons, and it looked like he was trapped in this chasm. In desperation he tried to get away by running up the steep hill-side, but was shot before he could escape. He now lies buried across the Watershed in Tweedsmuir kirkyard.

A final and tragic episode in the area came on 1 February 1831, when the mail coach from Carlisle to Edinburgh left the inn in Moffat, and headed into a blizzard that was building in strength. The guard was one MacGeorge, and his driver Goodfellow. Such was their determination to get the mail through that near the summit of the old coach road, now in the forest west of Annanhead Hill, they sent the horses back to Moffat and sought to continue the last four miles on foot to the inn at Tweedshaws. They never made it and a search party next day found their frozen bodies in a deep snowdrift near the summit. They are both buried in the old Moffat cemetery; this place has not been without sorrow and sinister association.

The Borders Forest Trust, with the ongoing support of the John Muir Trust, will shortly be continuing its innovative work by extending into this area. Having recently purchased Corehead

Farm, which covers much of the Devils Beef Tub; it will remove the sheep and start the lengthy process of planting native trees and recreating the ancient forest. Like the Carrifran venture this is visionary stuff, as it will be well beyond the life-time of those who are planning and planting the trees before the full effect will be seen. Future generations will benefit from this effort, and be inspired by it.

From Flecket Hill (463m) it is but a short descent to the A701 crossing, and the moor between the Watershed and Tweedshaws Farm is the uppermost part of the River Tweed SSSI – a roughly triangular area that includes the springs and burns that are the source of that fine river.

Three Local Authorities meet in the middle of the road at the highest point. Scottish Borders continues to the right, whilst to the left we bid farewell to Dumfries and Galloway, as South Lanarkshire takes over. The boundary then continues as the Watershed for the remainder of the Reiver March.

A very rough piece of ground beside the forest leads onto Bog Hill which, at 462m, is three metres lower than Little Bog Hill (464m). Did the cartographers get this wrong, or is it more likely just one of these quirks of tradition? A feature simply named 'pile of stones' is marked here on the map, as the route climbs to Hazelbush Hill and Clydes Nick. The route is in the forest for some 2km, but the Watershed itself is again clear of trees and planting. Nearer the top, the way opens out as the trees contour round the side of the hill. Clyde Law (546m) is then reached, and this represents a significant turning point on the Watershed. From Peel Fell to this point it has been a largely westward journey, but on Clyde Law it takes a new and decisive northward direction. In the traditional and anonymous rhyme:

> Annan, Tweed and Clyde
> Rise a' oot o' ae hill-side:
> Tweed ran, Annan wan,
> Clyde fell, and broke its neck owre Corra Linn.

A plethora of Dods, Heads, Shanks, and a Brae now stride northwards in fairly quick succession on this ridge, which maintains its height well, running parallel to the upper reaches of the Tweed. Commercial forest continues on the right up to the 500m contour, giving a varied and open strip that runs alongside the Watershed. Some naturally seeded native trees have taken advantage of this sheep-free zone and these serve to add variety and interest. On the left, the moors are clearly managed for grouse shooting, with a patchwork of burning to within about 100m of the Watershed line.

Tinto Hill now comes into view on the left, and stands out boldly above the upper Clyde plain and its fertile acres. This, the *red hill,* glows warmly in the afternoon sun; it is a great favourite for walkers from miles around.

A clear night spent camping high on the Watershed is sheer delight: before the moon appears a vast star-pricked dome creates an aura of mystery around and above. For there are the familiar constellations to be picked out: Orion with his belt, the Plough, the Pole Star, and the vast Milky Way stretching in one huge sweep from horizon to horizon. Beyond that, with the majesty of it all, we stare in wonder at the crystal clear experience. Later in the night, when the moon appears it all changes, as the stars fade and the whole landscape is bathed in silver light. The clarity of it, with the absence of urban light pollution, is captivating, and serves to delay the need for sleep – just sit in wonder a while longer, for this is special. And the flickering lights from the few settlements which can be seen are like distant campfires in the night.

The new day brings more delight, with Hare Cleuch Head (515m), Blacklaw Head (513m), Powskein Dod (536m) – pow meaning *head* and skein being *a knife*. These are quickly followed by Black Dod (548), Risingclaw Heights (507m), Wills Cleuch Head (539m), Whitecamp Brae (546m), North Black Dod (510m), and Culter Cleuch Shank (549m). There is a sharp contrast in these hills, between their almost smooth rounded profiles, and the steep ragged cleuchs that are cut into them at the head of most of the burns that lead off their tops. A dod is *a bare round hill,* and most probably comes from the Old Norse word *toddi,* meaning a *foothill.* This would suggest that the hills hereabouts got their current names after the disappearance of the woodland that once clothed much of landscape. They continue with Coomb Dod, (635m), Hillshaw Head (652m), and Gathersnow Hill (688m) before dropping almost 200m to Holm Nick, where a track crosses from the Coulter Water and reservoir to Holms Water. If time permits, a visit to the Glenholm Centre some 6km down the valley will repay the effort, with its wildlife information and excellent café.

Returning to the Watershed, Moss Law (571m) involves a steady climb on good firm short grass and heather. The next hill has a name with some interesting connotations; Culter Fell (748m) with a *coulter* being the knife part of a plough, and a *cooter* being given as the ludicrous name for a nose; an intriguing choice of possible meaning. The contour lines on the map show something very nose-like, and the view from further down the Culter Water presents a bold 500m high sharp wedge of hill, as if it were a vast plough ready to cultivate much of the flatlands of upper Clydesdale; nose or knife, either is apt.

A niggling confusion crops up here, with two different spellings of the name Culter to be contended with. The fell, the water, two mansion houses which lie ahead, and sundry local farms are spelt Culter, whilst the reservoir near the head of the Culter Water, is Coulter, and so too are the village, kirk and a couple of farms nearby. The Ordnance Survey has done a grand job in delineating which is which, but we remain puzzled.

Glenharvie Moss, Kingbank Head, and Dun Knees lead gently down to the sharp left turn on Birnies Bowrock (673m) before a steeper descent to the head of the Saddle Nick Burn, and a quick re-ascent to Scawdmans Hill (573m). The final top on the Reiver March is another hill with two names – take your pick, from either Black Hill or Gawky Hill (499m). I much prefer the latter, as the word gawk can mean to *flirt* or *to stare idly*. It's around here that the Southern Upland Fault is reached, and the ground falls away by over 250m towards the Central Belt.

The Reiver March has got our journey off to a good start, with a number of areas protected for their natural qualities, and a remarkable survival of unspoilt terrain as it weaves between the forest areas. Plans for the future will add greatly to this. Almost 95 per cent of this section is still a land ownership boundary and, being on the higher ground, will continue to benefit from its marginal status. With only two houses even close to the line, it is almost uninhabited, and the few roads which cross it are like minor punctuation marks. The rather prominent communication masts are intrusive but, who knows, in time advances in satellite and other technologies may render them obsolete. Hill, moor, bog, some rock, and all of the colours of largely natural vegetation are the overwhelming images which seem to sum up the Reiver March. And, when combined with all of the other sights and sounds of nature, it has indeed been a rich introductory experience.

As I stood on Gawky Hill, on the lip of the Southern Uplands Fault, I felt as if I was standing on a shoreline, with the higher solid ground behind, and a softer much lower vista ahead. It brought all the promise of a new horizon.

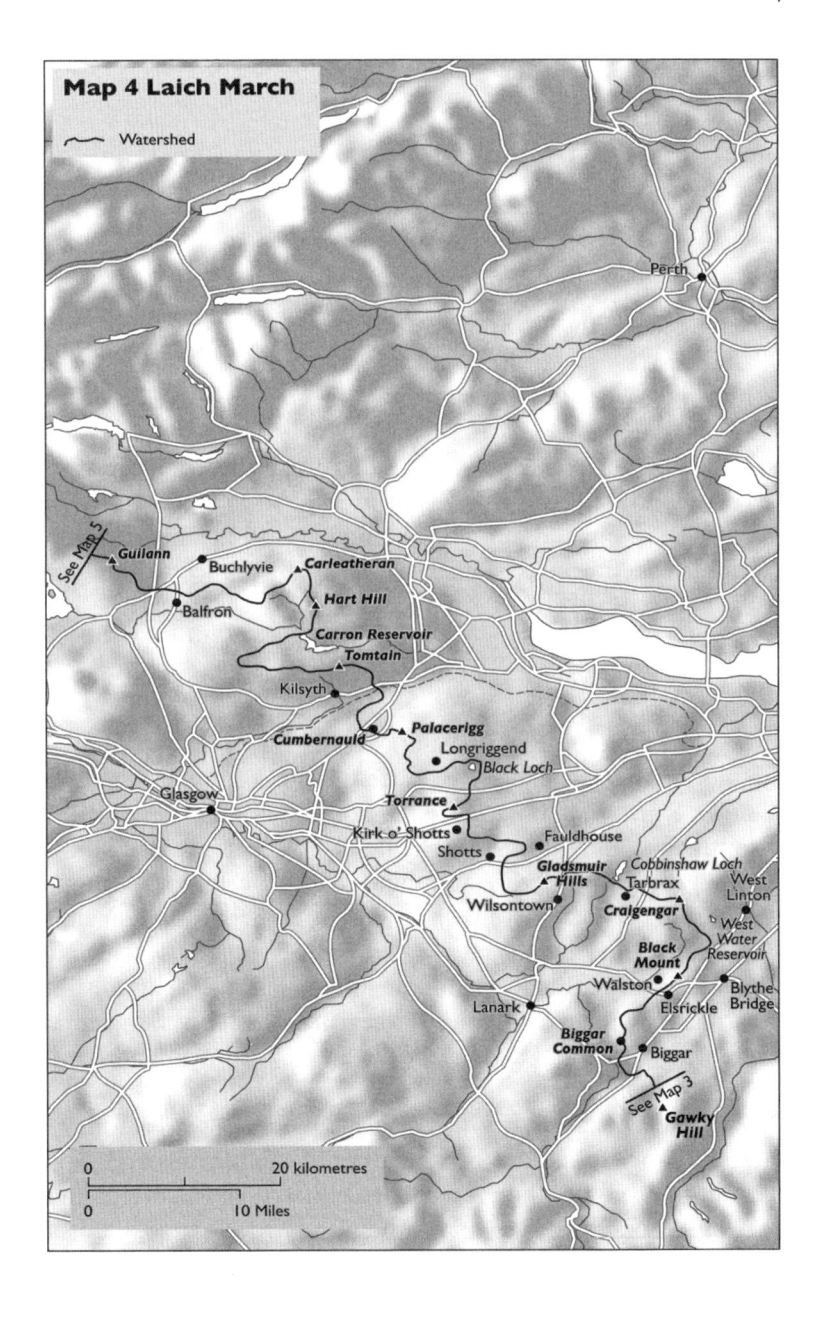

THE LAICH MARCH

Map 4 Laich March

CHAPTER THREE

The Laich March

The skylark sings where we have been,
Serenades the healing hand of nature,
And weaves a wilder, richer thread
Into the use-worn fabric.

THE DESCENT FROM the Reiver to Laich March on the steep north side of Gawky Hill is a rapid transition from upland to lowland terrain. The rough and more open landscape on the higher ground that has been left behind is quickly replaced by gentler, closer vistas, giving a comparatively enclosed feeling.

The next 175 kilometres of the Watershed's meander are across the rift valley of the Central Lowlands of Scotland, and is bounded by the two major geological faults. From Ballantrae in the south-west, the Southern Upland Fault sweeps north-east to Dunbar, with the Southern Uplands on one side, and the Central Lowlands on the other. Some 90 kilometres to the north, and running parallel to its southern counterpart, the Highland Boundary Fault makes a similar geological gesture, running definitively from Bute to Stonehaven. Between these faults, with the higher ground on either side, the rift valley exhibits a very different character. The average elevation is markedly lower, and the underlying rocks have distinctive origins, with coal, oil and iron-bearing strata. From this much of the heavy industrial activity in the area has grown, and left its mark in the landscape.

The underlying landform which we see in this area today is marked out on the surface by a number of smaller hills and single volcanic outcrops. As the subsequent ice sheets moved, and ground their way across the surface many thousands of years ago, they met resistance from these harder protruding volcanic rocks. The result of this is the distinctively undulating character of the Central Lowlands. Elevation, like wildness, is relative, and it is not difficult to trace the line of the Watershed as it marks the slightly higher ground from one outcrop to the other. This has played a critical part in maintaining its comparatively wilder nature along the way. Higher ground, poorer soils, and the more exposed location have left a largely continuous tract of wilder land above the headwaters of the rivers meandering from Gawky Hill to Guilan, west of Balfron. And the difference between the distances from fault to fault, as the crow flies is 90 kilometres, while the Watershed snakes its way over 175 kilometres; this illustrates the random line which geo-glacial time has left us.

Until the advent of Cumbernauld New Town in the 1950s, not a single settlement had established itself or developed on the Watershed, even in this more industrial and populated 'Central Belt'. This makes perfect sense of course; the exposed nature of the Watershed, and probable lack of a ready water supply, would make it the least attractive location for people to live and work. Its survival as an unpopulated strip is a welcome discovery, and one that offers a good prospect for further safeguarding or enhancing its wildness in the future.

Back to that rapid descent into the rift valley at Gawky Hill and, as the horizon closes in somewhat, the first feature to be discovered is Cow Castle, with its grassy mounds indicating the remains of an ancient fort. This motte and bailey was strategically placed to enable a watch to be kept on the crossing from Snaip to Kilbucho; the first low-level crossing possible round the northern end of these hills and fells. And there are the remains of at least six other such forts within a two kilometre arc of Cow Castle, which all point to the earlier importance of this area; one that was worth defending. The remains of Kilbucho Church to the east, which was abandoned in about 1804, suggests that this area was more populated at one time, and its original dedication was to a St Begha, who was the daughter of an Irish King, giving a link with the early Celtic church.

The boundary between the Scottish Borders and South Lanarkshire here swings away to the east of the Watershed, and doesn't rejoin the higher ground until Craigengar in the southern Pentland Hills.

Ahead and across the valley lies Shaw Hill (369m), which is preceded by a bog and a ruin. The flat-bottomed valley has a large area of bog to be negotiated, though in the greater scheme of bogs this one is at the lower end of the spectrum, and has probably been made more crossable thanks to some drainage. Parts of it remain as a wetland habitat, with all of the wildlife interest that brings. Halfway up the south-facing rough grazing on the other side are the forlorn remains of Threepland Backshaw Farm – a candidate for restoration, surely. The word threepland refers to a *debatable* or *uncertain place*, and backshaw to it's' location behind Shaw Hill; clearly it was never centre-stage in local life. Commercial forest on Shaw Hill has been planted across the Watershed, but the protected remains of some cultivation terraces and remnant areas of moorland terrain on either side of the forest roads, give a reasonable degree of wilder continuity, before the descent to the manse glebe, crossing by a minor road (the first tarmac for well over 20 km), and Coulter Kirk. The current kirk was built in 1812, but there is a record of a church on this site going back to 1170, and it has been continuously occupied as such ever since. The location was well chosen on a knowe overlooking the flat lands north east of Coulter village, and there is every reason to suppose that this same knowe was used and had significance in pre-Christian times. In JW Stevenson's book *At the Crossing of Scotland – the Story of Coulter and its Kirk*, we read:

> The glebe is, in fact, a watershed. The ditch-water at its eastern end and the water from the Baptism Well nearby (how far back that description goes no-one can tell) flows to Biggar Water into the Tweed and the North Sea; and the water drained westward three hundred yards distant finds its way by Culter Water to Clyde and the Atlantic.

Coulter Kirk is one of very few built on the Watershed and the

Culter Kirk. Worship on the Watershed.

present building with its graveyard and jumble of lichen-covered tombstones invites exploration.

To the west Culter Allers House, of 1882, is the mansion for the estate of that name which lies largely up the Culter Water. Culter village, at one time quiet and self-sufficient with its smiddy and mill, now lies astride the busy A702 and, remarkably for a small settlement, has a second mansion in its' midst in the form of Culter House. The Watershed can be followed by taking the back gate out of the churchyard, and along the remains of a path beside the high wall to the mansion parkland. Another gate then leads the Watershed across a tree-lined avenue running almost 2km north-eastwards from the rear of Culter House, where rough grassland and mature trees maintain an affinity with nature. After skirting a field towards Townfoot a retaining wall for the A702 must be negotiated. At this point the road is on the line of the former Roman road that had almost met up with the Watershed back at the Devil's Beef Tub, but they diverge quickly, with the Roman road heading for the woodland at the back of Kirkwood House.

The Watershed now experiences its first encounter with more fertile farmland as it travels north across fields and through woodland to meet the A72 just east of Wolfclyde. The *Ribbon of Wildness* here becomes a bit threadbare, where the wild link is dependent upon field boundary hedgerows and hilltop woods. This is a candidate for action in the future, to more clearly mark the Watershed and enhance its wildness with strategic planting.

Another field follows the crossing by the A72, and then comes the track bed of the former railway which closed in 1950. At this point the Watershed is a mere half-kilometre from the River Clyde, and the area of bog which it crosses is of particular interest. Sir Archibald Geikie, the pioneer of much of our geological understanding, maintained that there were at one time two Clydes. The upper river flowed east from here through the Biggar Gap to join the Tweed at Rachan, whilst the lower Clyde started its journey somewhere near the Falls of Clyde – though clearly as a much smaller river than the present one. Time and erosion found the two Clydes unite at Wolfclyde, and thus formed the river we know today. A number of writers have asserted that, at times of extreme flood, some water will spill from the Clyde across the modestly higher ground lying between Wolfclyde and Causewayend (now forming the Watershed), and find its way to the Tweed via the Biggar Water. This higher ground on the bog reaches no more than 3m above the level of the Clyde, and is therefore only a minor barrier. The level of the Clyde is about 199m, the bog just over 201m, and then the Biggar Water runs for some 3km at 197m eastwards from Fir Knowe. Major drainage works in the 18th century gradually transformed an extensive area of bog between Biggar and Broughton into productive farmland. The point at which the Biggar Water enters the Tweed is at 186m, a drop of only 15 metres over a distance of some 12 kilometres.

The normal course for a river, is for it to flow away from the Watershed, getting progressively further from it, as it gathers more volume and strength. So the Clyde's return to within a kilometre or so of the Watershed here, is most unusual. During the evolution of Scotland's river systems, what we now call the upper Clyde flowed east into the Tweed from here – had that persisted to the present day, the location of the Watershed would be rather different. This observation would undoubtedly hold true for a number of other river locations too, but we must take them as they are, with a degree of certainty that imminent change, is unlikely.

The minor road with barbed wire fences on either side is crossed, presenting either a challenge or the need to look for a nearby gate. A field is quickly followed by the ascent to Biggar Common, where the views open out and the terrain gets rougher underfoot. Biggar (meaning *soft land*) was elevated to the status of a Royal Burgh in 1451, and Biggar Common (388m) which, as the name implies, was at one time the common grazing, has been the site of occupation and human activity as far back as Mesolithic times. The current mix of moorland and commercial forest is comparatively recent though. The same storm that on the night of 28 December 1879 put paid to the Tay Bridge also decimated the mature forest that covered much of Biggar Common. More recently, some of it has been planted with commercial conifers, but much remains open moorland with heather and whin, rough grassland and a rich array of wild flowers throughout the summer season.

Deep-ploughing the land in preparation for planting in 1986 revealed some tantalising evidence of potential archaeological interest, which in turn prompted a number of field-walking surveys and subsequent excavations. A wide scatter of remains was found, and a number of damaged cairns were then excavated. These activities have shown that this elevated plateau was extensively used in the Mesolithic period. The empty moorland and forest of today gives a deceptive impression of its appeal to our earlier ancestors. This is by no means unique, as just about every hill top hereabouts has a cairn or fort on its highest point, often with evidence of settlement nearby; all pointing to a long period of extensive human habitation.

Fences present a frequent and varied array of barriers on the Laich March, later on the Northland March too, and I offer snippets of advice on dealing with this inconvenience along the way. I'm not damning fences altogether though; as it appeared the fenceline had been the saviour of the Watershed on the forest sections this March. But fences need to be addressed, both practically, and for what they represent. Fences are there for a purpose for both farmer and forester, and they are a costly item which will eventually deteriorate and require replacement. Walkers on the Watershed need to be mindful of this, as fences play a significant part in people's livelihoods; fences are to be treated with a bit of respect. And fences can fight back too! Delicate skin can be sharply abused with rusty barbs, and expensive outdoor clothing can easily come to grief. The point, at which you are astride the fence, when you are on neither one side nor the other, is the most delicate. So, taking all of these factors into consideration, my advice would always be to find a gate if there is one anywhere near to hand; no-one will think less of you for such a minor waver from the Watershed.

Where there is no alternative, the advice is to cross with care and in such a way as will cause no damage to either you, or more importantly, the fence – it is part of someone's livelihood. So, with rucksack off and lobbed over the top, walking poles poked through the lower wires, pick a location where the fence-posts are secure and wobble-free. Then climb over with due regard to the dangers listed above, retrieve rucksack and poles, and proceed in the knowledge that your actions have not been harmful. I will return to fences though, as they are a recurrent theme.

A number of farm steadings and houses lie on either side of the Watershed, as it heads towards Black Mount (516m), with fields, rough grazing and areas of woodland, where it is characterised by gently rolling countryside. The unoccupied nature of the line itself is only interrupted by the ancient cairn on Hyndshawland (308m) where the catchment of the Medwin Water starts, and the cottage at Harperhall, which is surrounded by acres of Christmas tree plantations. The need for weaving more wildness into the picture is evident along this stretch of the Watershed where the random areas of woodland would benefit from some additional planting of strips of native trees and hedgerows. This would give the rather threadbare *Ribbon of Wildness* more substance, and hence provide a more diverse habitat for birdlife and all that follows.

The River Clyde now swings west, as the Watershed moves north-east, but its catchment will continue to dominate the western side for a considerable distance yet, with the South and North Medwin Waters in this immediate area. These last few kilometres of the Tweed catchment will shortly call for a fond farewell to this familiar friend.

Walston School sits in an elevated and unlikely location almost on the Watershed, and serves a wide rural area including Walston on the one hand and Elsrickle on the other. A few fields further on, which also call for better planned planting, the route leads to the moors and to Black Mount. The fenceline is a clear guide to the summit, with its trig point and fine views. The hills of Broughton Heights and Drochil to the right, which John Buchan was so fond of, are framed by the valleys of the Tarth and Lyne Waters, which enter the Tweed somewhere out of sight behind a hill. Meanwhile, to the left, the large expanse of flatlands along the South Medwin paves the way for views over Dunsyre, famous for its blue cheese, and to Little Sparta, created by the late Ian Hamilton Finlay. The terrain here is clearly managed with grouse shooting in mind; with the areas of muir-burn to keep the vegetation short. Wild flowers are a delight here and, in season, the whole hill is ablaze with purple heather bloom. A steep descent is followed by a short and equally steep ascent onto White Hill (440m), where the fine views continue over Dolphinton, and back beyond Candy Mill towards Biggar.

A modern timber lodge has been built right on the Watershed close to Roberton Mains Farm. This holiday home, perched at over 300 metres, with fine views northwards towards the southern Pentland Hills, offers a blast of fresh air for the holidaymaker in this appealing location. Croft-an-Righ or *King's Croft* also sits on the Watershed beside the minor road to Dunsyre. The descent continues across fields and woodland towards the former railway and Garvald residential community. This is based round Garvald House, which provides a home for people with learning disabilities, and is organised on the principles of the Rudolph Steiner philosophy. It is an interesting collection of buildings – from the formal Georgian Garvald House to more recent purpose-built structures designed to maximise the quality of life, and care, of those for whom it is home. It has a kindly atmosphere, and those passing through the grounds will generally be greeted warmly by staff and residents alike.

The summit of Mendick Hill (451m) is just off the Watershed, and its east side is flanked by 65 hectares of SSSI. The vegetation includes over 100 species of vascular plants, on a strange landscape of eskers, kames and terraces which were left by the receding ice-sheet. This protected area is only a few hundred metres from the line of the Watershed. The views from here extend north-east along the side of the Pentland Hills above West Linton towards Carlops, with Edinburgh somewhere beyond.

Two ancient stone cairns sit astride the Watershed on the way towards North Muir (359m) whilst, just over 1km to the east of this, West Water Reservoir offers a delightful dancing light beside Slipperfield Mount. The reservoir, which was created as recently as the 1960s, is now the subject of triple protection in the form of an SSSI, Special Protection Area (SPA) and a Ramsar site. The protection has been brought in primarily as this is a notable wintering habitat for wildfowl, including pink-footed geese. The reservoir is followed by Catstone (448m), Fadden (566m) and Craigengar (519m) *crag of slime*, a significant point on the Watershed, for a number of reasons.

But first, across the Medwin Water, lies the Covenanter's Grave, which marks the site of the burial of one John Carphin. Mortally wounded at the Battle of Rullion Green in 1666, he fled across the hills and his final wish was to die in sight of Ayrshire, from whence he came. He was offered hospitality by Adam Sanderson at Blackhill, but declined, and pressed on. He died shortly afterwards at a place called Oaken Bush nearby, and Sanderson buried him on Black Law, from where the Ayrshire hills can just be seen. The gravestone was erected in 1841, a poignant link with a dark period in Scottish history.

The southern end of the Pentland Hills perhaps lacks the drama of the northern areas closest to Edinburgh. At this end, they are characterised by undulating heather moorland with few distinguishing features. The popularity amongst hill walkers and Sunday strollers of the northern Pentlands gives way to a wider emptiness here. A few traditional footpaths cross this way, but they are not busy. The main activity hereabouts would appear to be the very seasonal grouse shooting, and the moors are managed rather too severely for this purpose. Wide swathes of the heather are cut, or rather mangled, by some powerful tractor-borne machine in order to let the young heather shoots grow, on which the grouse so depend. This method of controlling the heather appears severe indeed, and lacks the subtlety of the more traditional 'muir-burn'.

At Craigengar we part company with both the River Tweed catchment and the Scottish Borders, as the West Water flows into the reservoir and then on to join the Lynne Water at Broomlee from one side of the hill, and Linhouse Water which joins the River Almond in Mid Calder flowing from the other side. The journey so far, running almost two thirds of the way round the headwaters of the River Tweed catchment, has covered some 162km from its start back on Hartshorn Pike and Craigengar is where the Watershed enters the Central Scotland Forest (CSF). To the right is the start of West Lothian, and this point is also the start of 328 hectares of SSSI with part SAC, of which 3.5km is on the Watershed. This area, which includes Bawdy Moss, is protected as upland heath and raised bog, with dry heath on the hill. One of the particularly pleasing discoveries in plotting the Watershed has been the number of SSSIs and other forms of designation, especially on the Laich March in this area. When taken along with the extensive Central Scotland Forest area, it becomes clear that over 50 per cent of this March is protected, or enjoys a proactive approach to its environmental regeneration, which will bring further biodiversity to the area in the future.

Maiden Hill overlooks the road with the strange name of the 'Lang Whang', otherwise known officially as the A70. 'Lang Whang' is seen to refer to a long stretch of narrow empty road – in this case from Balerno to Carnwath. A 'whang' is also a leather bootlace, so perhaps someone in the dim and distant past surmised that this road, which covers almost 20 miles almost devoid of any settlement other than the occasional farmhouse, looked a bit like a bootlace laid on the map. This is immediately followed by the 493 hectare Tarbrax SSSI, of which just over 1km is on the Watershed. This is a peat-land moss protected as one of the largest areas of its type in the UK, and marks the transition from a lowland to an upland environment.

Tarbrax, the *speckled tor*, recently won worldwide interest when two men were allegedly abducted by aliens on their way to the village. They survived, and lived to tell the tale, but the event has generated both interest and speculation in an area that might otherwise be described as unremarkable. This remote settlement, which is at the end of a side road from an unclassified road, owes its existence to shale mining and the production of oil. The prominent red shale bing just west of the village is the uncompromising legacy of this industry, which flourished here from 1864 till the mid-1920s. In time, the bing will mellow as it attracts a growing range of plant-life. The steeper slopes will be slower in this environmental evolution, but experience on other such waste heaps in West Lothian has shown that a rich array of plants – including heather and orchids, silver birch and rose bay willow herb, will eventually take hold. Much of the village of Tarbrax dates from about 1904, and although part of it was subsequently demolished, the remainder of it houses a vibrant community, whose most recent achievement has been the construction of a new community hall.

The Watershed has now entered an extensive area marked by the dreary legacy of mining for both coal and shale, quarrying, peat extraction, iron working, and land-fill. These industries and the other processes which they generate have had, and indeed continue to have, a major impact on the landscape. However as will be seen, nature conservation seems to exist strangely side by side with evidence of these activities, and the more recent regeneration of blighted land is having a real impact for the good. If we could look into the future, I suspect we would see a much greener, softer landscape across this area, in which biodiversity will have a high priority.

Cobbinshaw Reservoir has a natural appearance today, and the 62 hectare SSSI, which includes the water as well as the surrounding moss, is protected as moorland and raised bog, serving to reinforce the image of wildness. In readiness for the opening of the Union Canal, in 1822, a small loch here was expanded to provide a ready supply of water, which then found its way by burn and river to the canal when demand called for it.

There are the remains of the former railway station, on a branch for Woolfords and Tarbrax, at the southern end of Cobbinshaw Reservoir, and the debris of more shale mining beside it is evidence that this area must have been a hive of activity a century ago. The industry and prosperity has long gone, and the biggest sound now is from the express trains as they hurtle past, en-route from Edinburgh to the South, via Carstairs Junction. The railways which cross the Watershed present a bit of a challenge, as trespassing on them carries the risk of a hefty fine, as well as the inherent danger of being hit by a train. Thankfully, a metal footbridge was built here to enable the people of Woolfords to get to their station; this bridge is right on the Watershed, and recent maintenance is a positive sign as it serves a useful, if less hectic, purpose today.

Woolfords, a double terrace of former miner's cottages, looks rather lost in this isolated moor and commercial forest area, but it is clearly popular and offers affordable houses for those who can commute to work. The Watershed follows a rather straggled line of mixed woodland about 100 metres east of the settlement, and is then crossed by a minor road. At this point, the catchment to the left changes from the North Medwin, which flows into the Clyde south of Carnwath, to the Mouse Water, which enters the Clyde just downstream from Lanark. At the time of writing, the infrastructure is being created for the erection of a wind-farm to the right. It remains to be seen what impact this will have, but, paradoxically, since this involves the removal of commercial forest, there is every likelihood of more diverse habitats in due course.

South of Woolfords, at Wester Moshat, extensive opencast coal extraction operated for a few years but now the land is being reinstated. The strong smell of sewage in the area, as I passed by in 2005, was puzzling and unpleasant. As I subsequently discovered, this effluent was being spread onto the surface to put some nutrients back into the topsoil. The opencast enterprise has now moved a couple of kilometres west, to Haywood, and a gaping excavation of monster proportions has now been carved out of this part of the earth's crust. Hopefully, however, when the work is finished and the vast hole is filled in, something green will once again grow on these troubled acres.

The Watershed now enters an area of commercial forest, and roughly follows a fence line and forest track, with areas of open moor. It passes a feature shown as 'Hendry's Corse' – the latter referring to yet another corpse, but who Hendry was, and how he came to be here, is lost in the mists of the forest. Emerging from the plantation, another area of moor opens out before the A706 crossing, where an obscure reference to a 'White House', suggest either a toll-house or coaching inn was here in the past.

Just two kilometres to the south lies what remains of Wilsontown, the birthplace of the iron industry in Lanarkshire; established in 1799 by the three Wilson brothers on the Mouse Water, using local supplies of iron ore, coal and limestone. Such was the prosperity of this enterprise that, by 1807, the population of the village had increased to well over 2,000, in a settlement that included a church, school and bakery. Its remoteness from markets and ports was a disadvantage, however, and production ceased in 1812. It opened again in 1821, and under the new direction of the Dixon family, production continued until 1842, when it closed for good. Most of the last built remains were removed over a hundred years later, in 1946. In the 1970s, the whole area was blanketed with commercial forest, and so much of the evidence of industrial activity was obscured. However, a recent plan to reveal the site once again, and provide an interpretation of the industry that flourished here, has now been put into action. Trees have been cut down, and, in order to avoid any further major disturbance to what is now a site of industrial archaeology, helicopters were used to fly out the felled trees. The Wilsontown of today is a scattered sleepy community that offers little hint of its key place as the genesis of Lanarkshire's subsequent industrial prosperity. Something of its significance will be rediscovered, and the public will be invited to explore anew this area of industrial heritage.

Back on the Watershed is Leven Seat (356m). The area to the north and west has been the site of quarrying for over 50 years, excavating and processing fine silica sand for glassmaking and other specialist optical industries. The earlier areas of excavation which encroach onto the Watershed just west of the trig point are currently being used as a major landfill site, entered from the south. Plans for new areas of excavation to the west towards Muldron and the Gladsmuir Hills will see an expansion of the disturbed area. The plan however states that:

> The whole of the proposed extension (12ha) will be progressively restored to provide a mosaic of habitats and diversify the nature conservation interest of the site.

If the same approach is adopted on the reinstatement of the landfill area too, the longer term environmental prospects will be good.

Another short forest stretch on a ride along a dyke-line between two blocks of trees opens out onto an area of moorland that shows many sites of earlier excavation. But the healing hand of Nature has done its best to shroud the humps and hollows in greenery. A Water Board installation at the edge of the forest would suggest that some form of water supply comes or goes this way. On the B715 lies Climpy, a small and scattered village that had its origins in the mining days, but survives on the attraction of its very rural setting, for those who can travel to work elsewhere.

Black Hill and Black Law (311m) just about mark the highest points in an area of undulating moorland which has also seen its share of open-cast workings. It's most recent and current use dominates the scene. The Black Law Wind Farm which straddles the Watershed is one of the largest in the UK. Run by Scottish Power, its 42 turbines cost some £90m and have an output of 97MW. The site covers areas of moorland and rough grazing, forest and former open-cast coal extraction. A further 12 turbines will bring the output to 132.6MW. It was still under construction as I passed this way, and the security guard refused access to the several square kilometres on which the tracks and turbines were taking shape. 'It's a building site.' I was told. 'And you canna' come in'. Undaunted, I jumped a fence, headed across a bog, and found the line of the Watershed a little further on – beyond the security guard's influence. On Black Law, the drainage to the Mouse Water gives way to the South and North Calder Waters, which join the Clyde at Strathclyde Country Park and the M74/M73 interchange respectively. The boundary between North Lanarkshire and West Lothian now makes a number of diversions from the Watershed, and is generally to the east of it.

Electricity production from renewable sources of energy is both necessary and desirable, and wind turbines now provide a rapidly growing source of green power in Scotland and beyond. Their location is important in order to maximise the available wind, but visual and environmental considerations should also have a big part to play in the debate. The more elevated sites may be the best for wind, but these will also be the most visually intrusive. The Watershed is consistently on the higher ground, and therefore may not be the best location for wind farms from a visual perspective; and much has been written about the need to avoid planting turbines on the skyline. In spite of this, Black Law is well-sited; the surrounding landscape of low hills, moor and forest act as a good foil to what is a major industrial installation. It is a worthwhile use for the former open-cast areas, which will, in time, increase in biodiversity. The felled area of Sitka forest within the site will have much more environmental interest to offer in the future.

It may appear as if, thus far, the venture had been without difficulty, that the going was consistently good, that the hills were climbed with ease and always in good weather. That impression would be misleading. For there were days when the weather was unkind and visibility was poor, some of the steeper ascents were not easy, and

I often encountered terrain that was at the very challenging end of the spectrum. Bog, has of course, its many idiosyncrasies and deceptions, and I had frequent experience of them. Good boots and gaiters usually provided a dry, if nervous, passage. My gammy foot, the result of being crushed under the front wheel of a van when I was a small child, gave the odd arthritic twinge. And, as I discovered later, just after the completion of this epic walk and climb, the imminent onset of angina seemed to slow me down a bit.

So, quite naturally, there were days on which the unfolding achievement was tarnished; the journey lost its sparkle. I am one of life's great optimists – mostly seeing the best in things, I have a fair reservoir of determination, and I had the support of many good friends and my family. So the odds were stacked in my favour; I would defeat the dark days – whether physical or mental – and complete what I had set out to do.

By far the greatest challenge on the Laich March was, paradoxically, one of its great plusses. The areas of ungrazed moor, and those that were being regenerated following some kind of industrial exploitation, presented what was undoubtedly, the hardest going. As I sought to wade amongst thigh high star-burst clumps of emerald green moss, or lush rushes, picking a way through dense areas of self-seeded birch, or battling amongst a hostile mix of other rank vegetation; my short legs struggled. But in no way do I damn these areas, because they represent one of the finest features of the Laich March – Nature in triumph over the damage that earlier generations have inflicted on some parts of our landscape; the inexorable spread of wildness.

Lark Law (274m) may or may not live up to its name, for it is somewhat lost in a large Sitka forest, and a great line of pylons which marches across the Watershed here does detract from the scene, which then opens onto the edge of another area of former opencast excavation. This has been partially reinstated, and in time will become more attractive. On crossing the A71 at spot height 241m the wire fences start again bringing the need for agility and care, or the quest for a convenient gate.

One of the really heartening things about the line of the Watershed, is that it is generally so free of rubbish; it is largely unsullied by careless fly-tipping. Where it runs close to both Springhill and Tarbothie, however, a rough track crosses a stretch of open moor to a prominent former coal tip and is marred by all manner of domestic rubbish and builders' rubble. This one blot on an otherwise largely pristine ribbon is sad indeed, and reflects very badly on the surrounding area. A westward sweep close to Fauldhouse Moor takes the Watershed through one of the most mined areas in the locality. When I was a student at Moray House in the early 1970s, I did a placement in neighbouring Fauldhouse, and my survey project on employment in the town revealed that there were few jobs other than in the public sector and the various pubs and clubs in the village. The entry in the New Statistical Account of 100 years earlier, however, described a location of great industry, where at night the sky was lit up by the fires and furnaces, and there were boilers belching steam and smoke. It's quieter now; but there are even fewer jobs in the village.

On the seven kilometres of the Watershed between the A71 and the B7057, there were as many as seven different pits. Coal mining was the prime activity hereabouts, and providing accommodation for the miners was part of this. East Benhar mining village stood on Fauldhouse Moor a half-kilometre north-west of the Watershed, but nothing remains of it now, save for a few humps and hollows hidden amongst the Sitka plantation. Created by the Benhar Coal Co in the 1860s, by the end of that century it had a population of over 700 people, with its own school, mission church, miners' welfare society, and range of clubs and other activities. It survived until 1932, when the remaining population was moved to Fauldhouse, and the village was demolished. Thus, after 70 years, East Benhar, perched on its exposed and elevated position at almost 300 metres, came to an end. More recently, it has been referred to as, 'the lost village of East Benhar'.

At the B717 and a spot height of 250m, a trig point and further prominent Water Board installation mark the highest point on this busy road to and from the motorway. The Hassockrigg and North Shotts Mosses SSSI and SAC start here, with 1km on the Watershed. That these flat areas of peat land and raised bog are so close to Shotts is an anomaly in an otherwise disturbed landscape. It does show that the surveys to identify and designate such areas were thorough. An anecdote from a member of the Shotts Local History group is very appealing, he said:

> I know a farmer from Stane Bents in Shotts who said he could stand in the same place and throw two small bottles with messages in them. One would land in a stream going to the North Sea, and the other would land in a stream to the Atlantic Ocean.

The world famous Shotts and Dykehead Pipe Band has reminded the wider community of the existence of an otherwise neglected locality. As the mining and iron working ceased, the smaller industries and services which were attracted to the area in an attempt to fill the gap faced an uphill struggle. Unemployment may be high, and the town has in some respects had the stuffing knocked out of it, but the sense of pride that the Pipe Band epitomises shows that it has not lost its spirit. The Heritage Centre in the local library provides much of interest on the social and industrial history and traditions of Shotts and the surrounding area. And the existence of two SSSIs right on its doorstep are evidence that the area is not without natural interest.

Hillhouseridge Farm, which is less than half a kilometre from the Watershed to the north-west of Shotts and backs onto the prison of the same name, is home base to the Central Scotland Forest Trust (CSFT). About 91km of Watershed, from Craigengar to Holehead runs right through the middle of the forest area, and it would be reasonable to say that, whilst the discovery of the Watershed will add a valuable dimension to the work of the Trust, so too its work has already contributed in no small measure to the apparent wildness of the line. The forest is not one big area of trees, but a patchwork of smaller areas of woodland dotted about the landscape, and represents a big step along the way to the greening of the Central Belt. The idea of creating a Central Scotland Forest was conceived in the late 1980s, it was a bold and imaginative move, and undoubtedly paved the way for some radical changes to the landscape of Central Scotland.

Fast forward 20 years and the map of the forest area – stretching from Langbank in the west to Wilkieston in the east, and Dunmore in the north to Lesmahagow in the south, is now generously peppered with forest and woodland planting, creating a mosaic of rural and urban land uses. It is a landscape in the process of transformation by trees and all the benefits that they bring. The forest Trust's strategy for the period up to 2015 is both ambitious and achievable, and its scope has widened to include the environmental, social and economic imperatives. It acknowledges that the forest is making a big difference to the lives of people who live, work and play within its bounds, and boldly talks of its life-enhancing qualities.

The vision behind the strategy is equally positive and upbeat, with concepts which might well have been unthinkable in the past; recent success has clearly emboldened the Trust's belief in what can and will be done. With a vision of the forest improving residents' lives and people's perceptions of the area, communities now take a pride and express a sense of stewardship for the benefit of future generations. The Trust also aspires to create an environment that will in itself attract business investment and a growing population. Much of this vision is built on the richer biodiversity that the forest is already showing signs of achieving within its many landscapes.

The invisible thread which weaves its way across the Central Scotland Forest area is the Watershed and, remarkably, it seems to link a disproportionate number of pieces of woodland. With some 20 different areas on the Watershed planted by the Trust, seven Forestry Commission plantings, a number of private woodland initiatives, North Lanarkshire Council's valuable contribution in mainly urban locations, and the landscape reinstatement following industrial use, that vital thread can only grow and become a more visible and wilder ribbon.

Easter Fortissat Farm, like so many, is located just off the Watershed, and the name would appear to originate in covenanting times. A stone close to Fortissat House marks the place where the covenanters held an open-air preaching, when 40 people 'sat on the grass to hear the Word of God'. The Watershed then touches the Cant Hills, a ragged collection of small outcrops, with rather neglected areas of woodland giving way to some tantalising views in all directions. The peace is only marred by the constant drone of traffic on the M8 nearby. A second SSSI in the locality lies between these hills and Wester Baton.

What used to be one of the major roads between Glasgow and Edinburgh has now been demoted to the status of the B7066. Just west of here is one of the familiar landmarks for the thousands of people who travel daily on the M8, Kirk o' Shotts. This has recently undergone a major and much needed restoration, including its new flood-lighting, which is a beacon for the congregation's faith and determination. The other rather more uncompromising landmark is the soaring TV transmitter mast, which is now accompanied by an array of other smaller dishes and masts and on which the age of electronic and other communication so depend. Another river catchment handover occurs here, as the Almond, which flows into the Forth at Cramond, gives way to the River Avon.

One of the delights on a clear day for the residents of Harthill to the east was to go for a short walk up to Polkemmet Moor (prior to the advent of the current shroud of Sitka). From this vantage point they could see the distinctive outline of Arthur's Seat in Edinburgh on the one hand, and Goat Fell on the island of Arran on the other. Looking south, Tinto stands out prominently on the skyline, whilst to the north-west the profile of Ben Lomond could be identified. With its distant views, and the earlier reference to messages in bottles from Stane Bents farm, many local people in this hitherto abused and exploited area of Scotland have a keen sense of place in the bigger scheme of things. The distant landmarks are, in a sense, familiar, and the significance of living on the higher ground is appreciated.

M8 Crossing. Thousands cross this way each day, intent on some more urban destination.

Crossing the M8 could have been a big challenge because it is one of the busiest roads in Scotland but, thankfully, a strategically placed bridge, almost on the Watershed gives, an easy and safe crossing. It is far from peaceful, as the lorries and vans grind past beneath the bridge, their drivers no doubt anxious to complete their journeys. Immediately across the motorway, the remains of mining and contemporary quarrying have torn chunks out of the Watershed; action is needed to ameliorate the savage effects of these activities. The moorland around Duntiland Hill and Black Hill, with the other transmitter pointing skywards, gives views west to Roughrigg Reservoir and east to Forrestburn Reservoir; these stretches of water add welcome interest and reflected light to the landscape.

Torrance plantation presents an obstacle because the true Watershed has been planted-over, but with care a route through can be found using the rides and tracks. Once in the open again, the line runs close to both the Forest farm and quarry, and rough grazing land across to Raiziehill by the A89 gives firm dry walking. Plans to reinstate the Bathgate to Airdrie railway, which are now being implemented, may have some impact on the route here. However if the existing bridge is retained, it will give continued access to the track which runs north from here in a strip of mature woodland. Beyond the track, the Watershed crosses moor and rough grazing towards Wester Whin. Both Easter Whin and Holehousemuir must be counted as sitting almost on the Watershed as it swings round the eastern side of Black Loch. The area round the loch, with the exception of the Limerigg side, is a fine mix of moor and moss, and the SSSI and SAC on the west side has been designated on account of its peatland and mire vegetation habitat.

The Watershed weaves a strange route across the B825, around the back of the Limerigg primary school; it then enters some woodland and emerges again through a modern bungalow before recrossing the road and disappearing into the woodland beside the loch. The exit from that woodland is across a track and onto an area of rough grazing before recrossing the B825 once more. Here it enters an area of former industrial blight, in which planting with a mixture of broadleaved and coniferous trees have created an appealing habitat.

The opening scene of Shakespeare's *Macbeth* is set on a 'blasted heath'; an apt description perhaps for the next seven kilometres, which has suffered much. Both open and deep mining, recent peat extraction, landfill and fly tipping have all left their tide-marks in this place; a sad legacy. One notable and now scheduled feature is a nearby coal tip which has been nicknamed 'the Mexican Hat' – listed as an Ancient Monument. The prominent and uncompromising installation of a water treatment or storage facility atop the minor ridge does nothing for this landscape, and the area where peat extraction has so recently ceased is like a moonscape ... with water. There are moments of hope, where remnants of nature or regeneration give a clue to what is possible. The Longriggend Moss SSSI, with 38 hectares of blanket bog notable for its sphagnum moss and bog cotton, lies adjacent to the Watershed. And the areas of broad-leaved woodland planted by the CSFT 10 years ago have created a colourful and diverse habitat. The landscape in this area may have been of little consequence in the past, but the green shoots are just beginning to add some value to it today. Extensive areas of ungrazed moorland presented some tough walking, as the tussocks of mosses, like starbursts in every hue of green, were at least knee-high, and the area between them was soft underfoot.

Onwards towards Greengairs and we are not quite out of the blight yet, for this is the site of a former opencast mine that then became one of the largest landfill sites in the UK. From 1996 the methane from this decomposing rubbish has been collected to power a 3.8MW electricity generating plant – enough to power 2,000 homes. Some judicious planting round and on this will, in time, soften the edges. Greengairs village is sadly typical of so many former mining communities, in that it has rather lost its reason for being, and cries out for major investment. A rather dejected-looking modern pub, ironically named 'The Heritage', sits close to the Watershed at the eastern end of the village, but new housing in the process of construction across the road would suggest a glimmer of optimism. Here the Luggie Water and River Kelvin catchments take up the task of draining the landscape to the West, and empty into the Clyde opposite Govan. On crossing the B803, the line weaves past some scattered farms and ranch-style houses in poor farmland towards Fannyside Lochs and an altogether more interesting landscape. The name Herds Hill (178m) harks back to more rural times and occupations, and it is here that the River Avon catchment ends and that of the River Carron starts. Both enter the Firth of Forth at Grangemouth, the former beside the chemical works to the east of the town, and the latter on the western side of the docks.

Fannyside Moss, beside the loch of the same name, is a 33 hectare SSSI and SAC of active blanket bog and much of it is an SPA too, protected as a roosting and feeding area for geese. Such is its significance that the protected site has recently been extended in area.

Fannyside Loch. Nature excels in this untamed spot 'twixt Greengairs and Cumbernauld.

Palacerigg Country Park was established in the early 1970s, and has developed round the objectives of conservation, environmental education and countryside recreation. Large numbers of trees have been planted to create a sheltered environment for the wildlife. This includes thriving populations of roe deer, badger, fox and hare, as well as sparrow hawk, kestrel, long-eared and short-eared owls. The popular interest is also served with the valuable collection of rare breeds, visitor centre, café, play equipment and golf course, with the visitor centre heated by one of the few new generation wood-burning boilers in the area. The people of Cumbernauld have developed a strong attachment to 'their' Country Park, which has the Watershed running right through the middle of it – perhaps there should be a plaque to this effect on the bridge that spans the duck pond.

The descent towards Cumbernauld by Greenside runs through an area which will see extensive new house building in the years ahead. This provides an excellent opportunity to weave the Watershed into the plans from the outset, and provide a green corridor for the people of Cumbernauld to get to Palacerigg. To the left lies the Luggie Water and, further over to the right, Cumbernauld Glen, with its converging burns. Both Scottish Wildlife Trust (SWT) sites, these areas offer rich habitats of established and ancient woodland; a pincer movement of broadleaved trees coming to within 1km of each other from either side of the Watershed. The view across the valley presents a different picture, and a bit of a challenge – where is the Watershed in this very urban looking sprawl. With flats, roads, warehouses, a railway, schools and the bulk of the Civic Centre colossus presiding over the scene, it would seem unlikely that much of the wildness of the Watershed survives.

The original Cumbernauld village with its ancient kirk, mansion and general local self-sufficiency grew up a full 2km north east of the Watershed, well clear of the higher ground. It met some of the needs of travellers from Glasgow to Stirling; but was a quiet village. All that changed in the post-war years, when the urgent need to counter the squalor and overcrowding in Glasgow led to the creation of Scotland's five New Towns. These promised employment and prosperity for what became known as the 'Glasgow overspill'; people ready to be decanted from the slum tenements to a greener and better planned environment.

Fifty years on, much has been written about the success or otherwise of this piece of town and social planning, and Cumbernauld has, at times, been centre stage in this debate. But this book offers a particular perspective of Cumbernauld. The view from the Watershed as it makes its way nervously between the flats and tower blocks, roads and urban infrastructure is encouraging. Cumbernauld's image from elsewhere in Scotland is unjustly marred by just one major building: it's Civic Centre. This uncompromising edifice, on the top of the hill for all to see, does merit the 'Plook on the Plinth' award which it has received on more than one occasion. Look elsewhere though, and much of the New Town, which started life in December 1955, is well designed, with open spaces and woodland, and a good separation of pedestrians and cars. Plotting the Watershed through this was revealing. Although ground levels have been greatly altered in places, and it's hard to find, let alone follow, the contours with accuracy, it transpires that the Watershed at least in part, is marked by a thread of remnants of established strips of woodland and hedgerow. New planting adds significantly to this thread, to the point where the intrepid Watershed explorer is never more than 100 paces from greenery, some of it pre-dating the advent of the New Town. The initiative for this must be credited to the former New Town Development Corporation, but the North Lanarkshire Council has picked up where the Corporation left off. The Scottish Wildlife Trust is doing its share, with both enthusiasm and popular involvement, and the advent of the Cumbernauld Country Park to the north of the A80 will establish a large permanent green wedge – the community input to campaigning and planning for this has been impressive, generating a welcome sense of local ownership.

The route passes Greenside and crosses the railway at Lenziemill, just west of Cumbernauld railway station. The railway embankment is a corridor of greenery, and links with a small block of woodland east of the adjacent factory. Across South Carbrain Road lies some new planting which in turn adjoins a strip of established woodland and hedgerow remnant, which then climbs the hill north to Beechwood Court. At Hillcrest Court and crossing the Central Way footbridge it is clear that ground levels have been significantly altered, but fairly recent planting continues the green theme, and maintains the environmental interest. Dropping northwest to St Mary's Primary School and crossing Downfield Road, another broad green sweep of SWT woodland is entered before it traverses the A80 (shortly to become the M80) about half a kilometre east of the footbridge. The footbridge will do fine, for it provides a safe crossing of the dual carriageway; woodland on both sides would be calm and green were it not for the ever-present noise of the traffic.

A well-sited strip of mature trees going up the hill alongside Balloch Road almost completes the leafy link with the scrub at the top of Craighalbert Road, and the site of the former quarries which are largely surrounded by whin and gorse. Craighalbert Centre, the nearby church at Airdriehead, and a mosque mark the Watershed here, before it picks up the line of a former road between old hedgerows heading east past the two primary schools with their windmill capturing the plentiful supplies of airflow on this ridge. A footpath between the continuing remains of the hedgerows heads east passing the Roman altar stone and prominent water tower to Dullatur Roundabout, where a broad strip of woodland takes the route alongside the golf course towards Mainhead Plantation. Skirting the eastern end of the golf course, the Drumcap Plantation and Westerwood Hotel, the Watershed is then bisected by the high fence round the airport; a minor clockwise detour is necessary.

World Heritage Site – the Antonine Wall. The northern extremity of the vast Roman Empire.

THE LAICH MARCH

The line of the Antonine Wall, which has recently acquired UNESCO World Heritage Site status, is shrouded in mature woodland here, and this is crossed prior to the drop across the main Edinburgh to Glasgow railway and the Forth and Clyde Canal. Prudence must surely prevail, and so a detour along the Antonine Wall, with its mature trees, and a safe crossing of the railway by an underpass before Netherwood Farm, and then the canal at Wyndford Lock is necessary. When the canal was built, it utilised an area of wetland and loch at the head of the River Kelvin. This also involved the construction of embankments and drains, which further confuse the landscape. The most likely point at which the true Watershed crosses the line of the canal is about 1km west of the Wyndford Lock.

The Forth and Clyde Canal opened in 1790, closed to through boats in 1963 and fully re-opened again in 2002. It is 56km in long and provides a link with to the Firth of Clyde at Bowling, 40km to the west, whilst 16km to the east, at the mouth of the River Carron, the canal links with the Firth of Forth. The new link with the Union Canal at the Falkirk Wheel is a few kilometres closer. Most of the canal banks, and in some places a wide band of woodland beyond, are a haven for wildlife, and provide a narrow corridor of relative wildness that runs almost intact from coast to coast, and City to City. Here at Dullatur Marsh this wildness has been recognised and designated with the 90 hectare SSSI remnant of the Kelvin Valley marshes, and protected for its swamp communities that include species such as butter sedge, water horsetail and marsh cinquefoil. The Watershed crosses this valuable habitat.

The line is then crossed by the A803 close to Auchincloch before picking up on some mixed woodland and then swinging round by Mailings and Meadowside across rough grazing fields. Banton Loch, about 1km to the west, like other reservoirs close to the Watershed on the Laich March, was created to provide a water supply for the canal, and for iron-making further downstream. A line of pylons incessantly buzzing in damp weather, dominates the scene at this point, and a last look at the remains of mining is a reminder of earlier activity. Occasional trees and ragged bits of woodland soften the ascent towards the pine forest at Doups. Just over one kilometre from here, on Denny Muir, is the SSSI with 197 hectares of flushed grassland and fen vegetation, which includes deer grass, cowberry, and horses-tail cotton grass. The ascent is a breath of fresh air, both literally and metaphorically, as the urban spaces of Cumbernauld diminish and the more open spaces expand. A car park and viewpoint has been provided almost on the Watershed, where it is crossed by the minor road from Kilsyth to Carron Bridge, and the vistas are indeed worth appreciating. For the walker, there is better to follow; the extra 120m to the top of Tomtain (453m) – *the hill of fire* – fully repays the effort. A generally northward progression is marked here, with the advent of Stirlingshire to the right.

Tomtain provides the first panorama across the Campsie Fells and much of the central belt; a magnificent vista. In the Campsies, the Watershed takes another of these great S-shaped configurations, as it swings west for some 15km round the headwaters of the River Carron, and then 9km eastwards back across the western end of Carron Reservoir to Cairnoch Hill. A short progression north round the head of the Endrick Water is then followed by a 7km swing back west before dropping off *the end of the nose* at Stronend. These hills are certainly less busy than they were in the past. Whole generations of walkers from Glasgow served their apprenticeships hereabouts, and there were youth hostels to cater for their interest. The late Tom Weir spoke fondly of his early hill-walking days in the Campsies in the 1930s. He could see them in his mind's eye, if not literally from his home and work in Glasgow, and like many of his band, got the first bus or train possible out of town after work on Friday; they headed for the hills. With the advent of widespread car ownership though, walkers can readily get much further north into the dramatic mountains, and the Campsie Fells are the quieter for it. The recent and very popular advent of mountain biking will change that in the forest, and it will be interesting to see how the facilities for this growing outdoor activity are developed in the area.

The Watershed in the Campsies offers a fine walk with a purpose, with appealing vistas opening round all the points of the compass.

THE LAICH MARCH

As the route sweeps westwards and again east round the head of the Carron and Endrick Waters, the surrounding landscapes also take in the upper reaches of the River Kelvin to the south, and the vast amphitheatre of the upper Forth to the north. All this places the Watershed at the heart of the narrowest and busiest 'waistline of Scotland'. It is suggested that this area will play a key part in enabling species to migrate northwards as the impact of global warming becomes more evident.

From Tomtain on a clear day, the east-west orientation quickly becomes evident. To the east, the meandering upper tidal reaches of the Forth are framed by the steep escarpments of the Ochil Hills to the left, and the lower hills above Falkirk and Linlithgow to the right. This picture points further past Grangemouth towards the Forth Bridges and the more open water beyond. Edinburgh lies somewhere there in the uncertainty of a mild haze on the horizon. Looking west, across to the urban mass of Glasgow, and somewhere between Eaglesham Moor and the Kilpatrick Hills, the glint of light on the water picks out the Clyde as it changes from river to firth; the sight, or at least the hint, of salt water to both east and west, demonstrating the two facets of the Watershed.

In the coll between Tomtain and Hunt Hill, the Chapmen's Graves are marked on the map. A chapman was a peddler, and it could be that they came to grief in poor weather here, the highest point on an old route between Carron Bridge and Kilsyth. They were buried where they perished, with their graves marked by two small mounds of stone lying just north of the dyke.

This ridge has a familiar feel, with plantations of the Carron Valley Forest to the right, and open hill and moor to the left, with a fine continuation of the vistas which started so well on Tomtain. After Hunt Hill, Garrel Hill (459m) and the well named Lunch Knowe, it is time to stop and ponder the views to the south. Cumbernauld is growing less prominent with distance, its fringes merging with the surrounding woodland, while beyond, the great masts at Black Hill and Kirk o' Shotts point skywards. The graceful white blades of the wind farm on Black Law turn rhythmically in the early afternoon sun, and the southern Pentlands peter out gently where they almost touch the Clyde. Tinto stands sentinel to the south as a last link with Culter Fell and the Reiver March.

Trees and forests have become a recurrent theme on and around the Watershed and, as we will discover, this will continue to emerge from time to time. Although earning a living from trees in this upland kind of setting doesn't have quite the same cultural or romantic associations as shepherding, it nonetheless involves a significant number of people. From the time of the establishment of the Forestry Commission just after the First World War the work of the forester has been a big source of rural employment, and nowhere has this been more so than on the marginal upland areas. In the biggest growth period during the 1960s and '70s, new villages were established, often in locations remote from the more traditional centres of population. The life of the forester and his family was isolated and centred on a feudal style mono-employer settlement. The forestry industry was also very labour intensive, certainly by today's standards.

Times and practices have changed, it has become a much more mechanised business, and the forester has become more technically skilled; he is likely to spend much of his time in the cab of a machine that can do the work of ten men. His family will have found remote living unsuitable, and moved to the nearest town with all its facilities. Fencing, draining, planting, brashing or thinning, felling, extracting and stacking can all be done mechanically. Much of the work is now carried out under contract rather than by a company employee and, certainly within the Forestry Commission, the expansion has been in research, landscape design and ranger services. Earlier references to restocking plans show that, in many areas, the next generation of forest will be more people-friendly from the outset, and embrace the biodiversity mantra in sensitive or prominent locations. The forest worker will find himself planting more rowans and oak, hearing more birdsong, and working more closely with Access Officers and Rangers.

The commercial tree-line is generally around the 450–500m mark, and there are large areas of the Watershed that are above that bench-mark. Those restocking plans which were outlined earlier will see the unplanted areas along the Watershed expanded, and a genuine move towards biodiversity. More jobs will be created in the native forest or conservation sectors, much of this driven by the voluntary sector. And the opportunity for volunteer involvement seems likely to grow, creating the potential for interaction with the forest environment for those who spend much of their lives in urban settings. This is to be welcomed, it will foster a sense of commitment and interest from city dwellers of all ages; our interaction with this environment would be a sound investment for the future.

The surface of Birkenburn Reservoir, which was constructed as a water supply for the communities in the Kelvin or Glazert valleys gives back a dancing light, and enlivens the surrounding moorland to the left. To the north, lie the three related Bin hills, with their heads standing proudly clear of the surrounding forest cloak. Meikle Bin, at 570m, is the highest, but Little Bin sits close-by with a steep sided cleft separating it from its larger neighbour. And Bin Bairn nestles to the northern flank, giving a delightful threesome, whose names have amused generations of walkers and local people. A brief interface with East Dumbartonshire on the left follows for the next 6km.

Leaving the forest behind, a short climb onto the moorland summit of Lecket Hill (547m), and the views of the great conurbation of Glasgow and Lanarkshire spread out below the steep southern escarpments, and giving a stronger link here with the west. The descent to Moss Maigry, or *moss of the big paw*, beside the B822 Fintry to Lennoxtown road, involves a brush with a Sitka plantation. Emerging onto the road, and shaking off the pine-needles, the Muir Toll can be seen to the right, where a new house has replaced the crumbling toll-house. And, to the left, the Nineteentimes Burn can be seen flowing towards the Campsie Glen, and taking the puzzling reason for its name with it. A gentle ascent along the dyke onto Holehead (551m), the end of the CSFT area, in relation to the Watershed at least, has been reached. The line then enters Stirlingshire,

![Meikle Bin and Carron Reservoir]

Meikle Bin and Carron Reservoir. Where the true Watershed lies submerged beneath this sheet of water.

before a right swing onto open moor and Dunbrach. Here, the Glazert Water, which flows into the River Kelvin at Kirkintilloch, hands over to the Blane Water, which in turn joins the Endrick Water near Killearn.

Reaching Dungoil (426m) via a steep craggy descent seems to present another of those forest challenges, and it is indeed neither easy, nor needle-free, to find a way through. Short stretches of forest track help with the route finding onto the open ground around the summit. This is one of the few forest sites which has been planted without regard to the Watershed or any ancient boundary that might have marked it, and will in time be a sure candidate for action to leave a way through. A brief dalliance here does offer fine views along the northern slopes of the hills to the west. Swinging further to the right, the Watershed has now rounded the headwaters of the River Carron, and pushes east again to round the Endrick's upper catchment. Recrossing the B822 leaves the farm of Waterhead less than half a kilometre to the right. A short area of rough grazing comes next and, just missing the bog, it's back into the forest once again, with the choice of following an overgrown ride or clambering through an area of fallen trees. The forest road then runs for almost 1km along the higher ground before it is necessary to find some rides that offer a way through the more mature pines on the top of the hill before the descent to the Carron Reservoir.

Maps of this area prior to the construction of the reservoir show a boggy valley-bottom with the River Carron meandering through it, and one farm or dwelling right on the line. But the reservoir, built to provide a water supply to nearby industrial towns, flooded the valley, and a dam at both ends has served to increase further the volume of water it can hold. The larger dam is at the Carron Bridge end, and a lower one at the Randieford Bridge end. The lie of the land would suggest that, at one time, the upper part of the Endrick joined the Carron and flowed east, but glacial action scoured the valley south of the Fintry Hills sufficiently to cause a change in direction. Wildlife abounds on and around the reservoir, and in this hollow amongst the hills it is hard to imagine that it is in the middle of the Central Belt. Prudence again determines that a detour by the dam is necessary to rejoin the Watershed just east of Smallburn on the B818 opposite.

It is worth noting here that the Endrick Water SSSI and SAC starts 1km from the Watershed west of Gartcarron, thus protecting much of the upper reaches of that river. The remains of a motte and bailie structure lie right on the Watershed about 200m up the slope from the reservoir. It was here that William Wallace's loyal friend and great supporter Sir John de Graham lived. He died at the battle of Falkirk in 1298, and the poet Blind Harry wrote of '*Schir Jhone the Gryme's great bravery*'. He also wrote a lament that Wallace is alleged to have made over the body of his dead friend:

> My dearest brother that I ever had;
> My only friend when I was hard bestead;
> My hope, my health! Oh man of honour great,
> My faithful aid and strength in every strait.

The view of the valley, reservoir and surrounding hills gives some indication of why the castle was built here in the first place; it strategically guards this important crossing of the Campsie Fells. More forest then presents a new challenge, with the need to find rides, and roads, and the line of old dykes to get to the top of Cairnoch Hill (413m). Yet more forest follows in the descent, with the same demands, before a bog and the minor road is reached. A new wind farm on and around Hart Hill (436m) is quite an imposition from this angle, but from further afield, it is clear that the site is in fact well chosen. The surrounding hills almost hide the turbines, and act as a good foil. Earlsburn Reservoirs numbers one and two give more of that dancing light to the right, and the ancient cairn at Carleatheran (485m) in the Gargunnock Hills beckons to the north. The River Forth assumes the eastwards drainage at this point, and as the summit of this ridge is reached, another wide panorama across the upper Forth valley opens up. A few thousand years ago, this would have looked very different from today's patchwork of field, woodland and moss. The sea level was as much as 12m higher than at present, relative to the surrounding land, so a long inlet of salt water stretched west as far as Aberfoyle.

Below the crags to the north, the villages of Kippen and Gargunnock lie comfortably in the foreground, with the expanses of Flanders Moss and Blairdrummond Moss beyond. Doune, Callander and Aberfoyle nestle in the folds of hills on the northern fringes of this wet and boggy landscape, and the mountains of the Trossachs fill the skyline with their distinctive profiles. Winding this way and that through the mosses is the River Forth, with its ancient crossing at the Fords of Frew in the centre of this wide picture. To the right, extensive drainage programmes in the 18th century have created a more fertile plain, but to the left and around the Lake of Menteith, there are areas where little has changed, and the peat continues to form. This is a vantage point par excellence, with popular landmarks aplenty. Stirling Castle and the Wallace Monument stand proudly over the town, and Dumyat (418m) is the precursor to the succession of hills that make up the Ochills. The upper tidal reaches

THE LAICH MARCH

of the Forth are but 11km to the east. The route through the Campsies lies behind, with Meikle Bin and its family watching over the surrounding forest. To the south-west Earl's Seat (578m) hides the bold outcrop of Dumgoyne at the end of the Strathblane Hills. And further round stands Ben Lomond, meaning a *bare hill*, or a *beacon*: whichever seems the more appropriate. I much prefer the idea of a beacon.

On the long gradual descent towards the Spout of Ballochleam, the crags to the right have some fine names including Standmilane, Slackhavel and Slackgun. From the north, these crags are like a vast defensive wall some 4km long, and cast a threatening shadow over the farms and woodlands below. Slackgun gives emphasis to this defensive image, but in reality the only major incursion was by the drovers heading south via the Spout of Ballochleam – a waterfall on the Boquhan Burn. Some minor engineering work has sought to capture water from the west-draining burn, to turn it towards the Backside Burn and then the Carron Reservoir.

Stronend (511m) is surmounted by another ancient cairn and trig point. If the views from Carleatheran were good, then those from this vantage point are their equal. The mast at Bat a Charchel some 15km distant is a marker for the end of the Laich March, and an even fuller vista across to the hills and forests of the Trossachs is a delight. Above Balfron and Ballikinrain Muir, the crags lour over Sir Archibald's Plantation, and the village of Fintry straddles the Endrick Water below. The Campsies have been a fine experience with generally good walking, and plenty of opportunity to savour the full round of great vistas. And they have given both a look back at some of the earlier landmarks and a tantalising foretaste of what is to come. The 350m descent towards Mains of Glinn is steep and hazardous; it requires care.

A low lying bog dotted with birch trees would be much wetter underfoot had ditches not been dug to help the water make up its mind. Powside must sit almost on the Watershed, and, although the map shows a viewpoint at the intersection on the B822, the views seem tame by comparison with those from the top of the crags.

Balgair (183m) seems like a minor blip on the moor, but its quiet empty appearance today is deceptive. For it was here that The Balgair Cattle Fair flourished for almost 200 years, from the mid 17th century, until the advent of the railway in 1856. It is hard to imagine that this quiet spot, which overlooks the spread of Flanders Moss to the Trossachs Hills beyond, was for so many years the location of a major event with all of its bustle and activity. The main market was in June, but there were another three, in March, May and August each year. The sense of occasion and anticipation would have been lively, as the drovers started to arrive with their herds of cattle. Some would have been travelling for weeks and even months, as they brought the beasts from all over the Highlands and Islands, and the opportunity to rest and rekindle old friendships would have been welcome. Getting to Balgair Muir from the north involved crossing the treacherous mosses that stretched all the way up the Forth valley from Drip to Aberfoyle, but the most popular crossing was just east of Flanders Moss, at Fords of Frew. The sense of anticipation at the fair would have been heightened by the competition between the drovers as to who would get the best prices; how profitable would the venture be. With all of the noise and colour of the market, the scene would be lively. Then, all too soon, it would be over, and a different set of drovers would then head south with their cattle towards the Falkirk Tryst and onwards to the rapidly growing urban settlements of the Central Belt. Some would be bound for an even longer journey further south and perhaps cross the Watershed again at Mosspaul or Saughtree.

Just to the west of the plantation beside Balgair lies the Wester Balgair Meadow – a 20 hectare SSSI just over 1km from the Watershed. This is protected as a complex mosaic of unimproved grass and peat-land. A large stone at the side of the forest has the delightful name of *Wife with the Bratty Plaid*, a bratty plaid being a ragged plaid or shawl. And further on, the link with witches or old hags is maintained in the name of another big stone, the Carlin Stone. Across the moorland by Badenkep and Buchlyvie Muir, the Watershed is hard to follow in the very flat and largely featureless terrain. And this uncertainty continues to Cremannan Muir, with a long block of woodland standing right across the Watershed. At the A875 a spot height of 126m is decisive though.

Avoiding most of the scattered farmhouses hereabouts, the Watershed then meets up with Wester Camoqhuill and its close neighbour of Meikle Camoqhuill. These can be forgiven for intruding on the Watershed though, as the name Camoquill means simply *top of the hill*; the intrusion is honest.

Electric fences present a very particular challenge, not so much in the damage they can inflict on walker and gear, but in the shock and loss of dignity that they can cause. Unless you are brave, always assume that they are fully powered-up, and the voltage is waiting for you. They may only have one strand of wire, but that slim current-carrier can be much more of an obstacle that many strands of the barbed variety. The best place to cross is, of course, through a gate, if such can be found. If that is not possible, then pick a spot between two posts where there is most scope for a bit of 'sag' to be created, and if there is a convenient rock on one side, so much the better. Then you can use the rubber handles on your walking poles to make contact with the wire, and thus depress it sufficiently to cross. Earlier references to the mid-point of this transition hold very true here, and there is a very simple correlation between the length of your legs and the potential for real alarm and discomfort. It comes as no consolation to know that the voltage would cause no lasting damage.

The Bog of Ballat (70m) lies beside the track bed of the former railway to Aberfoyle and is the lowest point on the Watershed here. It was at one time to be the crossing point for a proposed canal that would have linked the Firth of Forth with the Firth of Clyde on a route to the north of the Campsies. Around the turn of the 19th century, when canals were all the rage, there were at least three occasions when this plan was aired, but on each occasion it came to nought. The canal route would have involved travelling up the River Forth from Stirling as far as the Fords of Frew (8m) just north of Kippen. From there a canal channel would have been constructed to cross at Bog of Ballat (70m), and then drop towards the Endrick Water west of Killearn (26m), and from there to Loch Lomond (4m). The final link with the Clyde would have been via the River Leven. One of the main disadvantages of this proposed route was that it would have been necessary for the canal to climb almost 25 metres higher than the summit of the current Forth and Clyde Canal. This rendered the proposal both impractical and uneconomic.

One other major piece of engineering which passes this way is all but invisible here, but it transformed the health and fortunes of the 'second city of the Empire' some 150 years ago. Then, as now, adequate clean water was the issue, and in Glasgow that was in short supply, and Loch Katrine was chosen to provide the water. The level of the loch was raised, and 26 miles of pipe and aqueduct constructed to convey the water to the treatment works near Milngavie. A subsequent addition to the water supply was added with the inclusion of Loch Arklet in the system. The big iron pipe lies just below the surface beside the Bog of Ballat and continues, in grand Victorian engineering style, to do what it was placed there for. Glasgow receives a plentiful supply of good clean Loch Katrine water. We will return to this later though.

The Watershed then continues westwards, avoiding every house and building along both the crossings by the A81 and the A811. Loaninghead sits on the left hand side by a few hundred metres, and Templelea a similar distance on the other. The brief encounter with more fertile farmland immediately gives way to moor and bog, with occasional strips of woodland or remains of hedgerow to punctuate the very gentle gradients. Bat a Charchel (229m) with its prominent mast and line of pylons overlooks the waters of Muir Park Reservoir. More featureless, but colourful, moorland on Moor Park and Tom nan Broc, *hill of the badger*, and the steep ascent onto Guilann (461m), bring the Laich March to as abrupt an end as it started back on Gawky Hill. For this is the meeting with the Highland Boundary Fault, and the geology dictates a very different terrain and landscape for some distance to come. This is also the point at which the Watershed enters the Loch Lomond and

Trossachs National Park. The West Highland Way (WHW) is less than 2km to the west, and the wide expanses of the waters of Loch Lomond lie nearby at Balmaha.

The emergence of the Watershed and its singularly wilder character has become something of a journey in itself. The revelation that so much of it is already protected or designated highlights its significance in our landscape in a way that, as far as I have been able to ascertain, has never been identified hitherto. With every national environmental organisation already focused on some part or parts of it, and many local agencies joining in along the way, there is a pressing job to be done in calling-up the common purpose. Although the Watershed is a single geographic entity, it doesn't exist in isolation from all that surrounds it, but rather its distinctive wildness reaches out in many places to touch other parts of the country, including, tantalisingly, the most populous.

Crossing the Central Belt may not be the most appealing prospect; indeed, the avid walker or climber might scoff at the idea. But, as we have discovered, the Watershed provides a route that naturally links the Border hills with the Trossachs, and all that lies beyond. The relative and actual wildness of it has remained very largely intact in this improbable setting, as by moor, planting and regeneration, the fine green threads of nature are woven into the landscape and our emerging ribbon. It binds the gentler wildness across the rift valley; it is the missing link.

RIBBON OF WILDNESS

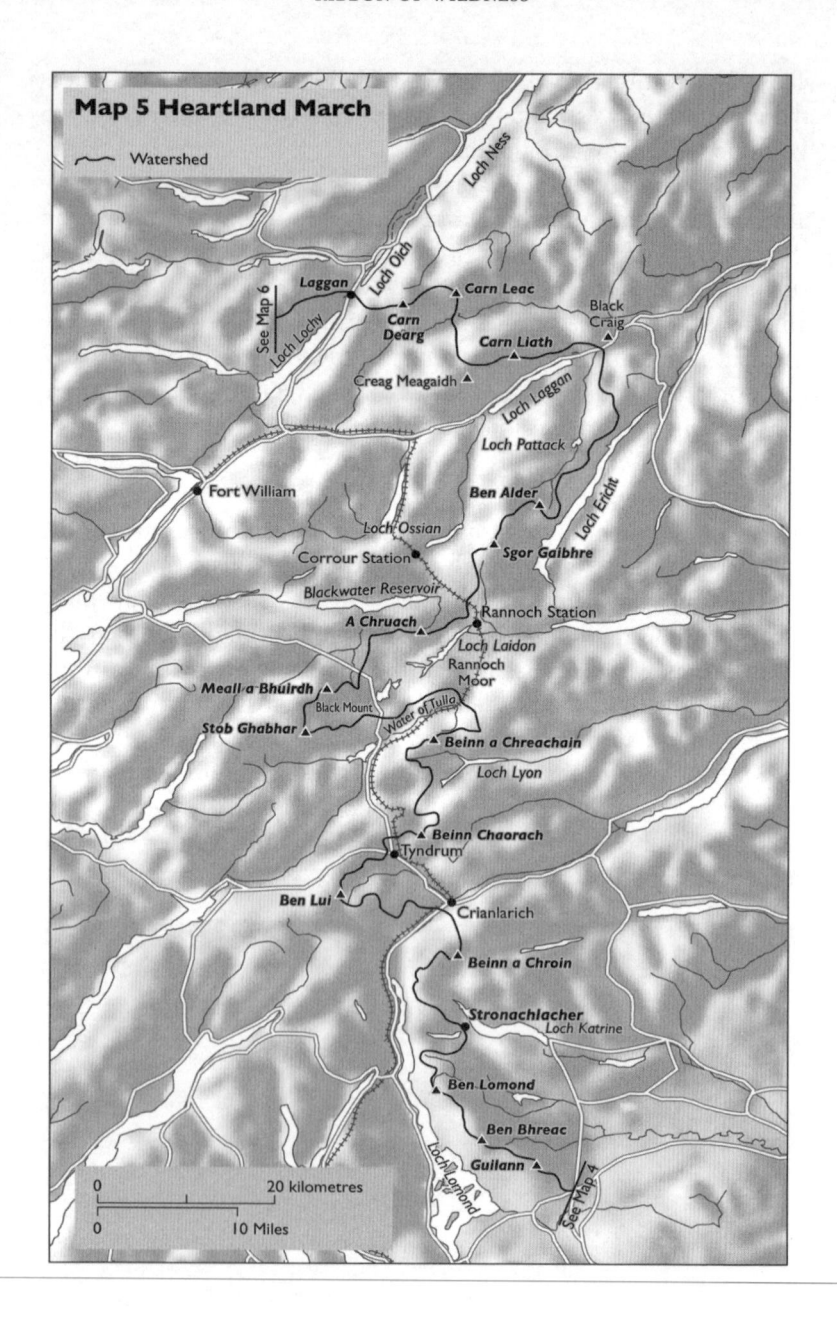

CHAPTER FOUR

The Heartland March

> So many familiar friends amongst these peaks and moors –
> Prompting memories and tales of great days-out;
> Now a new dimension unfolds in the quest
> For the invisible ribbon.

FOR THOSE WHO love Scotland's mountain environment, the Heartland March will come as welcome change from the less rugged, but none the less appealing, Reiver and Laich Marches. At an average elevation of just over 600m, and 240km in length, it offers a journey through both familiar landscapes and challenging terrain. Generations of hill walkers have found this general area easy to access from the main centres of population in the Central Belt, and enjoyed all of the delights and demands which these mountains presented. For those who enjoy looking rather than doing, the landmarks are well known too, as the West Highland Railway Line crosses and recrosses the Watershed five times. The A82 trunk road makes a similar number of crossings as it heads for Glencoe and beyond. And the West Highland Way passes within 2km of the start of this March, and subsequently crosses the Watershed at a further four locations on the journey north. So, by train, coach, car, and bike and on foot, there is regular point of contact to be had with the Heartland March.

A number of the most popular mountains in Scotland are to be found on this section of the Watershed. Whether it be for the *once in a lifetime* ascent of Ben Lomond, or some winter climbing on Ben Lui, or perhaps to experience a sense of remoteness on Ben Alder, the mountain experiences to be had in this area offer great rewards. They bring a feeling of more tangible wildness to the picture;

whether that is measured by what is there, or by what is missing, the conclusion would be the same. The wide views and the natural beauty of the terrain give a real experience of nature in the wild. In winter there would be few other footsteps in the snow, and in summer a distant figure somehow emphasises the solitude. The mountain hare may be cautious at our presence, but he is evidence (if such were needed) of the increasingly elevated environment that the Watershed has entered in the Heartland March.

The Highland Boundary Fault is a striking feature in the landscape, and the immediate increase in elevation moving northwards in this area is in the order of 150m. From Guilann the view across the southern end of Loch Lomond is a delight; the shores are forest-fringed, and boast a number of notable wetland habitats in places. The wooded islands stand out green against the blue or lighter waters of the loch. A distinctive image is the line of four islands which point decisively towards Arden on the western shore; Inchcailloch, Torrinch, Creinch, and Inchmurrin form a clear succession of hills poking out of the loch, and the pattern is continued on this side of the loch with Breac Leac and Conic Hill rising clear of the moorland. Turn through 180 degrees, face the other way towards the Menteith Hills, and another line of hills almost protrude from the green mat of Loch Ard Forest: Lime Hill, Drum of Clashmore and Ardrum draw another straight line running north-east. This is the Highland Boundary Fault, which starts in the vicinity of the island of Bute, and sweeps cleanly across Scotland to disappear under the waves of the North Sea at Stonehaven.

I was surprised to find little evidence of others having passed this way, for although Ben Lomond (974m) is amongst the most climbed mountains in Scotland, many of its neighbours are largely neglected. The ridge running along the eastern side of Loch Lomond would seem to offer a magnificent outing with relatively easy going most of the way. Guilann (461m) *the shoulder*, Stob a Chion Duibh, Beinn Bhreac (577m), Beinn Uird (597m) and Elrig provide a 12km succession of tops leading to Ben Lomond itself. Cashel Farm on the slopes of Beinn Bhreac is now billed as *The Forest for a Thousand*

Years by the Royal Scottish Forestry Society. This ambitious project is its' Millennium initiative, and the aim is to create a native forest running from the shores of the loch to the mountaintop, with the variety of different habitats that will entail.

The advent, in 2002, of the Loch Lomond and Trossachs National Park came after many years of debate about the need for National Parks in Scotland. The Watershed is quite literally the natural link between the two such National Parks, and the aims for the Park Authorities are:

- To conserve and enhance the natural and cultural heritage of the area.
- To promote sustainable use of the natural resources of the area.
- To promote understanding and enjoyment (including enjoyment in the form of recreation) of the special qualities of the area by the public.
- To promote sustainable economic and social development of the area's communities.

The Park Authority has to wrestle with the often conflicting interests which each of these aims stimulates. Not a year goes by without heated controversy in the press about the rights (or otherwise) of those who wish to drive speed boats on the loch, and every proposed development seems to carry with it lively argument about the apparent merits of catering for the car-borne public. Add signposting and way-marking, the need for jobs, quality of service, publicity and perception to the fray, and the passions will rise. Although Cairngorms National Park, which came a year later, generates many of the same issues, it doesn't have the issue of half of the population of Scotland living right on its doorstep. This factor creates its own special range of pressures and expectation.

I am very much with the need for the park in the first place, even if the Park Authority faces a difficult task in reconciling all of the conflicting interests, the park sits firmly astride Watershed, and takes in some very fine landscapes. Their beauty touches on the paradox of natural: man-made, or man-altered, but that is a familiar theme in many other locations. What seems important here is that there should always be a net gain to the landscape quality, and many of the 'developments' hereabouts seem to be achieving just that. A combination of Cashel Farm, the work of the National Trust for Scotland on and around Ben Lomond, SNH's designated woodland areas, the RSPB and its care for bird habitats, the Park Authority, and a plethora of small environmental groups, are all working together and doing their bit.

The view of the park from the ridge running ever higher towards the summit of Ben Lomond is fine, and seems far from any controversy; the only passion it raises is a love of wild places and all that they represent.

Beyond the dark green carpet of forest to the right lies the rim of the upper Forth catchment area and the hills that had first appeared from back at Carleatheran in the Campsies. The view along the north side of the Ochil Hills points the eye down Strathearn to somewhere near Forgandenny. The panorama along the western side of this ridge takes the eye from Loch Lomond to the hills beyond. Somewhere in their folds, lie the sea lochs of Goil, Gare and Long. As the light changes, the loch gives back so many different shades and patterns; its only constant is variety.

This is the point at which Scotland was once only 16 kilometres wide – 11,000 years ago the sea lapped on a shore just west of Aberfoyle, and Loch Lomond was a sea loch. The higher sea levels of the time created a somewhat different environment, but any anxiety that the top two thirds of Scotland could have been separated and formed the island of Highland Scotland can be dispelled, for it would have taken another million years or more to glacially grind away the 380m high ridge at Moine Eich which separated the sea loch to the left (Lomond) from the sea loch to the right (Forth). However, it is interesting to speculate on the very different Scotland we would inhabit if such a change had occurred.

As the Loch Lomond and Trossachs National Park embraces the Watershed – or perhaps it is it the other way round – a wealth

Peel Fell. The starting point, on the Kielderhead and Emblehope Moors SSSI, and home to a herd of apparently contented feral goats. Looking north-east across the lower Tweed Valley.

Greatmoor Hill from Cauldcleuch Head. Fence-line on the Watershed, with forest on one side and rolling open moor on the other, and Maiden Pap in the distance.

Craik Cross crossing. Where the Roman Legions passed en route to Newstead close to what is now Melrose. A mountain bike trail joins the Watershed here, and offers both challenge and excitement.

Grey Mare's Tail from Andrewhinney Hill. Looking across the upper reaches of the Moffat Water to this popular National Trust for Scotland property.

ABOVE
Culter Fell from Glen Holm. Close to the Southern Uplands Fault where the Watershed's Reiver March ends, and the Laich March begins.

RIGHT
Carrifran Wildwood. The Borders Forest Trust in partnership with the John Muir Trust has started the process of transforming this whole valley with extensive planting of native trees.

Threepland Backshaw. A forlorn ruin that poignantly exemplifies the growing emptiness of the line of the Watershed.

Tinto Hill from Biggar Common. Mature pine trees frame the vista across the upper Clyde valley to this familiar landmark and ever popular hill.

Cumbernauld woodland. The Watershed's eye view of Cumbernauld retains much of its greenery, never more than a hundred paces from woodland.

Forth and Clyde Canal. Flanked by wetlands, the canal towpath is a favourite for walkers and cyclists.

Cairnoch Hill across Carron Reservoir in the Campsies. In an amphitheatre of forest, water and moor, it is easy to forget that this is in the middle of the urbanised Central Belt.

Stronend from Kippen Muir. A quiet scene now, but the former Balgair Cattle Fair would have created a much more lively bustle of activity.

North side of Ben Lomond. The most southerly of the Munros, but very few of those who reach its summit venture into this emptiness.

Ben Lui and its neighbours. A ragged and rocky arc of popular tops where the Watershed bids farewell to the Clyde valley.

Round Auch. This dramatic horseshoe bend on the West Highland line is ringed with dramatic tops, articulated here with snow.

Glen Etive from Clach Leathad. A party of friends and family joined me for a final day on these tops, where we sampled the wildness together, and shared in the success of the whole venture.

Train crossing towards Rannoch Forest. Built here on a raft of brushwood, the railway crosses the Watershed five times. At this point it courts the wide expanse of Rannoch Moor.

Loch Ossian rainbow close to the Watershed. Looking east from near the youth hostel towards the distant Bealach Dubh – the 'pot of gold' was surely the discovery of the *Ribbon of Wildness*.

Loch a Bhealaich Bheithe between Ben Bheoil and Ben Alder. A small herd of deer which were standing in the shallows made off at my approach.

Carn Liath on the edge of the Creag Meagaidh National Nature Reserve. A rusting gateway to nowhere in particular, with the Cairngorms forming the distant horizon.

Crossing the Watershed at Laggan on the Caledonian Canal.
The 'summit' of the Canal now gives little indication of the challenge which
the builders faced in carving a trench through the hard rocks.
Transition from Heartland to Moine Marches.

Ben Tee with patterns in the evening sky.

Sgurr na Ciche in the 'Rough Bounds' is a formidable spectacle;
a long walk-in, and an equally long trek-out, but an immensely rewarding ascent.
Photo: Jim Manthorpe.

Cloud shadows across the hills of Killilan. The Watershed here
traverses one of the remotest areas in the country; a long distance
from anywhere, and a stunning solitude.

The Fannichs. Mountain and loch, with the sun catching the snow on the south-facing slopes.

Evening passion over Coigach from the Cromalt Hills.

The broken edge of Conival.

Glencoul from the lower top of Beinn Uidhe. Looking across another vast and majestic emptiness.

Carn Dearg. Where there is a pause in the Watershed's northward progress, and it swings boldly east across the magnificent Flow Country.

The Ben Griams – Beg and Mor. Typical Flow Country with Loch Rimsdale in the foreground.

Beinn Rosail and Palm Loch. One of the worst horrors of the Clearances occurred close to this apparently idyllic spot. Neil M Gunn gives an evocative account of this in his *Butcher's Broom*.

Ben Alisky. This modest but delightful hill barely raises its head amid one of the largest expanses of Ramsar sites in the UK.

The Stacks of Duncansby – Muckle, Peedie and Tom Thumb. These fine pinnacles provide a fitting guard of honour alongside the last few kilometres of the Watershed, as it hugs the clifftop, and the call of the seal echoes round the crags.

Duncansby Head. Where the fast flowing tides in the *Strait of the land of the Picts* interrupt any further Watershed on mainland UK.

of other designations come into play. Cashel Farm regeneration project, encompassing 2,173 hectares of mountain, moor and rock, provides an apt, if unconventional, gateway to the park. The eastern boundary of the National Scenic Area then works its way up from the loch-side to join the Watershed on Beinn Bhreac, and this is followed by the Loch Lomond National Memorial Park, which is a tribute to those who died in the two World Wars. We have also come onto the popular National Trust for Scotland property, and the SSSI area has started at Moin Eich. There is nothing ambivalent about the status of this part of the Watershed.

A number of the environmental or heritage organisations with properties on and along the Watershed seek to enhance the visitor experience by employing Countryside Rangers. Their roles vary according to the nature and purpose of the agency, and the particular objectives that are being pursued on the habitats, but there areas that are common to most.

The image of the Countryside Ranger with weather-toned complexion, unhurried stride, and dog at heel, is one that many would aspire to; the job appears to have much that our largely urban-based lifestyles and desk-bound careers cannot match. Adverts for these seemingly idyllic posts are always over-subscribed by both the suitably qualified, and the keen amateur alike. The job-spec calls for an extensive knowledge about flora and fauna, as well as excellent people skills, because an interface with the public in all its diversity will both reward and test in equal measure. Finally, all of the fencing and drainage, planting and lopping, counting and measuring will add to the need for a wide spectrum of practical skills.

There is more, because an ability and commitment to working in partnership with other environmental organisations can provide an even greater value. Involving people, especially the young, through programmes like the John Muir Award, puts learning, fun and sustainability firmly into the picture. Yes, the image of the Countryside Ranger is an appealing one, the potential fulfilment is great, and the impact on public enjoyment of the countryside is manifest.

Of the many thousands of people who venture up Ben Lomond each year, the majority then return the way they came by the footpath crossing at Moin Eich and hence to Rowardennan with its car parks, hotel, youth hostel, and campsites. But the Watershed continues northwards via a steep descent to Cruinn a Bheinn (632m) where the NSA ends (for now), and then to the head of Gleann Gaoithe. A track to the left zigzags down through a remnant of Atlantic oak wood to Cailness at the side of the loch. To the north, a line of hills running west to east is the start of a horseshoe round the head of Loch Arklet. After Cruachan (536m), Beinn Uamha (596m) provides an excellent, vista of the upper reaches of the River Forth catchment. It is a complex gathering of waters, rivers and lochs, which evolve into the full flood of the Forth itself above Stirling; it is like an inverted tree with many limbs and branches. The Kelty Water starts the headwaters of the grand complex on Beinn Breac, and the Duchray Water starts life a little further on around Cruinn a Bheinn and Gleann Gaoithe. A number of burns that feed into Loch Chon then become the Water of Chon and widen into Loch Ard after a short distance. At its outfall, it is joined by the Duchray to form the upper part of the Forth, and the Kelty joins in the flow above Flanders Moss.

On the narrow causeway between Arklet and Katrine, the Watershed is a mere 500m from the latter at Stronachlachar. Prior to its enlargement, to quench the thirst of the population of Glasgow, the shores of the loch would have been some distance further east. Its western end is fed largely by the Glengyle Water and, at its outfall; a small flow is maintained into the Achray Water. This is but a short run though, as it becomes Loch Achray after little more than a kilometre. Achray then becomes the Black Water, which in turn becomes Loch Venacher, and finally it evolves as the Eas Gobhain and joins the River Teith at Callander.

There is something fascinating in looking at all of these river systems from the higher ground – from above, for it runs counter to the convention of starting the journey of discovery from the river's mouth. The analogy of exploring a tree from the twigs and branches downwards offers a novel and very different perspective on the tree and its structure.

The theme of trees and forests is recurrent, and around Loch Katrine lies the immense 9,500 hectare project being taken forward by the Scottish Forest Alliance partnership. This will see a 20-year programme of native woodland regeneration, restoration and planting, interspersed with areas of open habitats. Key agencies in this ambitious effort include the Woodlands Trust for Scotland, Forestry Commission, RSPB, BP, and Scottish Water, which owns much of the area. The natural beauty of the Watershed terrain around Lochs Katrine and Arklet will be enhanced, and the objective of improved biodiversity will progress significantly in the years ahead.

Yet further on, at Parlan Hill, a final contribution to the upper reaches of the Forth comes from the River Larig. That in turn spreads to become Loch Voil which empties into the River Balvaig at Balquidder and then joins Loch Lubnaig south of Strathyre. The changing names and identities continues as this becomes the Garbh Uisge which tumbles merrily down the Falls of Leny, and joins with the Eas Gobhain above Callander, where they become the River Teith, which joins the River Forth close to Drip Bridge, just upstream from Stirling.

Meanwhile, on the western side one single very large feature has dominated the scene of the Watershed. Loch Lomond, the largest body of water in the UK, was formed as the ice sheet of what is known as the 'Loch Lomond Re-advance' finally melted and left a barrier of glacial debris across what was to become the loch's southern end between Balloch and Drymen. The long trench scoured by the glacial action filled with water, forming the loch. And although this action had taken place over the lip of the Highland Boundary Fault, it didn't obliterate it completely, as the chain of islands referred to earlier bears testament. The surface level of Loch Lomond is a mere 4m above sea level, so the drop from where its waters exit at Balloch into its entry to the Clyde in the shadow of Dumbarton Castle is of little significance.

It was worth getting the full picture of the major water catchments in this area, where the change from burn to river, river to loch, and once more to river, gives a wonderfully varied landscape. The view of this splendour is let down by a line of pylons which marches uncompromisingly across the Watershed just below Beinn Uamha, taking the output of Cruachan and Sloy hydro-electric power stations to their destination in Glasgow. Beneath the pylons, both the B829 and the Watershed traverse the narrow strip of land between Loch Arklet and Loch Katrine before meeting the first of only three houses on the entire Heartland March. All of the water from Loch Arklet formerly drained into Loch Lomond at Inversnaid but, with its level raised, much of it now crosses the Watershed to be added to Loch Katrine for Glasgow's water supply. On its way to the treatment works near Milngavie it recrosses the Watershed at Bog of Ballat.

One of the environmental benefits of this area's use as a water supply catchment is that farming practices are firmly controlled in order to avoid any form of pollution. And this is being taken a step further, with stock numbers being reduced to the point where trees will regenerate naturally.

Loch Katrine is the setting for two major, if somewhat different, romantic associations. Rob Roy was born at Glengyle, now at the head of the enlarged loch. His deeds of theft, lawlessness and attempts to provide his own 'fairer' form of justice to the local scene, have given him an endearing image, he is popularly seen as being a loveable rogue.

And Sir Walter Scott immortalised this area in the poem *The Lady of the Lake*, with some of the action taking place on Ellen's Isle near the eastern end of the loch. Written in 1810, he reworked the Arthurian legend and set the story in the Loch Katrine area. Like much of his work, it is an epic tale, which is by today's standards somewhat over the top in plot, character and language:

> Not Katrine, in her mirror blue,
> Gives back the shaggy banks more true,
> Than every freeborn glance confess'd
> The guileless movements of her breast.

But it caught the popular imagination, turned the Trossachs into Scotland's very own Lake District, and generated a new tourist industry. Others took up the theme with all its romantic imagery, including Franz Schubert who wrote the delightful *Ellen's Songs*.

When the West Highland Railway saw its first passengers in 1894, a new chapter in popular tourism for the entire corridor between Glasgow and Fort William opened up. The guide to this new railway entitled *Mountain Moor and Loch*, which was published in the same year, gave the traveller, starting from Kings Cross in London, a vivid introduction to the wild and romantic beauty that lay ahead. This line came late in the railway building era, but its advent had a significant impact on all of the communities it connected with. Although Stronachlachar is not on this line, it was none the less affected by the activity which the railway generated. A popular journey for people from Glasgow in particular was to sail up Loch Lomond, from Balloch to Inversnaid, where a coach would then provide transport to Stronachlachar. At this point the traveller was given a choice of either continuing by coach to Aberfoyle to connect with the branch-line there, or of taking another boat eastwards along Loch Katrine, and a further coach to Callander to link with the train there. A number of large and imposing hotels were built to provide accommodation at each of the points of change, and the building at Stronachlachar stands today in the woods just above the pier, but no longer functions as an hotel. In the railway guide referred to earlier, there is an appealing description of what the traveller will discover at, or rather from, Stronachlachar:

> The view from Stronachlachar is magnificent, as the eye follows the course of the gleaming water, in which the surrounding hills seem to stand inverted, into the very heart of the Perthshire Highlands.

This is a timeless image.

Although a number of the necessary links in this journey no longer exist today, and the traveller to the area is almost certain to arrive by car, there are still a variety of opportunities to be enjoyed in which Stronachlachar will feature. The steamship the *Sir Walter Scott* still plies its way in the summer season, starting from the pier at the eastern end of the loch. This journey is a popular day out for many people, and the experience of travelling without the normal sound of an engine, only the 'phut, phut, phut' of steam, is rather special. A variation on the theme is to bring or hire a bicycle and cycle to Stronachlachar on the private road along the north side of the loch, and then sail back. And the walk from Trossachs pier to the tearoom at Stronachlachar offers yet another appealing possibility.

Sterner stuff is called for, with the ascent to Garradh (559m), *fence* or *dyke* and, the rugged ridge along the north side of Loch Arklet to Maol Mor (684m), *big bald head,* with its trig point, and Beinn a Choin (770m), where the Loch Lomond NSA rejoins the Watershed. A clutch of fine hills around Cruach Ardrain (1,046m) make for excellent walking with the odd minor scramble for good measure. Parlan Hill (666m), Beinn Chabhair (933m), An Caisteal (995m), *the castle,* Beinn a Chroin (942m) and Stob Glas, (813m), *grey hill,* give some tantalising views towards Ben More and Stob Binnean, *pointed hill.* The Watershed then heads away northwards, but not before affording one last look back towards the Forth. It's been a long way since Craigengar in the south Pentlands, and the transition from moorland environment at the start of the Forth to one of mountain and rock at the departure from it, is striking.

Cruach Ardrain feeds three different river systems. Its west flank drains towards the River Falloch which in turn ends up in Loch Lomond, whilst water from its eastern side is bound for the Forth by way of the Inverlochlarig Burn, Loch Voil and Loch Lubnaig. And, finally, its north face drains towards the Tay by way of the River Dochart. A remnant of Caledonian pine forest on the northern slopes of these hills in Glen Falloch is now being given some protection, with regeneration slowly beginning to take place; the isolated grandmother trees are gradually being surrounded by infants of the same stock, but of a very different generation. And a short stretch of SSSI taking in Meall Dhamh (814m) and Grey

Heights (685m) represents the start of the River Tay catchment, which will be with us for some time.

A final descent to the railway and the A82 is through commercial forest, with a footbridge on the Watershed giving safe passage just over half a kilometre from Crianlarich, with its station and platform café. Crianlarich is largely a railway village and owes much of its earlier existence to the fact that it was a railway junction. The railways from Callander and Crieff combined to bring trains up Glen Ogle from the east, and the West Highland Line offered journeys to Fort William and Mallaig or Oban, with a return south to Glasgow also on offer. Although the loss of the Glen Ogle link in the 1960s has narrowed the choices, there is still a sense of occasion as the north-bound train splits in the station, with one half destined for Oban and the other for Mallaig.

The first house in the village on the A82 is some 150m east of the line, and the youth hostel and other services give a brief brush with domestic activity before the next ascent along the forest edge to Craw Knowe (466m). Just before Kirk Craig, the West Highland Way crosses, and on most days little knots of people can be seen, many of whom proudly regard this long distance route as their great challenge; they walk on with great resolve, and a few blisters. Ben Lui (1,130), *mountain of the calf*, presides over its near neighbours Beinn Dubhchriag (978m), *mountain of the black rock*, and Ben Oss (1,029m), *mountain of the stag*, where a National Nature Reserve spreads round Gleann Auchreach and the Cononish to the right, with an increase in native trees once again being the prime conservation aim. These hills around Ben Lui have a rugged profile, their corries being a favourite haunt for winter climbers, with the ice and snow in the north-facing Coire Laoigh and Coire Gaothach, *windy corrie*, lingering later than elsewhere in the area. To the west the vast Clyde catchment has been our companion since Clyde Law on the Reiver March and here we bid it farewell. An intriguing and exceptionally lengthy 'minor' watershed branches off to the left on Ben Lui, it crosses the Crinan Canal en-route for Sron Uamha at the tip of the Mull of Kintyre;

that challenge can wait though. From the top, a fine collection of rivers including the Awe (with its loch of the same name), Lochy and Orchy, which together empty into Loch Etive opposite Bonawe, then take over. Running steeply to the north, Ciochan Beinn Laoigh is part of a rapid 700m drop from top of Ben Lui to the bealach below, where the NNR also ends.

It will be some distance before the Watershed tops the 1,000m mark again, and two steep descents to rail and road crossings are familiar sights to travellers on these routes. Beinn Chuirn (880m) and Meall Odhar (656m), *dappled hill*, sweep in an arc round the head of the River Cononish, and the location of spasmodic attempts at mining gold in the glen. On Sron nan Colan (590m), *the companion's nose*, a right-angled turn to the left brings the Watershed down through an area of extensive debris from many years of former mine workings.

The railway branch which leads to Oban must be crossed with great care here and traffic on the A85, as it speeds across our path, should be given time to pass too. Houses on the Watershed are an extreme rarity on the Heartland March; the second house lies on the northern side of the road, and the third is some distance off. The remains of a dyke run up into the forest at this point and take the Watershed clear of the trees, where a somewhat rickety fence-line takes over and leads to the top of Beinn Bheag (655m). Another right turn brings the line down the side of the forest and yet another crossing by the A82. Unfortunately the conveniently placed bridge over the railway has been removed, so a very careful listen for the clickety-click of an approaching train is called for once more. The West Highland Way crosses again, with its random groups of brightly clad walkers heading to Tyndrum or to Auch.

Although I have said that historical references to the Watershed are few, and none refer to it in its entirety, *Mountain Moor and Loch* does allude to something significant here:

> About a mile beyond Tyndrum the line crosses the county march between Perthshire and Argyllshire, at an elevation of 1,025 feet. The boundary is the great watershed of

THE HEARTLAND MARCH

Scotland, and we find the mountain torrents now pouring westwards to the Atlantic through Argyllshire, instead of eastward through Perthshire to the German Ocean (later renamed the North Sea).

There is a later reference to the railway crossing the Watershed above Gorton, and the flow eastwards towards the German Ocean. These quotes would suggest that there was some awareness of *the* Watershed, or *the great* Watershed, in the late 19th century.

Rapid and unremitting are the most fitting words to describe the ascent that lies ahead here and, remarkably, a fence has been created and is maintained to within a short distance of the summit. After almost 600m of scrambling, the top of Beinn Odhar (901m) is reached, where the only thing to do is take a break and take in the views. Scan the wide panoramas north across the Auch railway horseshoe to the rocky crown atop Beinn Dorain's steep-sided cone, south down Strath Fillan to Stob Binnein and its neighbours, east to the Breadalbane Hills shielding Loch Tay, with Ben Lawers peeping over the Tarmachan ridge, and west over Dalmally, Loch Awe and Cruachan. That is only part of the vast 360 degree picture as seen from this rocky topped hill, for a dozen other well known landmarks punctuate the wide-screen in the middle and far distance; the list of Munros alone would be formidable.

The going on these hills now that the initial height has been gained on Beinn Odhar, is a joy to experience; mostly firm and dry, and flowing easily from top to top. Beinn Chaorach (818m) with its strange remains of some mini electric fence network to keep the mountain hares in (or out) leads on to Cam Chreag (884m) and the end of National Park on the Watershed after 82km. The wildness of the Watershed is by now gathering in both evidence and conviction. The trio of Beinn a Chaisteil (886m), Beinn nam Fuiran (802m) and Beinn A Chuirn (923m) ride boldly above the Allt Kinglas Water and the forlorn remains of Ais-an t-Sidhean, and face the rocky rear of Beinn Dorain, *hill of the streamlet,* and Beinn an Dothaidh with their 300m deep bealach between them. Strath Tarabhan to the east leads down steeply to Loch Lyon. The great Gaelic poet Duncan Ban MacIntyre 1724–1812, who was born in the hills south of Stob Gabhar, lived in Ais-an t-Sidhean for a number of years. One of his abiding poems is in praise of Beinn Dorain, and his verse in Gaelic is as follows:

> An t-urran thar gach beinn
> Aig Beinn Dobhrain:
> De na channaic mi fan ghrein
> 'S I bu bhoidhche leam.

> And the English translation:
> Honour beyond each ben
> For Ben Dorain:
> Of all I have seen beneath the sun
> The most glorious ...

The site of a chapel dedicated to St Duthac lies nearby; it provided shelter for travellers on the ancient crossing from Auch to Glen Lyon.

On Beinn Chaorach. With random rocks strewn across the summit.

Beinn Achaladair ridge (1,038m), *mountain of the soaking field*, with its other two spot heights of 1,036m and 1,002m is a turning point, as it reveals a new world across the Water of Tulla to Rannoch Moor and all that lies around and beyond this watery expanse. Its northern flanks above the railway are designated as SSSI, where the ancient forest has been saved from further loss, and is now making a slow comeback. This side of the Water of Tulla is shared with Beinn a Chreachain (1,081m), *mountain of the clam shell*, and the dramatic crag-ringed corrie amphitheatre focuses on Lochan a Chreachain. Some determined glacial grinding scooped out this hollow which then filled with water – dark and sinister on this north-facing slope; the going is good though, firm and dry on short grass and some rock.

The Watershed has another six kilometres to travel before it gains the most easterly point on the journey around the headwaters of Tulla. From Creag Mhor (788m) it weaves hither and thither to Meall na Feith Faide (826m), *hill of the longest bog* – though I suspect that there could be many other contenders for that accolade – and the erratic route along the Local Authority boundary (County Boundary sounded so much better) continues to Meall Buidhe (907m). Here there is a sharp 130 degree turn to the left towards the point where the railway starts its descent towards Rannoch Station, and the Rannoch Forest comes right up to the Watershed beside one of the largest areas of very black liquid peat hag ever seen. The trailing deer footprints in the firmer areas show that they are undeterred by this dark mire. As the Mallaig train trundles past on the 'floating' track, the area of surrounding moor quivers nervously, but it has done so for well over a 100 years and not sunk yet; a wonder of engineering in this isolated spot, the author of *Mountain Moor and Loch* was confident that it will last 1,000 years.

The 52km journey round Rannoch Moor starts on Meall-a Ghortain and ends on Sron Leachd a Chaorainn, within sight of Loch Ossian. Much of the area contained within this circum-navigation is designated and protected as SSSI, and the general

West Highland Line at 'The Great Watershed of Scotland'.

impression is of a vast hollow, a crater even – part moor, part loch, and surrounded by an irregular ring of higher ground, the Watershed. Although there are four points at which the lip of this crater dips, there is only one outlet, at the north-east end of Loch Laidon, close to Rannoch Station. During the last Ice Age, an enormous dome of ice lay above Rannoch Moor. The vast weight of this ice actually created a bigger hollow in the earth's crust; it compressed it like some weight being exerted on the skin formed on a bowl of custard. But, as the ice melted, the level of the land rose again, as if it gave a great sigh of relief.

One of the big challenges that I faced throughout what I then referred to as my *watershed epic*, was how to avoid the risk of being overwhelmed by the notion of one big long, and perhaps, unremitting trek. That would have trapped me in mental drudgery, and solitude would not be a good place to have such an experience; the whole venture may have failed.

From the outset though, I had broken it all down into more

manageable chunks. Firstly, it was spread over a nine month period from January to October – largely to fit round work, family and assorted voluntary sector commitments. So the outings ranged from three days in winter, to around two weeks in the height of the summer, and all I had to focus on, on each outing, was contained on the maps that I had with me. The travel plans for getting to the start, and returning from, each outing were prepared. Whilst a number of good friends and family gave valuable support in this, and public transport helped too, I found myself hitching (with much success) on many of the journeys. Clear goals were set for each day, in terms of route, distance and planned campsite. So what started as one very big venture was then packaged into smaller bite-sized outings. In order to avoid overdoing it, and to enable me to carry no more than a maximum of seven days supplies at any time, I had a one day break in the middle of the longer outings, with pre-arranged food, map and clothing pick-up points.

Accidents notwithstanding, I knew that the greatest danger to not completing the journey lay in either poor preparation, or by losing heart, and being overwhelmed by the size of it. I would like to think that I planned in order to avoid these hazards. I undoubtedly discovered a bit more of myself in undertaking and completing the venture. Clearly I had most of the necessary outdoor skills and experience, and my general approach to the journey was sound. On reflection, I am now conscious of the determined streak that I either liberated or discovered in myself; where and when better to realise this, than through a challenging interaction with Nature?

I digress though.

The journey along the northern side of the Tulla gives two very different impressions. The Tulla glen is fairly straight and increasingly steep-sided as it descends over 12km towards Loch Tulla, with Gorton Bothy near the head of the glen. Rannoch Moor, by contrast, is a confusion of water, bog and moor, with very few distinguishing higher points. Loch Ba and Loch Laidon stand out amongst the many other smaller and equally irregular lochs. Before the next A82 crossing, a number of small hills dimly distinguish the divide between Tulla and Rannoch, some marked by nameless spot heights only. Glas Bheinn (501m) stands at an acute angle across the Watershed before the descent to the A82, where a mast and re-ascent to Meall Mhor, with its sad monument to a dead climber, is then followed by Meall Beag before the short drop to the West Highland Way. The line of the old military road at the other side of the wood is the last crossing before the succession of tops that comprise the Black Mount.

If the circumnavigation of Rannoch Moor were an environmental feast, the next 11km would be the main-course. The rough and ragged arc round the headwaters of the River Ba is often described as 'a fine day out', or even 'one of the more challenging and rewarding mountain groups to be climbed in the area'. Although the West Highland Way marks a temporary departure from the SSSI area, the names of these hills together ring like a litany in the Munroist almanac. Beinn Toaig (834m), Stob a Choire Odhair (945m), *peak of the dun corrie,* the lesser known Aonach

Rannoch Moor from Black Mount. When a mile-high layer of ice melted, the surface of the land rose, as if with a great sigh of relief.

Eagach ridge (991m), *notched ridge*, Stob Ghabhar (1,090m), *peak of the goat,* which marks the end of the Awe system of drainage and start of the short and dramatic River Etive catchment. There follow, Aonach Mor, Clach Leathad (1,099m), and finally Meall a Bhuirdh (1,108m), *hill of the roaring,* where the crest of the hill suddenly reveals an unsightly clutter of ski installations tumbling down the north side to White Corries. But the Watershed steers a more north-easterly route, and descends towards the West Highland Way by Leacann nam Braonan and the final A82 crossing, where the SSSI restarts.

The 4km trek across the moor towards Black Corries Lodge, on terrain where few contours are marked on the map, involves cautiously picking a route between a succession of lochans and meandering burns which are almost indistinguishable from the surrounding bog; Rannoch Moor at its best. WH Murray, who inspired and informed a whole generation of climbers and outdoor enthusiasts, advocated a challenge here: swimming all the way across Rannoch Moor, via this tangled network of peaty burns and lochs. Whether he ever did this himself is not recorded, but a popular challenge is to canoe across, with relatively more canoeing than carrying. The definitive route across this confusion though is to keep Lochan Mathair Eite to the left, and Lochan Gaineamhach to the right; there should be firm moor between. Black Corries Lodge is about 100m west of the Watershed, and sits on the track from Kingshouse Hotel to Rannoch Station. North from the lodge, the line does a partial ascent of Meall nan Ruadhag (647m,) *hill of the young roe,* but veers east towards the A Cruach, *the heap* or *stacks,* ridge, before the summit. Lochan Meall a Phuill lies closely in the bealach before the next ascents onto Meall a Phuill, Stob nan Losgann (629m), *post of the toad or wretch,* and Stob na Cruaiche (739m) itself. With its trig point there comes the feeling that a new chapter is opening, with tantalising views north over the Blackwater Reservoir towards the Mamores and all of the majestic tops around Ben Nevis.

Scattered along the A Cruach ridge are a number of large granite boulders, which the retreating ice-sheet abandoned where they lay. Legend has it that some of these were used by the local clansmen to prove their strength and superiority in a kind of mountain-top bowling match, whilst some were allegedly used to ambush the enemy passing on the ancient route between Coe and Rannoch 300m below. Meall Liath na Doire, *hill of the grey thicket*, the final top on the ridge, presents a vista across another area of watery bog towards the next major goal which marks the end of the Rannoch circumnavigation – Sron Leachd a Chaorainn (737m).

A passing train heading south disappears briefly into the snow tunnel which is a mere 200m south of the point where the railway crosses the Watershed for the last time. It would be prudent to use this tunnel as a safe-crossing point. A short distance up the side of Sron Leachd, *nose of the grave,* lies, a further crossing as the track from Rannoch to Ossian passes.

Most climbers and walkers have stories to tell about the effects of the weather on their experiences on the hills; the weather is a major factor in determining how the day will fare. The late

Boulder on A 'Chruach. A friendly creature stands guard on the northern rim of Rannoch.

Kenneth Robertson was passionate about the Scottish mountains and, after over 60 years of climbing experience, he sought to make sense of it all; to somehow sum up all that it had given him. He had a few comments to make on that strange combination of the weather and the memory:

> When I think about my life on the hills, I remember chiefly those experiences that brought delight, and I often make lists of the hills and mountains that have given me so much, not always with clear skies, sometimes in wild and stormy weather. But often it appears to me that I walked in the sun along high ridges empty of human kind, in a perfect world.

He went on to acknowledge that the memory can play tricks whereby: 'The dark days drop through the filter, into forgetfulness.'

The weather on the Watershed is of course at the wilder end of the spectrum. With its location on the higher ground, it is more exposed, and lying generally to the west, it is more affected by the Gulf Stream coming from the south-west. The rainfall throughout much of its length is as much as three times that of the east of the country, the average January temperature is several degrees colder, and the cloud lingers longer. From this, it would be fair to conclude that it is less hospitable, and therefore harder to enjoy to the full. However, the words wild and stormy, are for many people synonymous with a great day out, which is rewarded with a feeling of having achieved something really worthwhile and memorable. The invigorating or challenging experiences which such weather can bring must be seen alongside the full atmospheric panoply.

In the same year that I ventured along the Watershed, Lorraine McColl completed a continuous unaided full round of the Munros. Over half of the days for her challenge were spent in a combination of poor visibility and at times, difficult conditions, whereas, only a third of my days were in poor visibility and just two in truly bad weather; in one sense at least, I was fortunate. Weather forecasts do help us to prepare or plan for the hills, for a period of a few days ahead at least, but they cannot remove the randomness in the bigger picture of the Scottish weather; nature will often have the last blow – or should that be 'laugh'? Weather isn't just about wind, mist and rain though, for there are crisp clear and sunny days in which you feel you could almost touch the hills on the other side of the valley; days when you imagine you can hear the silence, and night in these high places is breathtaking too. Then there are those stunning moments when the clouds part or the veil lifts, and suddenly there is a whole new world at your feet. Or there are those summer days with strong winds and no rain, which bring their own noisy challenge. Snow and ice add a further dimension to these weather scenarios; blizzard, white-out, crystals, sculpted forms, and mystery footprints, each create a new landscape. A note of caution though, as there are a few locations on the Watershed that would be treacherous in such conditions and where experience and the right equipment are essential.

Having met fewer than two people a day on average whilst on my trek, I found that solitude was my companion for most of the way. There is a tangible spiritual experience in walking or climbing alone (within the bounds of prudent safety), and this becomes heightened when it is over any sustained period of time. This very personal interaction with nature and the landscape has a special quality. I don't believe that it is in any way unsociable, but rather it offers time, place and space to be quite simply *at one*. For most people this is very different from the every-day hustle and bustle, and is therefore both refreshing and provides renewal. And where better to find this renewal and perhaps awakening of the senses, than in a state of self-reliance surrounded by wildness? The Watershed has plenty of that most valuable character and quality.

This solitude is indeed a very personal experience, and much has been written about its spiritual value in an otherwise largely secular Western world. I will leave it to others to more fully discuss and expand on this, but I appreciated it immensely and can vouch that the Watershed is *the place* to find lots of it.

And back on the journey, as each major top is reached it seems to herald some new vista, or to close an earlier chapter in the story.

And so on Sron Leachd a Chaorainn the view north is along the ridge to Carn Dearg (941m) and Loch Ossian beyond, with its remote and ever popular youth hostel. To the right, the 22km of the waters of Loch Ericht point straight for the southern Cairngorms and, beyond the far end of Loch Rannoch, Schiehallion stands head and shoulders above its neighbours. A couple of lochans high on the ridge seem to defy the logic that water must always drain to the lowest point, and their ripples dance in the afternoon sun, as if to celebrate this defiance. The end of the Blackwater and start of River Lochy system – including, the rivers Spean, Pattack, Roy, Turret and Gloy – is reached with the summit of Carn Dearg, where a right turn now focuses the attention on Ben Alder. The vast peat hag moors to the right are in marked contrast to the clean lines of Ossian and the valley of the Uisge Labhair, *loud water*, to the left. Amongst the trees at the head of the loch, the new granite and glass shooting-lodge, built from the profits of milk packaging, catches the evening sun. It is certainly no more incongruous than any other shooting lodge and, to my mind, provides a worthy new interpretation of the genre.

High ground is maintained with the succession of peaks which precede the descent to the Bealach Cumhain, *narrow bealach*. Sgor Gaibhre (955m) and Sgor Choinnich (929m) are separated by the Bealach nan Sgor, and the steep sided ridge continues along Meall a Bhealaich (865m) and Beinn a Chumhainn (903m). The view across the Bealach Cumhann to the western shoulder of Ben Alder seems strangely foreshortened, and makes the slope on the other side of this rapid 250m drop appear to be much steeper than it is in reality. It is the start of the next SSSI.

David Balfour and Alan Breck crossed this way in their desperate flight across Scotland in Robert Louis Stevenson's *Kidnapped*. With a bounty on their heads, they had travelled east from Loch Ossian, and were heading for Loch Ericht, whilst being pursued by dragoons:

> 'Well then, says he, let us strike for that. Its name is Ben Alder; it is a wild, desert mountain full of hills and hollows ... and the next moment, two of the ghillies had me by the

arms, and I began to be carried forward through a labyrinth of dreary glens and hollows and into the heart of that dismal mountain of Ben Alder.'

To the right of the bealach, the Alder Burn drops rapidly to Alder Bay on Loch Ericht, and the supposedly haunted Ben Alder Cottage bothy, which lies close to the shore. A short distance above it, on the steep side of the valley, is a cave in which the fugitive Prince Charlie is reputed to have hidden. It is a well chosen site, as it is effectively concealed amongst the rocks, and its elevation and position provide good views to the west towards Rannoch. No army in search of their quarry could venture unobserved on the Loch Ericht side or by descending from either the Bealach Cumhain or the closer Bealach Breabag. On Ben Alder, *mountain of the rock or water*, the summit plateau provides an excellent walk after the steep climb, and the first top at 1,056m is followed by the boulder-strewn summit of 1,148m over a kilometre later. Each summit opens splendid new doors on to the lie of the land, and invites a pause for a brew-up and gaze across to distant horizons. The Watershed is getting close to the 'heart of Scotland' – as defined by the Ordnance Survey, no less, the point which is furthest from the sea in every direction is in the Dalwhinnie area near to the head of Loch Ericht. And Ben Alder is undoubtedly the best vantage point on our journey to consider the more complex water catchment and drainage patterns of this part of the Scottish Highlands.

The Watershed, that simple east-west divide between the Atlantic Ocean and the North Sea, lies much closer to the western seaboard throughout much of its considerable length. Indeed, there are sections which are further west than the briny penetration of several major sea lochs; Lochs Linnhe, Hourn and Broom all venture further east than parts of the Watershed in the Rough Bounds, the western Fannichs and Rhidorroch. At some stage in its evolution, Scotland tilted, with the east side generally dipping towards the North Sea, and the west rising in part from the effects of the Moine Thrust. It is this tilt which has, more than anything, put the

Watershed where it is; the backbone or spine of Scotland is much more to the Atlantic side.

The views eastwards from Ben Alder cover much of the Cairngorms, looking beyond the north-south watershed at the Pass of Drumochter to that part of Scotland centred on the Cairngorm plateau, from which a number of other river systems radiate, like the buckled spokes of an ancient wheel. Although the Spey and Garry/Tay groups rise far to the west of this, moving clockwise in a great watery dance round the mountain mass, the Deveron, Don, Dee, North and South Esks, the Isla and the Black Water take more than half of the rain that falls on the Cairngorms, and debouch it into the North Sea. If this pattern seems less than clear from the high summit of Ben Alder, perhaps the knowledge that it is there nonetheless, adds to the variety and complexity of our Scottish landform.

To describe in any detail the view from Ben Alder would take much more than this rather hurried narrative allows. But, like so much of the Watershed's view of Scotland, it is a full compass vista of lochs and peaks, valleys and bogs, with moor, forest and rock only fading slowly to where the wide horizons merge with the even wider skies. For its entire plateau summit, covering the best part of a square kilometre, the whole mass is hemmed in by a total of four bealachs as lines of demarcation from its neighbours. The Bealach Cumhann to the west is followed by the sinister Bealach Dubh to the north. On the eastern side, the Bealach Beithe with its lochan of the same name, lies in the 400m shadow of the craigs and end with the Sron Bealach Beithe – the 'nose' of that bealach. And, finally, the Bealach Breabag marks the divide between this hill and the next on the route. There are a large number of marked crossings by road, track, and rail, but this track exceeds all others for elevation; at 834m it is by far the highest.

A fair challenge for the fit would be a race round Ben Alder using these passes, which would offer a 20km route starting and finishing at Culra Bothy. Another nose appears in the form of Sron Coire na h-Iolaire, an immense amphitheatre of precipitous rock on the Loch Ericht side of the run up to Beinn Bheoil (1,019m), *mountain of the mouth*. The sparse vegetation on this ridge gives firm terrain, easy walking and a clear sense of the Watershed as the lochan runs along 400m below on the left, while Loch Ericht is over 650m below on the right.

There have been a number of different theories as to the exact location of the centre of Scotland. Prior to 2002 the two main contenders were Newtonmore, where a stone was confidently placed to mark the spot, and Braes of Foss – 5km east of Schiehallion. These two locations are some distance apart so, in 2002, the Ordnance Survey (OS) decided to resolve the issue once and for all. Earlier methods had included trying to measure the point that is furthest from the sea in every direction – using a map, ruler, pin and string. Now the immediate problem with this method is that Scotland is not a neatly rounded or bounded landmass: it has appendages and inlets aplenty. So the OS decided to use a method which involves calculating the centre of gravity of a mass – a summary of this complex method can be found in Wikipedia! And the conclusion is that the centre of Scotland is at NN6678471599, this is 14.5km east of Beinn Bheoil, on the eastern shoulder of Sron na h-Eiteich, about 300m from the railway and A9, just under 2.5km from Dalnaspidal Lodge.

The proximity of the centre of Scotland at Beinn Bheoil gives a vivid picture of the Watershed's wide meanderings.

The mystery of the body of a young man propped against a rock near the summit, who was found to have been shot, remained for a number of years; as every single piece of evidence which might have identified him had been removed. Who was he, why and by whose hand did he die, and why did he die in such a remote location? Eventually, following a feature on *Crimewatch* and an international appeal, he was identified as being from France, but much of the mystery still remains.

The popularity of Ben Alder and its near neighbour comes as no surprise. Paths on the Watershed are not plentiful, but for a short distance below Sron Dreineach (another nose), it takes the path heading down towards Culra Bothy. A bog beckons though, and all to soon it is necessary to venture a little to the right onto Meall Mor (527m) and Meall Beag (518m), as the Watershed makes its way between Loch Pattack and yet more of Loch Ericht. A conveniently placed bridge over the Allt a Chaoil-reidhe gives ready access to Culra Bothy, which offers good shelter and the likelihood of the company of fellow walkers or climbers for the night. If they have brought some coal for the fire, so much the better.

Back on the Watershed, and the track which crosses to the new Ben Alder Lodge prior to a climb through the forest and onto the moors leading up to Meall Leac na Sguabaich (846m). Here, the end of Tay and start of Spey catchment occurs. The Fara ridge stretches north east towards Dalwhinnie, but the Watershed presses north to Beinn Eilde (674m) and, 2km beyond, it enters Cairngorm National Park. The next 16km represent a major milestone or two, for, in addition to providing the link between Scotland's two National Parks, this also holds the half-way point on our 1,200km journey.

Between the Falls of Pattack and the Dark Gully, the boggy moorland beyond Bienn Eilde is exchanged for forest. The deer fence presents the usual challenge, but a gate or stile near the river

Culra Bothy. Close to the 'centre of Scotland', but definitely away from it all.

offers an alternative. Although the going in this area of forest is not particularly difficult to negotiate, a compass bearing is prudent to help steer towards the cleared area round the abandoned village of Druim an Aird, from where some smaller clearings and old dyke lines help; the brief glimpses of distant hillsides which come and go between gaps in the trees are reassuring. Here the Watershed meets the divide between Feagour and Loch Laggan on the left, and Strathmashie and the Spey on the right and it is somewhat confused here, as a concrete water channel runs right across it bringing water from the River Mashie on the east side to the River Pattack to the west. This in turn flows into Loch Laggan at Kinloch Laggan, where a magnificent sandy beach forms the entire eastern end of the loch.

The effect of these engineering works has been two-fold. In addition to transferring water across the Watershed, it has in a sense moved the Watershed almost a kilometre to the east. Secondly, the concrete channel is impossible to cross, with sloping sides and deep fast-flowing water. The A86 crossing is a brief interlude before the difficult ascent through the forest of Creag Ruadh (560m), towards the trig point above Loch na Lairige.

The short Glen Shirra, on the right, looks unassuming and the view beyond to tree-fringed Loch Crunachdan could almost be entirely natural. However, some 50m beneath your feet, a tunnel takes much of the headwater of the River Spey across the Watershed to Loch Laggan. Downstream, these waters were used to generate electricity for aluminium production, but, as that has declined, the excess power is now fed into the national grid.

As the Creag Meagaidh National Nature Reserve starts on Meall Ghoirleig (526m), so too the National Park ends on Coire Dubh (916m).

Most visitors to the Creag Meagaidh, *bogland crag,* NNR enter by the 'front door', at Aberarder Farm by the shores of Loch Laggan. If their visit is for a mountain day, they then climb rapidly onto a great horseshoe of peaks surrounding the Coire Ardair with its crag rimmed lochan; Munros aplenty. And the crags in this north-east

Loch Laggan. Setting for the other *Monarch of the Glen*.

facing corrie are a great favourite for winter climbers, as the snow and ice give good conditions away from the effects of sun and melt. Since the establishment of the NNR in the mid-1980s, the aim of reviving the land by restoring natural plant and animal communities has led to a remarkable transformation, simply by reducing the deer numbers.

The Watershed follows the northern rim of the NNR area, giving another classic example of its role as a boundary. Our way in, though, is by the side door from Coire Dubh and the A Bhuidheanach ridge to the rock strewn Carn Liath (1,006m), *grey hill*. A couple of steep cols then punctuate the elevated route by Meall an t-Snaim (969m), Sron Coire a Chriochairean (991m), and the lesser summit of Stob Poite Coire Ardair (1,051m), *peak of the pot of the high corrie*. The route then heads out of the back door of the NNR to the north, and into a different kind of landscape.

The boulders and low ridges of rock along the line from Meall Ptarmigan (815m) to Creag a Bhanain (849m) end on the promontory of Sron Nead, which asserts itself over the surrounding moor and bog in the area where the Roy and Spey rise, to left and right respectively. The contrast between the firm high ground and the lower and much flatter terrain is indeed striking, and the Watershed is marked across this soft morass by the remains of a fenceline which appears to be slowly disappearing into the bog and vegetation. Loch Spey, to the right, heralds the start of that great river, which pauses only briefly in Loch Insh, before continuing its rapid and majestic course to finally enter the Moray Firth at Spey Bay. The mouths of most rivers have been tamed and constrained by either cultivation or development, but the River Spey, with its annual cargo of rock and gravel when in spate, still thrashes about as if it refuses to guarantee any particular line of exit to the sea.

Glen Roy, to the left, has long been a source of fascination, with its almost unique pattern of 'parallel roads', which follow the contours right round its mid and upper sections, and the side valley of Glen Turret. All sorts of fanciful and romantic theories were offered to explain how these 'roads' got there, and there was much speculation as to their purpose too. Although the more recent and accepted explanation, that they are the beach-terraces left by different loch levels as the glaciers melted and receded, lacks any mention of giants or any of the great mythical characters from history, they are still to be marvelled at. The uppermost reaches of this pattern extend to within less than a kilometre of the col at the Watershed between Roy and Spey, and these headwaters are linked by a narrow band of sssi. Also a short distance to the left is Luib-Chonnal Bothy, at the confluence of a number of burns, which faces the dramatic and often musical White Falls; a description that speaks for itself.

Thanks to the quality of the solitude that I have already mentioned, there was plenty of time to reflect on this notion of wildness as a continuous phenomenon throughout the journey. The emptiness was of course heightened by the infrequency with which I met other people, and the remoteness of much of the route seemed to put real distance between my independence and the rest of humanity. It was in this private little world surrounded by nature, that the notion of the title crept in on the scene; the conviction, that what I had encountered was a continuous state of relative wildness. And this wildness seemed to flow outwards along ridges to other mountain tops. Although the maps I carried didn't include anything beyond the sheets that I needed at the time, I knew just about enough of the wider geography of Scotland to visualise the secondary watersheds between the major river valleys, running off at right angles and finally dropping into ocean or sea.

Exploring an entire river from source to sea or from the point where it enters salt water to its genesis in the hills is a fascinating experience. As part of Journey for the Wild, with the John Muir Trust in 2006, I walked all the way up the River Dee, from Aberdeen with its harbour and enormous oil industry supply vessels, to the Pools of Dee in the Cairngorms. The busy water-borne industry, which keeps the oilrigs and pipelines flowing, soon gave way to suburbs and quiet farmland. Mature woods framed each wide sweep in the river, and, in many places, its banks were manicured for salmon fishing. The progress upstream was punctuated by towns and villages that had grown up and depended on the river and its tributaries, and occasional bridges marked the links between one side and the other. Mysterious deep pools, a linn or waterfall, shingle banks and long tumbling shallows all added to the immense variety of a the river, as it got slowly and perceptibly smaller. The upper pine woods were replaced by open mountain meadow and moor, as the vistas opened out to the steeper slopes and rocky tops. The final part of the journey up into the confines of the Lairig Ghru alongside what had become not much more than a small burn soon led to its source among the boulders and harebells that fringe the Pools of Dee. Though not on *the* Watershed, it was an excellent way to see where our rivers fit into the wider landscape.

To the north of the col between Spey and Roy, lies another of these areas which is marked on the map as a forest but lacks trees, as the deer and sheep have eaten any natural attempt at regeneration. Culachy and Corrieyairack Forests together stretch towards Glen Tarff which in turn leads to Fort Augustus at the southern end of Loch Ness. My first memory of any association with this erstwhile area of forest goes back to the 1960s when my imagination was fired by a broadcast by the late Fyfe Robertson. With his highly individual style and nasal delivery, he spoke passionately about the Corrieyairack Pass and its military road built in the 18th century by General Wade. I resolved then that I would visit this strange place as soon as practicable, to see for myself the road climbing to just over 770m, with its bridges and zigzag sections. I knew little of Wade and his roads at that time, but the very idea that a road should be constructed in such an elevated and remote location had captured my imagination. So, a few years later, I did venture up from Fort Augustus and, at the summit of the pass, was alarmed by a weird sound; I was on my own, so the scope for being spooked was unfettered. I eventually located the source of the strange whining noise as being a small rather ugly new building which I reckoned must have something to do with the transmission pylons that also cross the pass here. Cautiously I ventured closer to the building not knowing what to expect; it all seemed so incongruous, after all, and Fyfe Robertson's earlier account of why and how this pass was crossed by a military road merely added to the sense of mystery of the place. Eventually, the cause of the strange noise was narrowed down to a small wind-speed gadget fixed to the end of the roof; as it whirled round in this breezy spot, it made a whining groan – there would be no let-up in the wind hereabouts, I surmised. This is the Beauly to Denny power line, which is scheduled for a highly controversial 'upgrade'. But that is of course a misnomer – a dishonest one at that – because many of the new pylons will dwarf what they are due to replace. These plans certainly lack vision, and will, I suspect, go down in history as crass.

The Corrieyairack Pass, which rises to almost the same elevation as some of the hills round the summit, is watched over by Creag a Chail (760m) and Carn Leac (884m), where the end of the Spey catchment hands over to the River Tarff drainage area. Beyond Glen Tarff lies Glen Doe and the Allt Doe Water, where Scotland's most recent hydro-electric scheme has been constructed. It has won plaudits for its environmental sensitivity, with the dam carefully hidden amongst the hills and only visible at close quarters. Between Carn Leac and Poll-gormack Hill (806m), a strange double line of deer fences running in parallel rather dominates the scene, and poses the question as to why two fences so close together were necessary. Although there are many sections of the Watershed in which fence lines prevail, some are redundant, and so gradually disintegrate. Where they have been replaced, most of the remains of the earlier version have been removed, and in only a few locations are there foot-catching strands of rusting wire lying around; these should be cut into short lengths and taken off the hills altogether.

A wide area of rugged peat hag and bog, where the scant remains of a fence have all but sunk, then crosses to the prominent Carn Dearg (815m). Although perched close to the edge of the deep Great Glen trench, a final 3km of undulating moorland precedes the rapid descent into the upper reaches of the forest and a horse-shoe round the Allt an Lagain. Here the Creag nan Gobhar (497m), *crag of the branching river,* (497m) demands a final ascent prior to more pine needles down the back of the neck, and through the forest to the crossing of the old railway track just north of Laggan.

Arriving at the Great Glen is auspicious; it marks a juncture that is just past the half-way point on the Watershed, with in excess of 600km down and just over 500km to go. This offers an appropriate interlude in which to reflect on the experience to date. The three Marches already covered have been very different in terrain and character, but the common factor has been their wildness. There has been evidence of some of the major episodes in the creation of Scotland, and its evolution through fire, ice, water and time – *the abyss of time,* indeed. The journey has included some 50 areas with conservation or biodiversity objectives, mainly comprising the many different designated areas, and a number of key conservation properties. The recurrent theme of trees and forest has provided a glimpse into the landscapes of 7,000 years ago, and given a tantalising image of what parts of it will become once again. Our journey has provided a unique, comprehensive and unfolding vista across much of Scotland south of this fault-line; down great river valleys and lochs, over moorland both familiar and obscure, and by shaded bealach and wide mountaintop.

Solitude with Nature and the skylark have been our beguiling companions.

THE MOINE MARCH

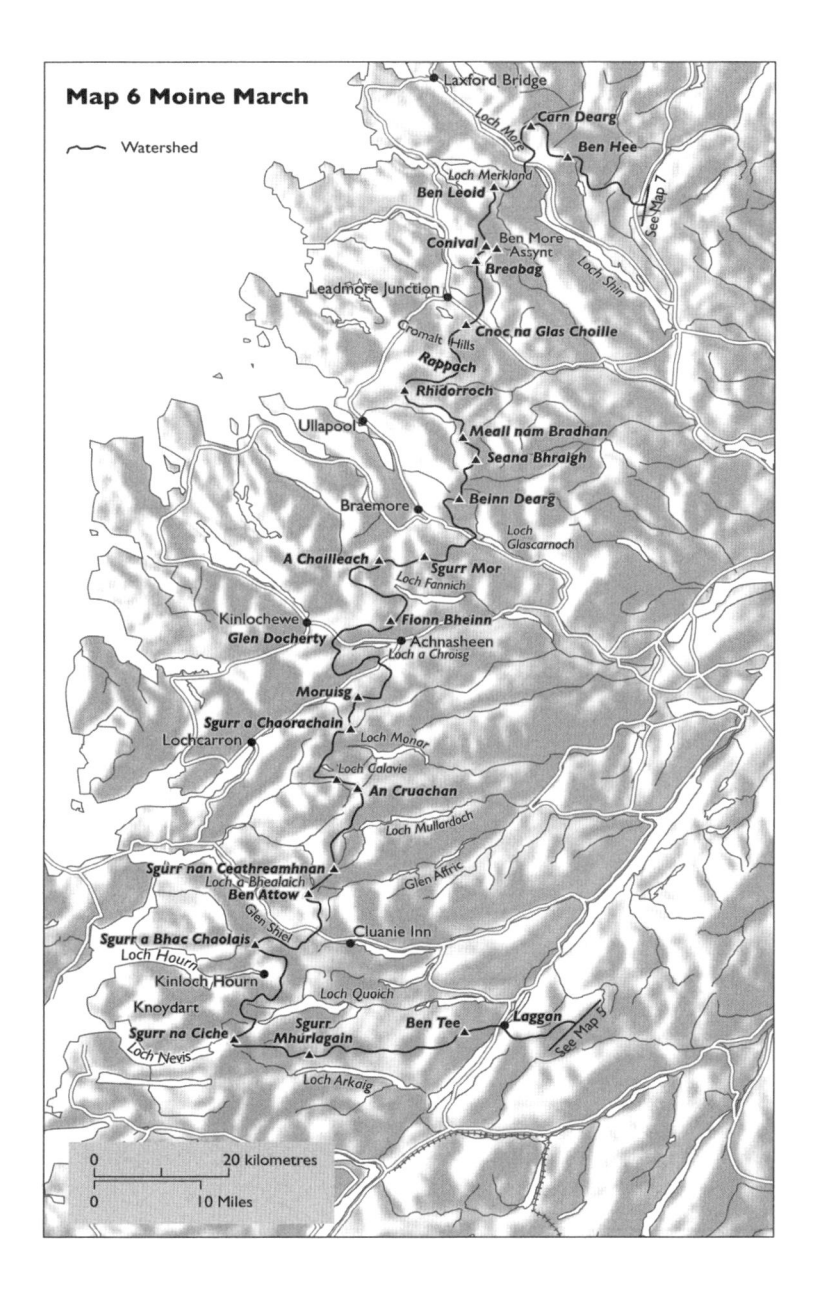

Map 6 Moine March

～ Watershed

CHAPTER FIVE

The Moine March

Solitude,
And a distant coast,
Grandeur,
Amongst peak, crag and loch,
Weather:
The anthem for wildness.

THE MAJESTY OF THE Moine march is without parallel; the unfettered drama of the mountain scene gives it special appeal. With 27 Munros and a fine succession of related tops, the average elevation of 595m presents a continuous unfolding kaleidoscope of vistas across to the western seaboard, the Minch and beyond. The eastward panoramas are punctuated by long lochs and glens pointing towards the North Sea shore and, in a few locations, the topography offers a brief glimpse of salt water on both sides simultaneously. Almost 50 per cent of the 330km is designated, and the emptiness of the terrain is reinforced by the infrequency of road crossings. With an average of over 40km between them it has (almost) escaped the motor age. The 28 footpath and track crossings occur at an average frequency of every 12km. Although it doesn't altogether escape the presence of communications masts and pylons, there is not a single house or barn directly on the entire length of the Moine march.

From Carn Dearg the steep, sharp profile of Ben Tee hints at a very different terrain on the far side of the Great Glen, and from Beinn Bhan this anticipation is intensified; there is a tangible sense of something dramatic just ahead. There is time for a brew-up beside the cairn though, and it is here that the immensity of the Great

Glen appears in all its splendour. A vast trench almost 500m deep and, at this point, over a kilometre wide has opened up in front; Creag nan Gobhar is on the brink.

If it can be said of a geographic feature that it has attitude, then this is it. Formed over 400 million years ago, it sweeps in one assertive and very straight fault-line, running directly from coast to coast. Its genesis was a vertical split in the earth's crust, in which the northern section moved about 100km north-eastwards relative to the southern land-mass; thus adding a further element to the three-dimensional jigsaw of Scotland. But of course that wasn't the end of the story, because it created a natural line of weakness for the glaciers to work on, and work on it they did, as they ground away the sharper edges of the fault, and gouged out what became a series of lochs, including one of the deepest loch trenches in the country. This long slow process almost cut a channel which would have linked Ocean and Sea, for it reduced the highest point in the glen to a mere 35m above sea level. Fast forward to about 6,100 BC and an underwater rock-fall on the Storegga Slide just off the Norwegian coast caused a tsunami in which there was a 21m surge which swept up Great Glen at least as far as the top of the top of the locks system at Fort Augustus. Consider such a large body of water sweeping along a confined space, and it would have had even more impact around the head of Loch Ness than on the open coast.

In my earlier comments on the early mapping of Scotland, and posing the question as to when it might have been possible to plot the Watershed with a fair degree of accuracy, I considered the Great Glen crossing as a critical point. Closer examination shows that Loch Ness is at an elevation of 17m, Loch Oich is 32m, with a slightly raised level to assist with canal navigation, and Loch Lochy at 33m. The Watershed crosses Great Glen between Loch Oich and Loch Lochy at 35m, close to Laggan Church, and the descent through the forest from Creag nan Gobhar is greatly helped by a conveniently placed ride crossing two forest tracks and the former railway track-bed on the way. This transition from Heartland to Moine is indeed the most spectacular, and creates a fine sense of occasion for the approach to and descent into the Great Glen. From the former railway, the Forestry Commission boundary below Bruach Buidhe, which runs at an angle between two cottages to meet the A82, seems to mark the Watershed. The construction of the Caledonian Canal in 1822 altered the landscape by raising the level of Loch Oich, changing the line of some burns, excavating the trench for the canal, and the creation of embankments from the spoil. One of the effects of raising the level of the loch was to create an area of fen at its southern end. Now known as South Laggan Fen, these 11 hectares of wetland are designated as SSSI and lie very close to the Watershed.

So the Great Glen is a straight, low-lying strip of land and water running from Fort William to Inverness – a convenient and traditional line of communication. Long before General Wade built his military road through the glen in 1727, to link the three Forts – William, Augustus and George – a well-used track passed this way. The canal followed a hundred years later, and the railway almost a century after that, but that was short-lived, coming too late and not providing any through route between the settlements at either end. The A82 was largely a creation of the 1920s and '30s, though there have been further improvements to it since the war. The canal builders faced a major challenge at 'the summit' at Laggan, where they had to cut through a formidable area of hard rock; but the softly wooded appearance of this location today gives not a hint of the difficulty that they encountered. And, bringing the travel story up to date, the creation of the Great Glen Way in 2002 has given walkers and cyclists a varied and interesting, but not too demanding, coast to coast route through the hills. At Laggan, it follows the path through the trees on top of the embankment, and on a sunny day the dappled light makes for a delightful journey.

Loch Lochy Youth Hostel is no more, but an enterprising local resident has bought the building, refurbished it and renamed it the Great Glen Hostel, and it is hoped that he will prosper where SYHA struggled. The exact line of the Watershed is not easy to determine here due to the altered landscape, but it would seem, once again,

THE MOINE MARCH

Crossing by bike in the Great Glen at Laggan. Dappled light on a traveller across the Watershed.

that there are no houses or other buildings right on the line, the closest being about 100m away. A detour of some 300m via the swing bridge at the south end of Loch Oich is necessary, as swimming the canal is not to be recommended. And the choice is then to either cross some rough grazing immediately across the canal, or to join the minor road nearby. Just beyond the North Laggan Farm, a steady ascent leads onto the moors before Ben Tee (901m) probably from Beinn an t-sithein, the *sharp* or *cone shaped mountain*, or much more appealingly, the *fairy mountain*. On the way some remnants of juniper cover give a hint at how it would have appeared were it not for what John Muir referred to as 'hoofed locusts'. But, in fairness to the sheep, I suspect that deer will have done their bit too.

There are deer fences and then there are deer fences, and the one just before the Lochan Diota is a formidable construction, with great big iron posts drilled and leaded into the bedrock; it doesn't wobble. The well rehearsed procedure for getting over just such a deer fence is deployed, and once again it works a treat – with no damage to fence, clothing or dignity. On Ben Tee a new vista to Glen Garry and Glen Kingie is revealed. The view out over Loch Garry to the hills and intersecting valley beyond is once again filled with promise.

Most people are content to climb any particular mountain once or perhaps just a few times, but I came across a truly remarkable record for Ben Tee, with 1,048 ascents by one Richard Wood. He lived and worked in the area for many years, and developed a particular affection for this peak. The challenges and ever-changing weather, the light, surface vegetation and wild flowers, the rich birdlife, and different approaches all combined to ensure that no two ascents were ever really the same.

The fine ridge of Meall a Choire Ghlais, at exactly 900m, can only be reached after a steep but familiar descent and immediate ascent – 350m down and very much the same back up again, but mostly on good firm grassy terrain. The ridge offers a pleasant pretty level walk on dry rock, giving a pleasing break from the earlier exertions, and time to take in the views. Some last vistas of the

Great Glen and all around; Loch Ness catching the light in one direction, and the hope of seeing Ben Nevis soon in the other. The fine succession of tops which take the Watershed on this 60km sweep westwards from Carn Leac in the Heartland, right into the Rough Bounds of Barrisdale, is decisive.

Loch Arkaig soon comes into view on the left, and takes up the task of receiving the very generous rainfall of this area, before pouring it via the short River Arkaig into Loch Lochy at Bunarkaig. At less than 2km long it must be one of the shortest rivers in Scotland. The passing glaciers did a neat job on and around these hills, for they are all shapely. Lochan Fhudair lies at the bottom of another 500m deep trench before Meall na h-Eilde (838m), and the bealachs on either side of Meall Coire nan Saobhaidh (826m) have been named as Bealach Choire a Ghuerein and the Bealach Carn na h-Urchaire respectively, with the latter being a reference to something or someone having been shot. The next tops are about white and black, with Geal (*white*) Charn (804m), followed by Carn Dubh (*black*) (604m). Between Sgurr Choinich (749m), with its steep eastern side, and Meall Lochan nan Dubh Lochan (567m), lies the first encounter with a quaking bog or flow, which needs to be crossed with care. It is a kind of hybrid between a loch and a moor, with parts of the mat of surface vegetation floating between areas of more open water. While treacherous for walkers, it is nonetheless an exceptionally valuable habitat.

Poor Meall Blair (656m) with its trig is just a *plain lump*, for that is what it means, but the loch of the same name is more appreciated, as it is protected along with seven others within the West Inverness-shire Lochs SSSI. Notable for two species in particular, the black-throated diver and the common scoter, the surrounding grass and heathland habitats provide ideal terrain for both nesting and brood rearing. The loch is deep, and the Watershed skirts its northern end beyond the Lochan Dubh. The craggy tops of Mam an Doire Dhuinn (564m), Druim Coire an Stangain Bhig and Sgurr Mhurlagain (880m) are a mild, if understated, precursor to all that will follow, but they do give the opportunity to look south over

Loch Arkaig, and the Pinewood SSSI on the hillside opposite. This protected area would surely have extended along the entire south side of the loch had it not been the unfortunate victim of a major fire during the last war, allegedly caused by the Commandos, who were based in Achnacarry House.

Fraoch Bheinn (858m) stands firmly on guard upon this westward sweep of the Watershed. The descent from Sgurr Mhurlagain, though dramatic, had been eased by the spur which leads down gently to the bealach, where the track from Strathan to Glen Kingie crosses. Strathan, now a small assortment of buildings which includes a former school, stalkers' cottages, kennels, farm buildings and the ruins of a barracks was, in an earlier existence, the centre of a scattered and more substantial population.

Tradition has it that there is buried treasure at Murlaggan nearby, valuables which had been destined to help fund the Jacobite cause. The supporters of the Stuarts never came to get it, or it arrived too late, if they arrived at all. On the other side of the Watershed, Kinbreack Bothy is only 2km distant, and offers good shelter for those passing through. It is one of those cottages hidden deep in a glen, with almost 700m of mountain towering over it on every side. For many months in the winter, the sun's rays never penetrate.

Fraoch Bheinn, *the heather hill,* is one of these tops. Its bulk is over 3km long, but less than half that in width sitting decisively astride the Watershed. And the line goes straight over the top – up 400m on the east side, and almost straight down some 500m on the west elevation into the bealach below. Once again route-finding becomes an all-consuming preoccupation – there are few places on the entire Watershed which present such a rapid ascent and descent.

An outlying spur of Druim a Chuirn (815m) is Sron a Tigh Mhoir, which brings another reference to a *nose* and *a big house,* though where the latter might have been, is obscure. After the quick ascent of Fraoch Bheinn, the next 10km is on a ridge which rarely drops below 700m. On the map, the line seems to flow effortlessly from top to top; from Sgurr Cos na Breachd-laoigh (835m) to the much snappier An Eag (873m) *peak of the notches,*

Sgurr nan Coireachan (935m) *peak of the corries*, then Garbh Chioch Bheag (968m), *peak of the little breast*, and finally Garbh Chioch Mhor (1,013m), *big rough place of the breast*. These provide an ascending litany of some of the very best names, but on the rock the line is anything but flowing. It lurches from pinnacle to outcrop, where the hand of nature has carved fantastic shapes and gnarled formations.

There is hardly time during the taxing route-finding to look to the left, where A Chuil Bothy sits almost surrounded by forest in Glen Dessary below, whilst Glen Kingie has been left behind and Loch Quoich is now lapping the northern tip of the ridge running off to the right, adding the plentiful rainfall to be turned into electric power.

Sgurr na Ciche (1,040m), *peak of the breast*, is another reference to the female form – its pointed ness must have been seen as a very youthful example. This prominent top is the start of the big National Scenic Area (NSA) of Knoydart, and the River Carnach which enters Loch Nevis at Sourlies, takes over. The guides say that there are three ways of approaching this formidable hill, impressive from any direction. The first is along the ridge of the Watershed, the second is the long haul up from Sourlies Bothy at the head of Loch Nevis, and the third is by boat across Loch Quoich. A sharp right turn is called for here, lest the Watershed should slide further west and drop into the sea. A former stalker on Glen Kingie estate spoke of this hill being at the very western extremity of the estate, and they felt that to go beyond would risk 'falling over the edge'.

This area brings the generally western location of the Watershed into sharp focus, with two sea lochs reaching out to touch it. The eastward penetration of Lochs Nevis and Hourn into Scotland's land mass is almost Norwegian: 'fjord' would be an apt description, certainly in relation to the latter.

Here is the Rough Bounds, the huge expanse and jumble of ridges and intersecting glens constrained only by the sea lochs, and inviting greater exploration. Knoydart peninsula is anchored in these hills of the Watershed, as if to remind it that it is still part of the mainland and not an island. Accessible only by a long walk in,

Loch Nevis from Sgurr nan Coireachan. One of the finest and most dramatic ridges of the Watershed.

or by boat to Inverie, it is one of the spiritual haunts of those who have fallen in love with Scotland's wilder terrain.

Knoydart was the last mainland outpost of a predominantly Catholic population – it's as if it was beyond the reach of the Reformation. All that came to an end in 1853, when over 300 of the people were herded onto the *Sillery* and shipped off to Canada. The clearances of Knoydart were a grim and brutal episode, and the only voice of protest came from the priest; a lonely voice in a big emptiness. A visit to Inverie today gives more than just a glimmer of hope that over 150 years of decline have come to an end. In the community buy-out by the Knoydart Foundation, and with the support of its partners, including the John Muir Trust, there is a new beginning. And this new beginning is driven by that compelling combination of place and people, environment and those who have the greatest stake in its future; the local population. Woodland regeneration sits side by side with modest but sustainable tourist development. There is a growing harmony between what people do in, or to, the environment, and the pressing need for economic and social development.

Careful route-finding is again called for here, picking a way north-eastwards by Meall Choire Duibh (740m), *lump of the black corrie*, takes a bit of care. As Loch Quoich gets closer some thoughts on its earlier form and subsequent alteration come to mind. The small loch was transformed into a 7km sheet of water when the hydro-electric scheme of 1962 was created. Prior to that event, a number of settlements near its west end, and a shooting lodge, clung to the shores. In the 18th century the outlaw Ewen McPhee lived on an island in the loch with his family. He had been arrested for desertion, but escaped and managed to avoid capture for 45 years; he lived to a ripe old age under difficult circumstances. He may have been helped by local people because he became something of a personality and folk hero. The Kinlochquoich Lodge was a favourite of people like Sir Edwin Landseer, the painter, and Edward VII, and it featured regularly in the weather reports as the station with the highest rainfall in the British Isles. The only evidence of its existence today is in spring when a lilac streak runs up the hillside to the north – for *Rhododendron ponticum* escaped from the policies and seems to be making a bid for Cluanie Inn. As the water level of the loch rises and falls, due to the demand for electricity and the seasonal fluctuation in rainfall, so a grey and white tide-mark mars the shoreline. But the other side to this is that the loch and a good number of other hydro-electric schemes in the Highlands do much to help meet our rising targets for renewable energy.

The smaller of the two dams is at the west end of Loch Quoich, and this raised a question as to whether it had been built on the Watershed, or to east or west of it. With reference to a hydrographic map predating the construction of the dam, I was able to check-out the position. It transpired that the dam is indeed on the Watershed, or at most, a few metres to the east of it. Either way, it makes crossing the bealach an easy stroll, and the surrounding land, which was disturbed some 50 years ago for road and other construction purposes, has become a rich wild flower habitat; the orchids and thyme love it.

A dead sheep lying in the lee of the northern end of the dam ensured that I didn't delay, but set about the hefty ascent of Sgurr Airigh na Beinne (776m) with gusto. This top leads onto the Druim Chosaidh ridge, which presents a long succession of stone waves to be negotiated, as each one obstructs the way. The ridge ends with Sgurr a Choire bheithe (913m), a pulpit of a place projecting boldly westwards towards Barrisdale and the Knoydart peninsula. It presides over a change in the drainage in the Rough Bounds, with the River Carnoch, which empties into Loch Nevis at Camusrory, giving way to the River Barrisdale.

Sgurr a Choire bheithe is the westernmost point on the entire Watershed. A look at a map shows almost every peak in the area to be surrounded by *rocky doodles* – small billowing black lines in which the contours have been swallowed up; this is a vivid portrayal of what is to be found on the ground. At about 5km west of the head of Loch Hourn, it is very much in the heart of the Rough Bounds, and rough could not be a more apt description of all of the surrounding terrain. A somewhat tortuous ridge comes round from Druim Chosaidh, and drops steeply to a bealach before rising again just as rapidly onto Slat Bheinn. The word slat can either mean a *wand* or *penis* – perhaps chosen to give some gender balance after all those mams, chiochs and a ciche! In any event, it is a strange and primeval looking mountain; one of the wildest on the Watershed. It illustrates the almost unimaginable power of glaciation. For, although the ice-sheet sliced away much more mountain than it left behind, what we see is but the stump of the many layers of rock which once overlaid this grandeur. But here, the rocks look like they have only recently bubbled up out of the bowels of the earth, and the scant pockets of greenery have gained only the lightest toehold in the crevices and hollows. The great rounded haunches and slabs of rock make for fine walking and scrambling though.

Slat Bheinn sits like a giant stopper on the pass between upper

In the Rough Bounds. Where Knoydart is 'moored' to the Scottish mainland by the Watershed hills.

Glen Barrisdale and Gleann Cosaidh, apparently blocking the way from east to west. On its northern side a lonely track winds its way through between lochan and outcrop. Prior to the dam, this track would have run down towards the settlements which now lie submerged under the waves on the loch. It now loops round to the right along the side of Loch Quoich before returning west again by the small dam at the end of the loch. From there it rejoins itself at the remote Ambraigh, where a right turn leads to Barrisdale on the shores of Loch Hourn, and a left turn to Inverie, via the Mam Barrisdale pass and the Gleann an Dubh Lochain. For generations of walkers, the mere mention of these remote routes has had an air of pilgrimage about it – into the very heart of the Rough Bounds.

From our elevated vantage, we look down on a primeval landscape that truly lacks order, and out of that chaos, magnificence has been born.

Still to the west, over 1,000 hectares of upper Glen Barrisdale forms a rich and important pinewood habitat, with associated birchwood and moor, all protected as SSSI. The lichens in this site are particularly important, and because of the maritime influence, there is a wealth of oceanic species. Rough country continues along the Sgurr a Chlaidheimh (841m) ridge, and then drops just before Coire Beithe to one of the longest dead end roads in the country. This single track road from the A87 at Loch Garry takes a tortuous 35km to get to Kinloch Hourn, and the last 3km descends steeply to the sea in a route that would not suit the timid driver. Until the late 1960s the road turned off the old A87 at Tomdoun Hotel, but the creation of the Glen Loyne hydro-scheme changed all that. The old A87 wound its way from Glen Garry to Tomdoun and then over the shoulder into Glen Loyne. From there it climbed to 435m before dropping to Cluanie Lodge and the inn of the same name. Glen Loyne was submerged behind a great concrete dam, the road was re-routed via Bunloyne to meet the A887, then across to Loch Duich by way of Glen Shiel. When the water level in the new Loch Loyne is low, the old hump-backed bridge on the former road emerges forlornly from a sea of peat.

The water draining from the north side of Sgurr Chlaidheimh which would otherwise have found its way to Kinloch Hourn is now captured in a culvert and directed east to add to Loch Quoich.

A line of pylons and inevitable mast tarnish the Watershed, which is just over one kilometre west of Loch Quoich, but in almost every other respect this landscape shows all of the wildness and primeval qualities of that surrounding the head of Glen Barrisdale. And this continuity prevails across a succession of very fine tops; Meall an Uilt Bhain (607m), Sgurr a Mhaoraich Beag (948m), *little peak of the shellfish,* and Sgurr Thionail (906m) give a real sense that the hand of man has not left much evidence. The track coming up from Kinloch Hourn to meet another in Wester Glen Quoich is but a scratch in an otherwise unmarred landscape. Looking across to the south side of the South Glen Shiel ridge gives a fine picture of a Munro-bagger's paradise. This side is clean-cut and almost devoid of crags, whereas the north side is a jumble of counter ridges and deep corries leading down to the valley floor. Munroists love this ridge for you will hear them remark that *South Glen Shiel gives as many as seven in one day*; I will return to this later.

A clear horseshoe round the head of Wester Glen Quoich takes in Sgurr a Bhac Chaolais (885m), where the westward drainage becomes the River Shiel, and then meets the Bealach Dubh Leac, *bealach of the black slab* or *grave*. This track from Achnagart Farm on the A87 to Loch Quoich or Glen Loyne climbs to 719m in just over 3km, and I have heard reports of groups on horseback fairly recently trekking this way. The first top on the south Glen Shiel ridge which is Watershed territory is Creag nan Damh (918m), *rock of the stags*, and this is the end of the National Scenic Area – but not for long. Of the five tops on the ridge which are also on the Watershed, three are Munros, and there is a rather pathetic and well worn track which bypasses the two that are not; a sad reflection on some erstwhile mountaineers. The idea that they should say 'if it ain't a Munro, then don't climb it' is definitely not in the spirit of this place.

The row of tops make a really fine regiment, with Sgurr Beag

(896m) followed by Sgurr an Lochain (1,004m), *peak of the little loch*, and Sgurr an Doire Leathain (1,010m), *peak of the broad thicket*, succeeded by Sgurr Coire na Feinne (902m). Here the change to the drainage pattern gives the River Cluanie to the west, and Loch Cluanie to the east. This forms the River Morriston, which enters the waters of Loch Ness at Invermorriston. Druim Tholaidh completes this ridge as the Watershed descends to the A87 crossing. Like every other deep bealach on the Watershed, the view from one side to the other is foreshortened in a very disorientating way. The opposite side always looks depressingly steep, as it seems to present the prospect of a very challenging ascent ahead. This is some quirk of perspective though, because the reality is never quite as demanding as anticipated.

Samuel Johnson and James Boswell spent the autumn of 1773 touring the Highlands and Western Islands. The *Journal of a Tour to the Hebrides* was published in 1775 and is Boswell's account of this somewhat demanding adventure. We are told that on 1 September:

> We passed through Glensheal, with prodigious mountains on each side. We saw where the battle was fought in the year 1719. Dr Johnson owned he was now in a scene of as wild nature as he could see; but he corrected me sometimes in my inaccurate observations.
> There, (said I), is a mountain like a cone.
> Johnson:
> No Sir. It would be called so in a book; and when a man comes to look at it, he sees it is not so. It is indeed pointed at the top; but one side of it is larger than the other. Another mountain I called immense.
> Johnson:
> No; it is no more than a considerable protuberance.

Close to this 'considerable protuberance' lies the Cluanie Inn, a favourite haunt of climbers, which gives ready access to the mountains on both sides of the glen. The A87 is the main road to Skye and, like so many main roads, much of the traffic is going somewhere

South Glenshiel Ridge. Boswell and Johnson here had a passionate discourse on the shape of 'a protuberance'.

else in a hurry, only affording passengers a cursory glance at the magnificent scenery on either side of the glen.

A strategically placed gap in the forest on the north side gives ready access to Meall a Charra (806m), *hill of the friend*, though much of the forest has now been felled, and it is hoped that the restocking will involve something a bit more imaginative and pleasing than Sitka. Such is the depth of Glen Shiel that the summit of Sgurr a Bhealaich Dheirg (1,036m), *peak of the red pass,* cannot be seen from the road below, but on Meall a Charra the gently rounded top of its larger neighbour comes clearly into view.

Two major National Scenic Areas meet on the Watershed, and run side by side for the next 11km, with Kintail to the left, and Glen Affric to the right. Kintail with its Five Sisters is a National Trust for Scotland property, which was purchased in the early days of that organisation thanks to the generosity and vision of Percy Unna. Glen Affric, which includes large areas of Scottish Natural

Heritage property, is famed and valued for its inspirational pinewood regeneration. From the summit of Sgurr a Bhealaich Dheirg, the vistas in every direction easily repay spending some time for a brew-up, with binoculars at the ready.

There is a natural change in the drainage pattern from here, with both River and Loch Affric flowing eastwards, which then become the River Glass at Cannich, and eventually enters the Beauly Firth at Beauly. That in turn becomes the Moray Firth, beyond the Kessock Bridge at Inverness. The retreating glacier left Cnoc Biodaig (361m), *hill of the dirk,* almost on the Watershed between Glen Lichd and Glen Affric. Four kilometres to the west is Glenlicht House which the University of Edinburgh Mountaineering Society use as a club hut – although it is a little more substantial than its name suggests. Just 1km east of Cnoc Biodaid is Camban Bothy which was first renovated in the late 1960s in memory of the climber Philip Tranter, who died in 1966, and who wrote the novel *No Tigers in the Hindu Kush*. He was the first to achieve what became known as the 'Glen Nevis Round', which involves climbing all nine of the Munros on the Mamores side of the glen, and then a further four ending on Ben Nevis, all within a 24 hour period. His was a significant contribution to Scottish mountaineering, and his death was keenly felt. Camban Bothy is a fitting memorial. Another three kilometres to the north east is Alltbeithe Hostel, one of the homeliest I have ever stayed in. On a coast-to-coast a few years ago I experienced a warm welcome in the hills there, and in the morning woke to see a small herd of deer grazing contentedly just a few metres from the door; a rather special occasion.

Back at Camban and the Watershed walk, I saw a fox at fairly close quarters, though I suspect it saw me first. Reckoning I posed no threat continued on its way unmolested. A fenced plantation of young native trees on the lower slopes of a mountain with two names – Ben Attow or Beinn Fhada, caught my attention. The wild flowers growing inside the enclosure were much fewer in number than on the outside. Without the grazing deer, the ground vegetation was taller and perhaps more rank, but the trees were doing well.

This is a fine example of a longer term benefit – yes, the wild flowers have diminished, crowded out by the longer grasses, but in time the trees will mature and attract a considerably wider range of birdlife in particular. The trees will add a new texture and seasonal colour to the hillsides, and there will have been a net gain in biodiversity.

Ben Attow, also known as Beinn Fhada (1,032m), *the long mountain*, stands sentinel at the eastern end of a block of mountains, which are in turn surrounded by popular through tracks from Glen Affric to Loch Duich at Morvich. Its long plateau summit is ringed with deep corries and slabs on three sides and, were it needed, it would make a magnificent lookout post offering fine clear views down several neighbouring glens. The descent to the north and the shores of Loch a Bhealaich is steep and requires careful route-finding. When I was about to set out on this stretch of my walk northwards from Glen Shiel, my elder son Kenneth asked me where I was heading for. I explained that it was into Kintail, West Monar and beyond, he remarked:

'Its quiet there, you won't see many people in that remoteness.'

How right he was.

One of my most recent and treasured discoveries has been a small booklet written by the late Kenneth Robertson. He has already been quoted; he was my uncle, and can be held responsible, in part at least, for inspiring my love of wild places and the mountains of Scotland. At the end of each year he produced for family and friends an informative and well-written account of his outings; these were always a joy to read. His little booklet on *The Wilderness* was for me a recent discovery, which opened a new appreciation of how he saw the Scottish mountain areas.

He called it a *Little Essay*, and started by considering the literary sources which will have helped to subtly shape our perception of wilderness. He draws on a variety of quotes including the Bible and Bunyan, Wordsworth and GM Hopkins, and from these gives the spectrum of wilderness as a terrifying or desolate place on the one hand, to its more romantic qualities on the other. Some would

Beinn Fhada from Sgurr a Dubh Coire. With Glen Affric on one side, Glen Licht on the other, and Five Sisters as neighbours, it is in good company.

argue that the wilderness or wild areas stand on their own, and that their qualities are source enough. In reality, like the quality of solitude, it is deeply personal; I find the undercurrents which literature provides are a worthy dimension to it. In any event, these sources are deeply rooted in the mountain culture, and their influence on everyone is both subtle and profound. Kenneth then touched on the old issue of wilderness and wildness, and acknowledged the difficulty of their definitions. It is all relative, he concluded.

I was delighted to find that of the six areas he chose and wrote about, three are directly on the Watershed, one is partly on it, one is next door, and only Cairngorm is not. Ben Alder, Affric/Kintail and northwards, and Beinn Dearg/Seana Braigh are the three that find the Watershed running right along their tops, in Knoydart/ Barrisdale it is the Watershed that almost anchors the peninsula to the rest of mainland Scotland, and Fisherfield/ Letterewe provides some major peaks to be admired from the Watershed. Of Ben Alder area he said:

Its inaccessibility is a large measure of its charm ... a wild country of moorland, peat bogs, hills and barren glens.

Whilst his comments on Affric/Kintail include:

This splendid tract of the Western Highlands covers a huge roadless area of mountains, lochs, moorlands and empty glens.

Those familiar with these areas will appreciate the sentiment, and no doubt wish to add their own perceptions.

Camping by the *loch of the bealach* is a special experience, as the sense of isolation and wildness is evident. Surrounded by magnificent hills, and with the sound of water lapping on the shore, this spot is almost perfect. Drifting off to sleep, with the knowledge that there are another three days of this remote living ahead, is soporific; Nature's own sleeping draught.

The River Elchaig has now picked up the drainage to the west, and it enters Loch Duich via Loch Long at Dornie, having plunged over the Falls of Glomach, still within the bounds of the National Trust for Scotland property. Moving northwards Sgurr Gaorsaic (839m) and Beinn an t-Socaich (910m) take the Watershed to its highest point at Sgurr nan Ceathreamhnan (1,151m), *peak of the quarters*. This marks the end of the NSA, as its boundary then follows the tops to the north of Glen Affric. A further change in the drainage from the Watershed also occurs here, with various burns forming the headwaters that empty into Loch Mullardoch, which becomes the River Cannich and then helps to form the River Glass at Cannich.

The journey northwards follows the Watershed through the middle of an immense area of isolation, with no public roads, a few through tracks and some very large estates. Kilillan and Benula together cover some 32,000 hectares in which nature and deer hold sway, with forestry and farming being generally nearer the periphery. As long as the owner gets a good bag of deer in the few days each year that he is resident, he is content to benignly let the

Skye from West Benula. Like a vast regatta in full sail on The Minch

wildlife prosper. The prominence which is the most distant from habitation is probably Mam Ruisgte, *the bared breast,* on the flanks of An Socach (1,069m), *the pert female*. This is over 15km from a public road in any direction. But to get there along the Watershed there are a number of tops to be taken including Stuc Bheag (1,075m), Stuc Mor (1,041m), Creag Ghlas (856m) and both the hill and loch, *of the file* or *tooth,* Sgurr nan h-Eige (657m). Loch an Droma is aptly named as the *loch of the ridge,* and lies beside the track from Iron Lodge to Loch Mullardoch. Iron Lodge is not what it seems, or at least what the name might imply, for the present building is not iron at all, but a 1980s bungalow. This incongruity in such a remote and magnificent setting has been abandoned fairly recently, and the elements are beginning to take their toll on its fabric.

Just beyond Carn na Breabaig (678m) the Affric and Cannich Hills sssi and Strathglass sac run alongside the Watershed. On Meall Shuas (732m) the westwards drainage changes to the River

Ling, which enters Loch Long at Killilan, and at An Socach, the eastward pattern is picked up by Loch Monar, *loch of the high ground*, which empties into the River Farrar and joins the River Glass at Struy. On An Cruachan (706m), *the hip*, the designated areas end. A number of tracks converge below An Socach, and the Maol-bhuidhe Bothy lies 3km to the west. Cnoc a Mhoraire sits almost in the middle of an area which is dotted with lochans and patches of bog, giving a difficult bit of route-finding to reach the *mountain of the hump*, Beinn Dronaig (797m).

In his book *Isolation Shepherd*, Iain R Thomson provides a valuable insight into life and living in the remote West Monar Forest area until the coming of the hydro-electric scheme in the early 1960s. The level of Loch Monar was then raised, and it grew some six miles in length, flooding much of the area around Pait and Strathmore at its western end and close to the Watershed. Iain Thomson and his young family were the last to live at Pait before it was demolished and the foundations disappeared beneath the rising waters. It was a remote life, which called for a degree of self-reliance that would rarely be called for today. Access to their isolated shepherd's cottage with its essential byre and hayfield, was generally by boat from Monar Lodge, and that at the end of a long journey up Strathfarrar from Struy. In the few years that he lived there, Iain gathered a wealth of information and lore about the area, its life, work and traditions, and has given a very valuable record of these.

I found that the sense of remoteness on this section was almost intense; any form of habitation was distant, and only those with a clear purpose would venture into this emptiness. So the glimpse into the herding and stalking life of the area of over 50 years ago, which Thomson's book gives, is a revelation. He writes of the many and varied experiences which both he and his predecessors had whilst living in the glens where the Watershed forms an arc round the headwaters. It is a tantalising story of a vanished way of life.

He recalls details like the group of Scouts that he met at Monar Lodge, and then transported up the loch by boat, along with a load of hay, to Pait. There they set off westwards with their handcarts, across the Watershed at the Bealach Bhearnais (600m) towards Achnashellach. In admiration, Thomson described them as 'hardy boys'. He recounts the story of a tramp who 50 years earlier, had set off on a similar journey, but in poor weather conditions. Having been fed and watered by the gamekeeper, he headed off into a snow storm, and the only evidence of his having been there came months later when some sheep dogs showed great interest in a lingering snow drift. His body was taken to Monar where it awaited removal by the police. No one had missed him, so his anonymity remains to this day.

The more romantic image of illicit distilling in the hills is associated with the inaccessible north-facing crags of Meall Mor. The father and son team of Alister and Hamish Mhor somehow outwitted the excise man, and for much of the mid 19th century produced a legendary local tipple close to the Watershed.

Iain adds a further touch of humour in his description of a funeral cortege from Pait which bore the remains of a 'matronly woman of ample size' to be buried on the shores of Loch Duich. The party assembled for the task included just about every able-bodied man in the area, and as they crossed the Watershed below the steep slopes of An Cruachan, they took it in turns to bear the coffin on their shoulders. The single and most important factor in achieving this was their 'fuel', which consisted of fair quantities of that illicit nectar from the still on Meall Mor.

This part of the Watershed may be quiet now, but at times in the past it saw all sorts of unlikely activity, including moving a thirty foot flat bottomed boat called *The Flyer*, which weighed several tons, from Loch Carron to Monar. It was in the late-1880s that this difficult task was carried out, with the vessel being variously dragged by horses past Bendronaig Lodge, onto Loch Calavie, and then by more horse hauling and loch floating, to be formally launched on Loch Monar at Pait. It then served the estate transport needs for many years. And then, in true Victorian style, a fence was constructed at the behest of one WL Winans, who was the shooting tenant at the time. He wanted to be sure of his bag, and resolved to ensure that 'his deer' didn't stray onto any other estate. So he ordered the construction of this fence with heavy iron posts to run all the way from the sea at Killilan. It took over two years and a small army of workers to build it and, during that period, probably had a significant impact on the local economy. I came across the rusting remains of the 'Great Fence' in the bog west of An Cruachan.

On a much sadder note, Thomson tells of a shepherd and his family who lived in a particularly remote cottage at the foot of Corrie Ghraigh-Fhear. The shepherd's three-year-old son died as a result of an accident, and was then borne in a home-made coffin, to be buried at Clach an Duich. The image of this tragic journey through the lonely country is sad indeed.

His final account of a Watershed related event tells of an expedition to retrieve some sheep that had strayed across to Bendronaig Estate. He and companion set off by Land Rover to drive by road all the way round the hills via Struy, Achnasheen and Achnashellach. By the time they got to this little settlement, they were feeling very thirsty, and stopped at the hotel for some liquid refreshment, by the time they left this hostelry, the day was getting late and Bendronaig was still some distance off. They got there in the gathering dusk and deteriorating weather, the older sheep were loaded into the back of the Land Rover, and then Iain set off on foot in the dark with the remaining 50 sheep. It was a grim trek through some wild and remote terrain, in which he became conscious of his own vulnerability. But, eventually, he recounted that it was with great relief he that he felt the track under his feet turn downhill, and could see the outline of the familiar hills of Strathmore.

These extracts are clearly worth the retelling, as they give a good flavour of the kind of human experience which must have taken place at so many of the Watershed crossings, even in the most remote and least populated areas. This experience on and around the Watershed was clearly at the more extreme end of the spectrum. Historically, life, labour and travel were simply all more difficult, and interaction with the terrain and the elements was more demanding. But these same factors that our ancestors had to contend with in the annual round of living and working are just what give it such appeal for us today.

Beinn Dronaig may be the *hill of the lump*, but it undoubtedly has its better northern side where the profile is more complimentary. The view from the track on the north side of Loch Calavie has great attraction, with the hill appearing to grow out of the bog at its eastern end and then rising steadily for over 500m in one long bold clean sweep. This would have been the very familiar, and perhaps reassuring, profile of the hill for those who used the summer shieling on the north shore of the loch. Meanwhile, the view of Beinn Dronaig from Lochcarron, as it rises behind Attadale, is framed beautifully by the hills and wooded slopes on either side. The people of that village must surely regard it as *their* guardian mountain.

The bealach at the western end of Loch Calavie is less than 20m above the loch and provides a short interlude between the steep descent from the beinn and the rapid ascent of Sail Riabhach (771m), the *brindled* or *grizzled heel*, by way of the *black crag*. Though the exact meaning of many of these names may now be elusive, those that can be translated almost without exception give a vivid description, full of character. I have a clear memory of the surprise that I got as I made my way up the gently sloping ridge towards Bidein a Choire Sheasgaich (945m), *little peak of the corrie of the barren cattle*. The short, sweet grass dotted with flowers was a delight to walk on, and the easier gradient gave more opportunity to fully appreciate these surroundings. So, ambling along almost in a trance, I was astonished to come upon two white ponies idly grazing at over 800m. Had they been mountain hares I would not have been at all surprised, but there they stood, heads down, having a sweet feed, as their tails swished languidly in the soft breeze. A very good and logical explanation was offered to me recently, as to why they were so high. It was outwith the stalking season, so their services were not needed for carrying deer carcasses off the hill. And, being wise beasts, they found that this high meadow was almost midge free; it made perfect sense.

At the bealach before Beinn Tharsuinn (817m) a distinctive stone

Loch Monar from Beinn Tharsuinn. Try as he might, the Excise Man could never be sure that he had eradicated every illicit whisky-still hidden in this majestic wildness.

dyke marks the Watershed, denoting an estate boundary. As I picked my way carefully down through loose scree and grass, I was intrigued to note how the dyke climbed straight up the other side, but gradually faded into the oblivion of the surrounding scree. Either the builders had had difficulty finding a firm enough footing for the dyke as it climbed a 45 degree slope on loose rock, or they failed to see the point of this demarcation and going any higher in such a remote place. The splendid ridge of Beinn Tharsuin curves in an arc with three marked spots on it. Short firm grasses with few outcrops make for easy going and the opportunity to take in the fine views; time for a brew-up. And it was here that I saw something else that almost took my breath away. I had walked for many hundreds of kilometres from that starting point on Peel Fell, along this east–west divide between an ocean and a sea, but had not seen both to the full simultaneously. Then, all of a sudden on Beinn Tharsuinn, the conditions were right – on one side I could see a glint of light catching the open waters of the Moray Firth, and on the other side the Minch gave back some of the afternoon sun; a special moment indeed. And, to added to this, the Minch looked like it had an ancient regatta taking place on it, with Skye billowing in full sail; ragged and clear, while Raasay kept somewhat in the shadow of its much larger neighbour, and the Small Isles trailed behind in this flotilla. All this called for an extended brew-up.

Just a few kilometres to the west is Bearneas Bothy, which is appreciated greatly by those who love these wild places and their splendid isolation. Their Bothy nestles just above the head of Loch an Laogh, the *loch of the calf*, and looks down towards the headwaters of what becomes the River Ling and the final link with Loch Duich. At the Bealach Bhearnais where those 'hardy scouts' reached an altitude of 600m with their handcarts, there is a significant change in the drainage westwards, as the headwaters of the River Carron come into play, which finally join the salt waters of Loch Carron at Achintee.

Monar Forest SSSI is entered at the bealach as the Watershed climbs the projecting and steep rocky shoulder of Sgurr Choinnich (999m) *mossy peak*. The principal and outstanding habitat feature that so merits protection here is the summit heath, but there are also snowbeds and dwarf shrub heath of note too. Both Sgurr Choinnich and its close neighbour Sgurr a Chaorachain (1,052m), *peak of the field of berries*, are like linked three-pointed stars on the map. The finely sculpted corries and the clear lines of the shoulders which separate them radiate from the summits. In *Hell of a Journey* Mike Cawthorne said of this:

> From the summit at 1,052 metres the crest continued westward along to Sgurr Choinnich, another Munro. This was the finest walking of the day, a mile of narrow ridge where for once we forgot the cold and discomfort and focussed on safe foot placements, delighting in the exposure of a misty highway a long way from anywhere.

The drainage to the east changes with simple clarity as one of these high ridges introduces the River Meig to the scene. This eventually flows through Strathconon to become River Conon and enters the Cromarty Firth at Maryburgh. Descending northwards needs care, as the vegetation and scree become loose on the steepest sections below Sron na Frianich (this *nose* is of Gladstonian character), and the SSSI is then left behind at the bealach to the west of Glenuaig Lodge. This descent also gives a very pronounced foreshortening experience, as the mountainside of Sgurr nan Ceannaichean (915m), *peak of the merchants,* opposite looked severe. However, true to earlier form, it is nothing more than a steady even climb, and on looking back to the descent, the same trick of perspective appeared.

The summit of Sgurr nan Ceannaichean (915m) may just miss the Watershed, but most certainly merits a conquest for its own sake as a very fine hill. The ridge from this top to Moruisg (928m), *the big water,* flows in a simple s-shaped double sweep on easy short grasses, with the crags being largely confined to the steep corrie to the left. The River Bran is now added to the complex of fine rivers to the east and joins the River Meig at Scatwell, but not before passing through the Achnasheen Terraces SSSI where, in the process of deglaciation, the finest outwash terraces in Scotland were formed. The river then meanders in familiar fashion along the floor of Strath Bran, enters and leaves a number of smaller lochs, and then finds itself being dammed to form Loch Luichart, from which it is put through a big pipe and a power station at Scatwell. Part of the final long descent to the A890 crossing is down a pronounced ridge like the prow of an upturned ocean liner, and then by Cnoc na Moine (600m), *hill of peat,* to cross the railway a kilometre southwest of the lonely cottage of Luib, meaning *the bend.*

Two ancient looking standing stones on the north side of the A890 keep guard over this crossing, as traffic makes haste to or from Loch Carron, but this is not generally the land of such monoliths, either singly or in pairs. Were they on the engineers' plans for the recent upgrading of this section of the road, or has some ancient giant placed them there to mark a long forgotten event in history

– who knows? A loop in the Watershed between this crossing and the next, above Glen Docherty on the A832, takes it into a new context, for although the route itself is unremarkable, the wider setting overlooks a very different landscape. The loop moves across a number of minor hills including Carn Beag (550m), with its trig point, and Beinn na Feusaige (625m). On Meallan Mhic Iamhair (499m), the westward drainage changes to the headwaters of the short Kinlochewe River which empties into Loch Maree, and finishes its journey to the sea, at Poolewe, by the equally short River Ewe. After crossing a shoulder of Carn Breac, the Watershed then swings round the Moine Mhor, *big morass,* and crosses to Carn Loisgte (446m). On the way it passes close to the top of the Coulin Pinewood SSSI, and enters the Wester Ross NSA, which encompasses an immense 145,300 hectare spread that includes Torridon, Beinn Eighe and Letterewe. Carn Loigste provides the ideal spot from which to view this stunning landscape of pinewood, loch, bare rock and sheer summits.

The profiles of these great mountains are simply breathtaking. Two kilometres of picking a way round and between a scattering of lochans and small outcrops then takes the Watershed to Bidein Clann Raonaild (466m), *the pinnacle* or *boundary of Clan Ronald,* where the view down Loch Maree, framed by Beinn Eighe and Slioch, is the stuff of the very best picture postcards. As the Watershed then descends eastwards to the next bealach, Glen Docherty, *place of scouring,* rises to meet it at the inevitable mast and the very recently improved A832. Loch a Chroisg, *loch of the crossing,* lies just to the east, and is a reminder of our ancestors' awareness of the lie of the land, and its significance.

A young plantation surrounded by deer fence on the north side of the road calls for either a bit of agility or a small detour to the left. But, once clear of this, the going is good, and the views open out again onto yet more of the magnificent landscape. The eastern boundary of the NSA moves north towards Dundonnell, and the Watershed heads eastwards in the direction of Fionn Bheinn, *white mountain.* Three tops along the way give increasingly fine views over Achnasheen

THE MOINE MARCH

Loch Maree from the top of Glen Docherty. Here the Watershed is on the edge of an iconic area.

and beyond to Strath Bran and Ben Wyvis near the east coast. Carn na Garbh-Lice (517m) is followed by Creag Dhubh, and lower down the slope to the left is the simply named Coire Bog, before Meall a Chaorainn (705m) is reached. The main summit of Fionn Bheinn (933m) is not quite on the Watershed, but most certainly merits a short diversion because it is there, and for its singular mountain quality. The route then swings north-east to the minor top (874m) before dropping steeply towards Toll Beag, and then north towards a big concrete pipe and track. This ugly construction contours round two sides of Fionn Bheinn to bring additional water to Loch Fannich for its hydro electric task. The pipe, which is at least two metres in diameter, and sits on a ready succession of concrete support cradles, is intrusive and undoubtedly one of the less attractive features of an otherwise worthy project.

From Fionn Bheinn over Achnasheen. The breach in the dyke gives passage to the mountain hare, and herds of deer.

The pipe is not the only big feature in this landscape though, as Loch Fannich lies at the base of a fine tight mountain group of the same name. The Fannichs provide excellent mountaineering opportunities, and are popular amongst a wide climbing fraternity. The approach to them is normally from the north, but the view of their south-facing profile, with Loch Fannich in the foreground, is impressive. Their height and mass are accentuated by the lairig, or *long deep pass*, which slices northwards from the head of the loch. If there is any water left over from the hydro-electric extraction at its eastern end, the water becomes the River Grudie which empties into Loch Luichart at Grudie. The shore of Loch Fannich comes to within about 500m of the Watershed, before it heads west once again onto Beinn nan Ramh (711m), *the hill of the oar*. This is a fitting description of this hill, as it is long and narrow, and the ancients must have had a premonition that the loch would one day fill much of the valley to the right. I had one of those simple and delightful experiences as I made my way steadily up the hill, when perhaps 50m ahead of me I saw one, then two, and finally five deer pop their heads over the top of a small rise straight ahead. They scrutinised me from their vantage point, and the daft notion that they had set up an ambush gave me great amusement, before they disappeared once again. Perhaps I wasn't worth the bother!

A hill named a *cockroach* seems unlikely, but there it is, An Carnan (446m), a low hump which, but for its name, would not merit a mention. To the left, a collection of lochans with a name including the word Moine denotes another morass, but fortunately the Watershed skirts the edge of this bog-hopping challenge. The approach to Groban (749m), the *top of a rock hillock* or *a mugwort*, is briefly just inside the NSA, and it provides a vantage west and north to Fisherfield and An Teallach. It is also very close to both the Ardlair SSSI and the Wester Ross Lochs SPA; a landscape of great worth. The drainage pattern changes with the march northwards, with the headwater burns draining to Loch a Bhraoin, and then via Gleann Mor and the River Broom to enter Loch Broom at Inverlael. Looking at the wider picture here, the mention of Fisherfield and Loch Broom is evidence of the distance travelled on this epic walk.

This is a good point to reflect on the immensity of the Watershed in the landscapes of Scotland; the words Leviathan and sleeping giant do seem apt in this case. Although there has been much by way of anecdote and human experience to relate, the concept of wildness is also taking shape too.

Immediately after Groban is the Bealach na h-Imrich *bealach of the flitting*, or *moving house*. At 440m and with no clear track crossing, it would be a hard route to use for such a purpose, but I prefer to see it as a flitting on the Watershed; moving into the Fannichs. At a second bealach above this, close to Ceann Garbh Meallan Chuaich is a rusty iron gate hanging at an obscure angle and marking pretty much all that is left of an old estate march fence. At this point the route joins a long, very pronounced ridge that has climbed cleanly from the end of Loch Fannich, at Ceann Garbh a Chaillich, and gives a fine walk up to A Chailleach (997m), *the old woman,* itself. On Toman Coinnich (935m), *little meeting* or *assembly,* the Fannich Hills SSSI is entered, and the *speckled mountain,* or Sgurr Breac (999m), is the last top before the lairig which cuts so cleanly through these hills, and the Fannich Hills SAC is reached too.

The path that crosses from the Dundonnell road to Loch Fannich climbs steadily up to this bealach. At about 550m there is still a fair way to go to the top of Sgurr nan Clach Geala (1,093m), *peak of the white stones,* and this ascent is sufficiently steep to call for a bit of route-finding to avoid some long slabs and crags running right across the face of the slope. A sharp ridge takes the Watershed to Carn na Criche (961m), which then continues round the head of the Coire Mor to Sgurr Mor (1,110m), *the great peak,* and the highest in this range. Surmounted by a large well-built cairn, this top presents magnificent views in every direction; time for a brew.

The drainage from here changes in both directions. To the east lies Loch Glascarnoch and the other headwaters of Glascarnoch River which then becomes the Black Water, and joins the River Conon just beyond Contin. And to the west there are a number of burns feeding Loch Droma and the Abhainn Droma in the Dirrie More. This burn then tumbles across waterfalls in Corrieshalloch Gorge before joining the River Broom. The view to the north is dominated by Beinn Dearg, and Ben More Coigach can just be picked out beyond the waters of Loch Broom. It would be so easy to stay and enjoy this vista for much longer, as there is a great deal to be seen. That east–west divide has once again become clearer, with salt water to be seen on both sides. The route to Beinn Liath Mhor Fannaich (954m), *the big grey mountain of Fannich,* is over some areas of boulder field, but, conveniently, a track has been organised by moving some stones to the side, creating a ride through the rocks. A small stone shelter has also been created beside this track using dry-stone walling; it is a neat and very robust construction.

The Watershed continues up by way of a steep, loose jumble of boulders onto Beinn Liath Mhor Fannaich (954m), then descends rapidly round Loch Sgoireach, lying snugly in its corrie, to Beinn Liath Bheag (665m) and past the east end of Loch Droma to the A835 crossing.

The A834 has become a major artery for almost all motor transport to the north-west coast and Lewis, with the ferry from Ullapool to Stornoway but a few miles down the road by Braemore and Leckmelm.

On his *Scottish Journey* of 1934, the poet Edwin Muir (1887-1959) passed this way, recording his observations as he travelled by car round a pre-War Scotland. His candid comments on his crossing of the Watershed would not have looked particularly good in a tourist brochure of the area, but the image he portrays is clear nonetheless:

> It was as if a vast hand were clumsily pressing down this silence; the density of the clouds kneading everything together with a soft enclosing movement. Heavy drops lay on every blade of grass like a cold sweat, and yet the little circle of visibility remained, as though a pocket of light had slipped down here and were continuously bracing itself and making a fragile vault. In that circle blunt-looking rocks appeared and disappeared now and then, producing an effect as abrupt as if they were living things that had stepped out of the cloud and stepped back again. But except for them there was nothing but the bleak glistening road, the tangled heather, and a perpetual almost audible drip-dripping of the bodiless rain, falling slowly from just overhead.
>
> After a long but busy imprisonment in this circle, I saw with relief that I was going downwards...

He had crossed the Watershed, and his imagery of the experience is indeed vivid; we have all been in that 'fragile vault'.

The southern shores of Loch Droma, *loch of the ridge*, would have looked rather different if plans in 1918 for a railway to Ullapool from the line at Garve had been realised. These plans followed the Garve to Ullapool Railway Act of 1890, and were led by Sir Montague Fowler of Braemore, one of the foremost railway engineers of the late 19th century. By then, however, the railway-building age had all but passed, and nothing came of them. Andrew Drummond's much more recent tale entitled, *An Abridged History of the Construction of a Railway Line Between Ullapool and Lochinver,* makes exciting reading, and certainly captures something of the challenges which the project would have entailed. If not a railway, then a reservoir, for Loch Droma is not what it seems. Originally it drained west down the Dirrie More past Braemore Junction towards Loch Broom, but the hydro-electric scheme of 1960 saw its western end dammed, and a pipe sunk through the Watershed at the eastern end to take the water to boost the new Loch Glascarnoch; another water pochle.

Although seeing the promise of what lies ahead on and around Beinn Dearg, *red mountain*, has already almost moved the journey forward, this bealach on the Watershed does merit a bit more attention. The name Droma has already occurred further back along the Watershed close to Iron Lodge, meaning *loch of the ridge,* its reappearance here is predictable, and it is still aptly named, in spite of the hydro-graphic reorganisation that has taken place here. To the east, Loch Glascarnoch is another Hydro Board creation and just below the dam is the Altguish Inn. I had taken a break in my big walk, and hitched a lift to Ullapool to get a caffeine fix and a bun; while hitching back, my lift commented in deep sonorous tones whilst slowly shaking his head, that the 'Altguish Inn is a strange place'. I then stayed the night in the adjoining bunk-house, and wondered at the comment; it was indeed perceptive! Westwards from *loch of the ridge,* and Dirrie More, the *great ascent* (or in this case descent), leads down to Braemore, *big upper part,* and for many travellers, this heralds the prospect of Ullapool and its famous Ceilidh Place, or the ferry to Stornoway.

The Fannich Hills SSSI and SAC come to an end right in the middle of where the Watershed reaches the road and, at the very same point, the Beinn Dearg protected areas start; they appear on the SNH *sitelink* website like two areas meeting as if to kiss in the middle of the A835; a wild romance, perhaps. From here, the approach to Beinn Dearg takes a swing westwards first by Meall Feith Dhiongaig (535m), where a track running for a full 3km on the Watershed can be followed. The path is a pleasant change to the usual rough going, but where it splits the route follows neither branch, but continues up the ridge to Beinn Enaiglair (889m), and then a right turn down to the bealach where the earlier path crosses. The immense boulders which lie abandoned here by the passing ice sheet all those millions of years ago suggest a hasty retreat. In reality, it was a much more gradual process, with the higher ground being the last to be free of ice. Iorguill (872m), *the uproar* or *skirmish,* is only won after a hefty climb through some rough and loose slabs, but the view westwards from the top as you regain your composure is prize enough.

From Iorguill the line of the Watershed moves north for about half a kilometre across a level pavement of slabs to meet the drystane dyke which runs along the top of the 350m cliffs beyond. This dyke is truly impressive, and must have taken much skill to construct. It includes some very large slabs of rock and is perched at the very edge of a steep drop marked by more *rocky doodles* on its northern side. Following the dyke eastwards onto Beinn Dearg (1,084m) it is necessary to take a bearing for the summit cairn, as the dyke misses out the summit before dropping steeply by the northern shoulder. The summit is a small plateau with a substantial well-built cairn; ideal for a well-earned pause and for more vista-taking delight.

Although I have said that I met relatively few other people in the hills, I was intrigued by the interaction between us. As a fellow walker got closer, there was always a brief uncertainty as to who would nod or speak first, but once this formality had been dealt with, there usually followed a brief discussion about the day, the journey or the weather; almost always affable, though rarely protracted, as each was on a journey of their own. In contrast though, some preferred to remain in their own little world; whether out of shyness

Beinn Dearg from Ullapool. Residents of Ullapool have a powerfully dramatic conclusion to their backyard.

or simple reserve, they passed seemingly unaffected by the presence of another human being. Yes, occasionally my upbeat greeting was carried off in the breeze, but that is the sometimes the way of solitude, and certainly no one is the poorer for it.

Descending north with the dyke as a useful guide, the ground is broken by slabs of loose rock and large boulders that look like they may have more tumbling yet to do. Here the Watershed is joined at the bealach by a path coming up from Gleann na Sguaib and Inverlael on Loch Broom, just 7km distant. Three fine tops in quick succession march the Watershed further north and all of the higher ground here has the additional designation of the Beinn Dearg SPA. Meall nan Ceapraichean (977m), *hill of the lumps* or *little tops,* is succeeded by Ceann Garbh (967m), and Eididh nan Clach Geala (928m), *covering, or web of white stones*, takes up the rear. To the right Glean Beag can be seen stretching east through a number of other glens of increasing size to join the River Carron at Amat Lodge before finally reaching the Dornoch Firth at Bonar Bridge. A track leads down to Glenbeg Bothy some 6km away – unusual, in that it is a bothy in two separate buildings; though each has its own appeal. Not to be outdone by the east, the drainage to the west also changes, picking up the headwaters of the Rhidorroch River, which enters Loch Broom at Ullapool, having become the River Ullapool along the way.

This area is well known to those who like the idea of coast-to-coast routes, as one of the shortest of these (at a mere 43km) passes this way: the Ardgay to Inverlael or Dornoch Firth to Loch Broom to give it its more precise salt water connection. One of the questions that I posed when talking to local people in the area concerned the economy; reconciling the conflicting pressures of development and conservation. For this presents the paradox of change and changelessness; land use and land-living. How can these areas, I asked, balance the needs of a viable and sustainable local population with its seemingly timeless natural beauty? Surely one of these must give? It is inherent in the tension between work and wildness.

> What I would hope for is for more visitors, but in sustainable numbers, who come to enjoy, and appreciate the area for what it is. The majestic drama of the landscapes is our greatest asset, which is here to be experienced, but with sensitivity. There is plenty of room for more visitors, to help with jobs and the economy, but their reason for coming is important – these landscapes can be a real inspiration.

Negotiating a route round some lochans, outcrops and the inevitable bogs had been only a minor distraction to the scene ahead, for beyond the bealach which is perched on top of the 250m deep Cadha Dearg, *red pass,* to the left, is Seana Bhraigh (927m), *the old mountain,* or *old upper part.* A short, easy ascent on good firm grass leads to the first top of 906m and straight ahead is the Creag an Duine, *crag of the man,* which becomes narrower and sharper as it gets closer to the end of a ridge, with a 300m drop on three sides. This may be a diversion, but it is well worth the taking, and it's easy to see how the crag might have got its name: it stands erect and bold as a single point jutting out towards the head of Strath Mulzie. It is here that the Corriemulzie River, which joins the River Einig at Duag Bridge and then the River Oykel at Oykel Bridge, makes a start. But back to Seana Braigh, and the Watershed runs to the higher summit to the north-west. A small shelter in the form of a circle of rough dyke at the top provides some protection should that be necessary, but in fair conditions the panorama is captivating.

The route from here leads into Rhidorroch along a low ridge between upper Strath Mulzie to the right and Glen Douchary, *the black and broken moor,* to the left – a very tempting track curves round between river and ridge, but it is most definitely not on the Watershed. Creag Dhubh (592m), Meall nam Bradhan (679m), *hill of the salmon,* and Mullach a Bhreun-Leitir (406m) give an undulating and at times rocky approach to the south end of Loch na Daimh, with a number of tracks and paths crossing, and to the east the Rappach Water joins the Corriemulzie to then become the River Einig. The Beinn Dearg areas of protection come to an end, but the Watershed then enters the north-eastern boundary of the Rhidorroch Woods SSSI and SAC. This is notable as one of the largest areas of native woodland in Ross and Cromarty, and contains the complete range of woodland types which are characteristic of the north-west Highlands.

Rhidorroch, *the dark hill slope,* is a strange and beautiful place; a world apart. Most landscapes can be read and even predicted, even on a first visit, but Rhidorroch defies that kind of logic. It is neither high nor remote, with parts of it almost in Ullapool's back yard. It isn't particularly well known by those from outwith the area and, indeed, it is invariably bypassed by visitors, who will have bigger and grander sites in mind. As I looked at the map and then tried to plot the Watershed I was baffled, especially with the area to the north of the Rhidorroch River. The contour lines are erratic and weave this way and that without any apparent purpose; they look like they were drawn by someone under the influence, or were blown by two opposing fans before the ink had dried. The watercourses meander hopelessly amongst this miasma and, in places, give up and form lochans. It takes attention to detail and perhaps the help of a magnifying glass to plot any link between any apparently higher points in this area.

Looking across at Rhidorroch from Creag Dubh it appears as a rippling sea of heather moorland, with a completely random spread of small tops to give it texture. Lochans punctuate the landscape, and give it both variety and interest. Like a number of other locations on the Watershed, the beauty is in the detail. And this becomes much clearer as the rather contorted line of the Watershed is followed in a great horseshoe round the perimeter. The contrast between the outer world beyond and the more enclosed little world within is palpable.

Three factors created this oddly beautiful landscape. Firstly, when these rocks were being formed, as layer upon layer of sand settled, and was compressed by subsequent strata, some layers were harder than others. Fast forward a few eons, and this multi-layered sandwich tilted to a fairly steep angle. And finally, another eon and an Ice-Age or two later, and this sloping mass had its top sliced off. The different layers and their relative hardness meant an uneven cut; more of a ripping effect. So the ice retreated, the vegetation came, soil and peat formed, and the hollows filled with water: thus the landscape of Rhidorroch, the *dark hill slope,* was formed.

From the low, narrow Watershed ridge between Loch an Daimh, *loch of the connection,* and a waterfall on the River Douchary, a gentle rise to the west leads up to three small tops that almost dance along the lip of a crag overlooking the Rhidorroch River to the south; Creag Ruidh, Creag Ghrianach *sunny craig,* and Meall nan Uan (426m), *hill of the lamb,* start the circumnavigation of Rhidorroch. The succeeding tops almost merge with their surroundings, and barely rise higher than the heather-clad ripples all around them. Meall Leath Choire (549m), Meall an Eich Ghlais (463m), Beinn Donuill (448m), and Cnoc a Choilich (416m) are the ones with names, but the lesser ones nearby have a strange anonymity to all but the local shepherds and stalkers. A river and a sea loch with the same name come next, but with different spellings, betoken a change in the short drainage to the west, with the River Cannaird which enters Loch Kanaird at Isle Martin.

Loch a Chroisg, *loch of the crossing*, (where have we come across that name before?) and Rappach, *the noisy place*, mark the transition between Rhidorroch and the Cromalt Hills, and as if to herald this change, Meall a Bhuirich Rapaig (474m), *hill of the bellowing stags*, comes first. Strath nan Lon is the *strath that is worthy* or *able*, and the Cromalt Hills are gentle and rolling, and not in themselves particularly striking. But with the easier going and the absence of an immediate eye-catching landscape, they offer that familiar opportunity to look. To the west an array of iconic and well-loved mountain forms further afield dominate their flatter surrounding terrain; the profiles are instantly recognisable. Cul Mor, Cansip, Suilven and Quinag, combine to give this area its defining image. Across the head of the Oykel, the great bulk of Breabag fills the horizon. And looking back, Seana Braigh with its north-facing pinnacle, *crag of the man*, appears to keep watch over an area that is almost devoid of man and his endeavours. The River Oykel now features in its own right to the east, and drains down through Strath Oykel to reach the Dornoch Firth at Bonar Bridge, while to the west a complex network of burns, rivers and lochs take over, which unite in Loch Veyatie, and then the River Kirkaig, which enters the sea at Inverkirkaig.

A few kilometres to the left, on the edge of the Cromalt Hills, a west-facing cliff on Knockan Crag tells the remarkable story of the geological history of this area, and of the efforts of two individuals to unravel the secrets bound up in these rocks. In the late 19th century Ben Peach and John Horne put forward a theory as to how it was that older rocks from the east of this line can be seen overlying younger rocks from the west. They concluded that a fault line occurred about 480 million years ago, internal pressure split the earth's crust along gently sloping lines, forcing rocks upwards and westwards over the younger rocks. This became known as the Moine Thrust, and whilst it is seen best here at Knockan, it extends all the way from the island of Eigg northwards to the Atlantic coast near Tongue. It is one of the causes of the tilt to Scotland's landform north of the Great Glen, and whilst the Moine march of the Watershed generally runs parallel to the fault, its influence affects the much wider landscape. Knockan Crag is a SSSI, and the large area immediately to the west of that includes the Inverpolly SSSI and SPA, covering many of the lochs in the vicinity, plus Inverpolly SAC, and the Assynt-Coigach NSA. No wonder then, that when the opportunity arose in 2005, the Assynt Foundation, with the support of the John Muir Trust, acquired 17,000 hectares of Glencanisp and Drumrunie Estates. This community buy-out is taking forward its plans for active conservation, access and education.

Just three of these gently rounded Cromalt Hills are on the Watershed: *the bellowing stags* of Meall a Chaoruinn (454m), Meall nan Imrichean (298m), which alludes to another *flitting*, and finally and appropriately, Cnoc na Ghlas Choille *hill of the green forest*, which is right on the Forestry Commission boundary. A mixture of rides and a track give a strenuous route through the forest to the A837 crossing, where an isolated cottage sits about 300m from the Watershed.

The initial mixture of open moorland and forest, with a deer fence or two by way of challenge, includes a number of ancient chambered cairns and a burnt mound, with a gap in the planting around spot height 357 which leads onto Ruighe Chnoc (369m). Here the Ben More Assynt SSSI starts and, within a short distance, the Assynt-Coigach NSA is also entered.

Sgonnan Mor, *the big lump*, is a less than complimentary name for the next top, but it was clearly given when viewed from the bottom, as the view from the top begins a succession of increasingly magnificent vistas. On Meall Diamhain the westward drainage enters the domain of the River Lonan, which enters Loch Assynt, then emerges as the River Inver, and eventually meets the sea at Lochinver. A series of deep, steep corries to the east of Meall Diamhain and Fuarain Ghlasa then start the approach to Breabag.

A sea of white boulders, some the size of small houses, litter the long ridge called Breabag (718m), *hill with cleft* or *little kick*. It is perhaps redolent of Carn Liath overlooking Loch Laggan, but the context is very different. Breabag is the wild introduction to an even greater wildness beyond. For the traveller it involves boulder-louping on a new and unprecedented scale. Every step has to be measured and considered, and the landing may not be just as steady as anticipated. A few solid areas are cut with great chasms, pointing almost straight down some 500m to the valley floor on the right. This is a landscape almost devoid of vegetation, which only serves to give the rock scape a brighter, whiter glare; it is unforgettable in its grand austerity. At its northern end Breabag Tarsuinn then drops steeply to a bealach prior to a breathtakingly steep and exposed ascent onto Conival (987m).

My night on Conival called upon my reserve of courage and fortitude. I was camped high, in a little hollow that offered little protection from the wind and rain. The noise that these made on my tent and the surrounding rocks, was formidable, so there was little prospect of any sleep. In the dark watches, the tent buckled and swayed, and a fine drizzle found its way through the two layers of fabric. Unable to sleep, I found that many, perhaps irrational, thoughts assailed. What if my tent disintegrated or I were to lose my maps? What if my waterproofs took flight to the next parish, or I was left without my supplies? How would I survive the night, let alone the next day?

I found that the arrival of the dawn, even though the wind had only abated slightly, brought a more rational perspective on things. The tent and all its contents, including myself, had survived; I would live to see, and walk, another day! Coping with such an assault though, and the effect that it had on me at the time, brought some of the potential hazards of this solo exercise into sharp focus. I certainly gained the satisfaction of survival from it, even if, for a while, it had all seemed dangerously fickle.

It will, I think, have become evident that I am captivated by the original meanings that the ancients gave to hill, mountain and loch. As I suggested in the introduction, these names serve to give a vivid picture of how our ancestors viewed their world and its major features. They clearly had an affinity with nature, and its symbolism could enrich their lives in a way that many would aspire to today. Some of these features in the landscape acquired mystical or religious significance for reasons that are now lost; but the names have been handed down and, thankfully, most can be interpreted. Conival, *the enchanted hill,* is one such. Although it is often eclipsed by its larger neighbour Ben More Assynt, Conival has a character and presence that merits a mention in its own right. The crown of quartz gives its rocky summit a distinctive appearance, it offers views to the River Cassley in the east, and to the west, Inchnadamph NNR with its caves in which the bones of long-extinct animals were found and which provides a link with wildlife in the area over 11,000 years ago.

A few of my encounters were with small walking or climbing groups in the care of a mountain guide; this was a reminder of the people who earn a living in the hills, and whose livelihoods depend upon a combination of the freedom to roam, the weather, their own skills, and a public that is willing to pay. Few mountain guides will have grown financially rich by their efforts, but most will gladly talk of the pleasure and privilege of working in such environments – despite the effect which the weather can have on their income; a rich experience in every other sense.

These guides need good equipment which is always fit for purpose, and each will have his or her own preference for make, model and maintenance. Qualifications to at the very least Summer Mountain Leader level are essential, and registration with the Adventure Activities Licensing Authority will be necessary for any work with the young or vulnerable. Add to that the need for disclosure checking, valid first aid certificate, and lists of 'Approved Providers' which most Local Authorities now require, a few memberships in order to keep up to date with best practice, and piles of paperwork and the job is less appealing than it had at first appeared. The work will vary according to the seasons, with perhaps the need to be able to turn a hand or foot to something else in winter. One of the key attributes is, of course, a good manner with people – the group I met somewhere back along the way were clearly trying the patience of their guide, with overindulgence the night before slowing the pace. But tact and good humour seemed to be winning through.

From Conival, the Watershed runs along the top of a narrow ridge northwards, with steep scree on either side; it is an awesome place. The sssi ends about one kilometre short of Mullach an Leathaid Riabhaich, where the westward drainage changes to some burns, which enter Loch Glencoul under the lee of the Stack of Glencoul, and its spectacular tidal flow under the Kylescu Bridge. The view to the north is exceptional, into a landscape that radiates wildness. A number of lochs including Loch an Eircill are perched on the top of steep crags, and seem to defy the laws of gravity. Not long into his winter journey from Sandwood Bay to Glencoe, Mike Cawthorne said of this area, as he crossed from Glencoul to the eastern side of Ben More Assynt:

> The path which had begun nowhere ended nowhere, tipping me into the middle of a quaking bogland. Ahead was an unnamed wilderness, a huge collecting basin for hundreds of square miles of rainfall. It is both a fortress and a trap. Defended on three sides by broken quartzite mountains and ribbon lakes, swollen rivers quickly cut off its southern exit. There is not the faintest echo of the outside world, one's natural inclination is to hurry across the trackless miles to seek the line of a stalkers' path, not because it would ease movement, but because it is something human to grasp onto.

He may have exaggerated the size of the rainfall catchment, but everything else about his observation rings true as the Watershed straggles northwards across this ragged landscape. A series of small but steep ridges get in the way of progress towards the next goal, and even between the ridges, the bog and tussock make the going slow. The shorter the legs; the more tedious the going! Thankfully Beinn Leoid (792m) with its trig at the summit offers some respite. The descent on the ridge to the east of this precedes the rapid ascent of Meallan a Chuail (750m), with its fine mixture of rock and grass, which makes for very pleasant walking. Lochs Merkland and Shin now capture the plentiful supply of rainwater, which then become the River Shin and enter the Kyle of Sutherland at Invershin. And a similar change to the drainage westwards focuses on Loch More, Loch Stack and the River Laxford, which join the sea at Loch Laxford. The end of the NSA comes at Lochain Meallan a Chuail which, like its neighbouring lochs, fills the bottom of a corrie scoured out by some serious glacial action. Meall an Fheur Loch (613m), *loch of the hill of the cattle grazing*, has Loch Cul a Mhill on one side and Fheur Loch (the cattle grazing reference), on the other. The final well-wooded descent from Creag an Sgamhlainn (464m) to the A838 just misses the north-facing crags.

At the bealach on the A838 between Lairg and Laxford Bridge, there is only a gap of 3.5km between the head of Loch Merkland and Loch More. A canoeist would only have to carry his canoe for a short distance on a paddling venture from Laxford Bridge to Bonar Bridge: a coast-to-coast with little portage and a wealth of fine scenery.

The final flourish on the Moine March is in a small knot of hills north of the bealach between Lochs More and Merkland. It was from these hills that Dave Hewitt took a route north-westwards towards Cape Wrath by way of Foinaven in his Watershed walk of some 20 years ago. His account of this journey, and the final few days in particular, is well worth revisiting. I found this little knot of hills to be something of a challenge, not because they are particularly high or any more rugged than anything that had gone before, indeed the going was fairly dry underfoot. Instead, the struggle was that Ben Tee and the end of Moine was in sight from the top of Creag an Sgambhlainn, before that wooded downward scramble to the road. It would have been so very easy to nip across in that direction, and just skip the knot: no-one would have known!

All temptation was suppressed, and a fresh resolve to reach the goal without deviation came into play. A young plantation protected by the necessary deer fence on the north side of the road presents both challenge and choice, and the going around this is firm with a steady pace needed. Two tops, Cnoc a Choilich (374m) and Meallan Liath Beag (527m), lead to Carn Dearg (797m) with its dry rock and grassy terrain. This is a turning point, with a radical change in the route from northwards to eastwards, for the drainage moves round from the west to the north. Here the waters collect into the Strathmore River which enters the Atlantic on the north coast of Scotland via Loch Hope, at Inverhope, near the mouth of Loch Eriboll. Cape Wrath is only 36km away and, also to the left, the Foinaven SSSI and SAC and North-West Sutherland NSA are close.

At the imaginary stop sign' on Carn Dearg, the ridge goes off to the right and descends steeply to the unnamed spot at 582m – this should be called Comhnaidh na Tionndadh, *place of turning*. It is followed by three tops that then take the Watershed on a very rocky ride to the track from Gobernuisgach, *branching river of the waters,* to West Merkland: Carn an Tionail (759m), Beinn Direach (688m), *the straight* or *upright mountain,* and Meall a Chleirich (628m). From there, a formidable descent of over 350m to the bealach and the track is followed by another rapid ascent to another *rough heel,* Sail Garbh (582), and onwards to the *fairy mountain* of Ben Hee (873m).

Moine is the apotheosis of our wander through the wilds. Here, the hand of man has had a gentle touch, and his footprint has been light. Devoid of house or barn, its long emptiness has heightened the solitude that every traveller will most surely covet. That same solitude is accompanied by everything Nature brings; it has a simple magical quality that is without equal.

The roll-call of great mountain names, both familiar and less so, has been matched only by the regular succession of designated and protected areas; some intimate and others vast. Together they tell a story of the supreme quality of the landscapes that they conserve. That there should be a single geographic feature, the Watershed, linking so many of them is noteworthy.

Map 7 Northlands March

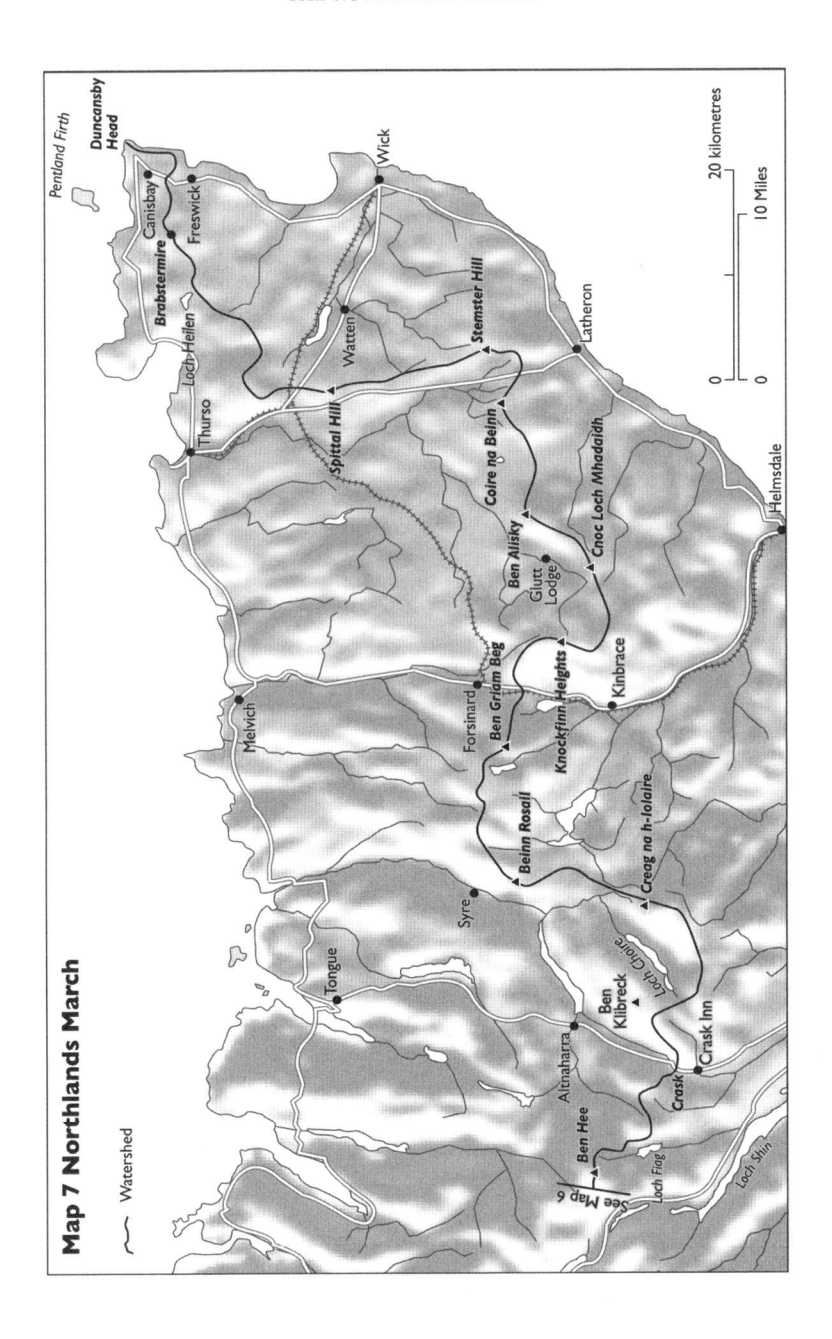

CHAPTER SIX

The Northland March

> Here, the waters' course is inhibited;
> Strangled by sphagnum.
> Yet it has its singular delight,
> As the wide skies and dancing light illuminate
> A landscape that is subtle, and
> Dressed with Nature's full palette.

AS I APPROACHED the start of the Northland March, I felt as though I was entering upon a great unknown, for though I felt that I understood mountains, what would I make of the forthcoming big bogs of the Flow Country? My earliest experience of a 'flow' went back many years to climbing and walking days in the Galloway hills, with the Silver Flow taking almost centre stage between the Merrick range and Backhill of the Bush Bothy. But that seemed small in comparison to what I saw on the map as I pondered the Northlands of Sutherland and Caithness. Put simply, I wondered how it would be possible, or indeed safe, to cross miles of this terrain, which was shown as dozens of lochans interspersed with random but frequent little tufts, and meandering burns aimlessly searching for a means of escape. Such is the Ordnance Survey depiction of these areas: it is like no other. I'd had a little flavour of it on the ridge to the north of Loch Lochy back in the Great Glen, but my memory seemed to have temporarily erased that experience, and the scale of what lay ahead seemed a little daunting.

Looking down from the summit of Ben Hee, when the mist lifted sufficiently, I could see my goal for the day – the tiny white dot of the Crask Inn a long way to the south-east. To be heading in that direction in itself seemed odd, for I had journeyed in a generally northward direction for over 850km from Clyde Fell. But here the Watershed takes a rather southerly direction before reaching its destination at Duncansby Head. The route appeared to take me between Loch Fiag on the right and Druim na Bad on the left – this may sound sinister, but it has a much more enchanting meaning, *ridge of the boats*.

When I subsequently researched the question of wildness in this area, I discovered that some 61 per cent of the 180km of the Watershed from Ben Hee to Duncansby Head is designated and thus protected. This is by far the highest proportion of the five Marches, and shows that there are landscapes and habitat features that are particularly worthy of protection. The one overarching document that covers much of this in addition to the 21 specific SSSI citations is the Ramsar citation entitled *The Caithness and Sutherland Peatlands*. This covers an area of 143,569 hectares, much of which is on and around the Watershed. Alongside this is the Special Protection Area (SPA) citation with the same title, which covers an even larger 145,517 hectares, and the Special Area of Conservation (SAC) designation. All these point clearly to the great importance of these landscapes, and the measures that are now in place to protect them.

The Peatlands of Sutherland and Caithness are important because they represent not only the largest and most intact blanket bog in Scotland, but also one of the largest such areas in the world. This is no ordinary pocket of bog-land then, but is of significance on the global stage. It has some unique characteristics in terms of the range of vegetation, surface pattern types, and the variety of rare species of wetland plants and animals. In particular it supports five per cent of the total world breeding population of greylag geese, and 18 per cent of the world population of temperate dunlin. But, impressive as that sounds, the sheer variety and numbers of other species found in this area is exceptional, and we will return to this at Forsinard.

It is worth noting again the rationale behind the assertion that the Watershed's northern terminus is at Duncansy Head and not anywhere else along the north coast of Scotland. The Atlantic Ocean wraps itself around the west and north of Scotland; it is the same body of water that laps all of these shores. The only obstacles to this are the archipelagos of Orkney and Shetland; they act as the divide between Atlantic and North Sea. There is geological continuity between Caithness and Orkney and, were we to wind the calendar back a mere 8,000 years, we would find Orkney to be a peninsula with no Pentland Firth separating it from the mainland. Frances Groome in his *Ordnance Gazetteer of Scotland* had worked this out over 100 years ago, and nailed the northern terminus firmly to Duncansby Head.

Cape Wrath beckons rather tantalisingly to the north-west, with the apparent terror in its name (a corruption though), its lighthouse, isolation, majestic cliffs, and the notion of a last outpost in Scotland. However, the Watershed has only one conclusion, and it lies 180km to the north-east, with its own special kind of landscape along the way.

Ben Hee with its twin tops of 873m and 851m heading-up the ragged Allt a Ghorm choire, is the point of transition between Moine and Northland; the jumble of slabbed rocks on the summits are in marked contrast to the softer textures that follow. A very steep descent of over 450m from the lower of these tops requires care, but at its base the journey has entered the Northland March. The average elevation is 240m, considerably less than the previous two marches, but that doesn't detract in any way, and it has many unique qualities.

The Druim nam Bad flow sssi, with its purple moor grasses, deer sedge and heathers, drains rather ponderously into or towards Loch Meadie and its subsequent burn entering Mudale which becomes Loch Naver at Atlnaharra; the sea at Bettyhill is a long way off though. To the right of Bad a Bhacaidh (446m), the drainage is in a southerly direction to Loch Fiag and the River Fiag. This in turn empties into Loch Shinn at Fiag Bridge, which then flows through a hydro-electric station at Lairg at the start of the River Shin, before journeying to the Dornoch Firth at Bonar

Bridge. A series of unnamed spot heights follow the Creag Dhubh Mhor (553m) and the Bealach na Creige Duibhe. The SSSI and Ramsar sites start at spot height marked 397m, and at 391m the River Vagasite assumes the drainage pattern towards the River Naver. There also the River Tirry, which drains into Loch Shin just north of Lairg, takes over. At Loch Eilanach the Watershed meanders in an apparently aimless fashion, struggling to provide any kind of clear divide, for it has well and truly entered upon the Cnoc an Alaskie (312m) flow. That there is a trig point here is remarkable, for it is a terrain of rampant peat hags and quaking bogs. The Ordnance Survey must have dug deep to find a sufficiently firm footing for its concrete pillar, though, as only the top third of it now raises its head above the surrounding morass.

Danger lurks on these moors and flows, even for the experienced. Some 50 or more years ago, a shepherd from the Mudale side to the north set off on a winter's morning to tend his sheep and, as the day progressed, he found himself in rapidly deteriorating weather conditions. With only his dog for company he struggled on, but the driving snow obliterated any feature that he might recognise; he was in great danger. After many hours, as he started to descend from the higher ground and thought he was heading for home, he saw a distant light and made as best he could for this beacon. He got to the door of the cottage, but it was not the one he had expected to find. The occupant of the cottage was surprised to hear a faint knocking on her door on such an evening but, as she opened it, the figure standing there collapsed. She tried to revive him, but to no avail. The shepherd lay dead on the doorstep of Fiag Cottage, over 12 miles from home and on the opposite side of the hill and moor from where he had set off. In the desperate weather he had become completely disorientated; he had crossed the Watershed. It is believed that his dog remained at Fiag, and never returned to Mudale.

Close to Cnoc an Alaskie a fenceline is picked up and offers some guidance as to the way forward towards Crask, but it can mislead or at least confuse. The fence-builder had to find something reasonably firm to drive the posts into, and it was that need, rather than the precise Watershed, that governed the line of the fence.

The Flow Country became something of a *cause celebre* in the environmental movement of the 1980s, and indeed this concern achieved a popular shout in the press, with even the tabloids adding their bit. What was at stake was one of the last major areas of blanket bog in Europe and a rarity even on the world stage; a particular type of habitat in which a special range of species of flora and fauna thrived, and in which, up to that point, our activities were having only limited impact. The unique and precious qualities of this area were brought into focus by a threat that had its origins at the other end of the UK. And it is interesting to note that the much more recent debate surrounding the wisdom of planting wind farms on peat bogs, and the carbon released in the process, would have added to this stramash of 25 years ago.

Rich people, or those that have become rich, like to hang on to their money, and they like to exploit every facet of any fiscal regime to make their dealings tax-efficient: in other words, they expect their tax advisors to ensure that they don't pay any more tax than they need to. Wise people, you might think. But when the cost of this 'prudence' is an environmental disaster, it is a flawed regime.

These *nouveau-riches*, many from the world of the media and communications, based variously in the South-east and with properties elsewhere in the world to retreat to, were advised that it would be 'tax efficient' to invest in trees. Their investment could be offset against tax over a significant period of time they were told, and so forestry companies were engaged to buy up land and plant commercial forests on their behalf. This practice was perfectly legal and indeed commonplace throughout the more marginal areas of the UK, where the economic decline in hill farming at the time was most evident. Generally, it was designed to assist our balance of payments over the longer term, by promising a reduction in timber imports, for if land could no longer support sheep and hill cattle, then why not plant trees instead? And the best investment would be where the land was cheapest to purchase – in the far north.

The drainage ploughs soon moved in, and carved their way across vast tracts of Sutherland and Caithness, surface water was immediately channelled away, and ridges of upturned vegetation and peat provided a supposedly good environment to plant Sitka and larch trees – by the million. In this much altered ecosystem, the bird population, and all the wildlife it depended on, disappeared.

There was a growing and vociferous concern at the damage being inflicted on this valuable habitat, and indeed, at the very cause of that damage. Environmentalists were incensed and campaigned, and the press picked up the story and ran with it. The inequity of tax avoidance (or efficiency) for the rich, and PAYE for the rest of us, made good copy, and it worked; the law was changed, and the tide of destruction turned.

So what is it like to walk across a 'flow', a quaking peat bog, or a floating mire? Well, it requires care, an ability to read a map, and good boots, in addition to quick-footedness (or perhaps quick-wittedness). The first thing though is to have some basic understanding of what the bog really is. It is a living, growing, evolving habitat in which water, peat, plant vegetation and more water are the main ingredients. Surface vegetation of mosses and grasses are loosely matted in an unusually liquid mix. In the wetter west the purple moor grass and bog myrtle predominate, in the slightly drier east of the Flow Country, it is heather and bearberry which are more in evidence. Sphagnum mosses are the most common plant species throughout; their lack of solid matter and ability to retain water are vital to the habitat. Rainwater falls on these and it is trapped, as there is very little drainage – nowhere for that water to go. In some places open pools and lochans are formed, and their margins are ill-defined. The occasional tussock of something seemingly more solid adds to the surface texture, whilst beneath this floating squelch is peat; peat still forming from the slowly compressing dead vegetation, and which could be many metres deep. In some places these flows are slightly higher towards the centre because of the build-up of water and vegetation which cannot escape. A number of key bird species are particularly attracted to this habitat.

One solution to the challenge of getting across to the other side of a flow – some of which cover several square kilometres, is to go round the edge; there is usually some firmer ground to be found there. But that could be deemed a deviation from the apparent line of the Watershed, so a direct crossing should be made. The first thing to do is 'experience' a flow by venturing on to as firm an area as possible. Stand legs slightly apart, and flex the knee and hip joints – but don't bounce! With any luck, your feet won't sink (far) and, as you get rhythm into these flexing movements, so to the ripples will go out round where you are standing. The surface mat of vegetation will undulate, with you in the middle of this pattern. This brings to mind both the image and the metaphor of throwing a stone in a pool, with the ripples radiating outwards; though in this case, you are the stone. This is alarming, fascinating and exciting – all at the same time. But it gives you a feel for the place and a sense of how it works.

Having tried it out, you then need to start reading the terrain round you – the types of vegetation and how firm they appear, where there are pools and open water to be avoided, where there are more solid humps that stand proud of the surface, where there are more continuous areas of hardened peat, and so on. Walking poles are a must, as they spread the load, help with balance, and provide something useful to prod and test the surface, and often what lies beneath it too. Keeping moving is a wise approach, but this needs to be tempered with constantly reading the surrounding flow, and picking a route to follow. The experience is exhilarating, and crossing dry-shod is the reward.

Though it was not my first experience of a flow crossing, Cnoc an Alaskie certainly put my skills to the test. The Crask Inn could be seen all the while; perhaps that was the incentive to get across expeditiously. Another obstacle loomed, though, a well-maintained deer fence and canal that crossed from left to right; a strange barrier in such a place. As I later discovered, this forms part of the Shin hydro-electric scheme, and channels water that would otherwise have ended up in the Naver, adding it to Loch Shin's output or out-pour.

This, then, is the last place in which water is 'pochled' from one side of the Watershed to the other. The channel requires care as the sides are steep, and the flow through it will depend on recent rainfall. A rough track which provides access from the road to this little piece of engineering also gives an easy climb up through a gap in the strip of forest to the A836, where the usual phone mast and clutter detracts somewhat from the scene. Right turn and, in about a kilometre, the hospitality of the Crask Inn awaits.

A Chraisg, meaning *the crossing*, is aptly named and, at 264m the traveller on this lonely road from Altnaharra to Lairg is conscious of its elevation. To the north, the Allt a Chraisg flows towards the isolated shepherd's cottage of Vagastie. And, to the south, Strath a Chraisg runs west from the Bealach Easach to become the River Tirry at the bridge below Crask Inn. This hostelry owes at least some of its origins to droving days, but sheep, not cattle passed through as recently as the last war. Large droves of sheep were gathered at Tongue, and herded by a small group of men with perhaps a dozen or more dogs over a three or four day drive by Loch Loyal, Strath Vagastie and Crask to the sales at Lairg. A real sense of occasion ensued, with large numbers of sheep, dogs, herds and dealers from all across the north of Scotland there to do business; business that could either spell good fortune for the next year, or despair. After the sales and due celebration, the drovers were then returned home, with their dogs, in the back of a lorry. The sales at Lairg are still a high point in the year, but the droving days are long gone.

Near the summit at Crask, on the north side, the remains of the Tinker's Cairn mark the place where an itinerant worker perished one January day in the early 1930s. A small band of labourers who had been working on relief road construction along the north coast had either been sacked from the job, or simply gave up due to the appalling conditions, and were heading back to Glasgow, from whence they came, on foot. One of the party was ill before they even set off, and there were frequent stops to enable him to catch up. A night in a barn at Altnaharra did little for their spirits and even less for their wellbeing, but they set off again towards A Chraisg in the morning. Just before they reached the highest point the one who had been ill succumbed. His remaining companions laid him out beside the road where the snow would quickly cover him, and headed onwards to Lairg to report the loss. A pauper's grave and anonymity were his final lot.

Throughout the summer season though, the moors around Crask are alive with flowers and birdsong, bog cotton and moor grasses flow gently in the breeze. And, with wide views to the distant hills in the west and wider skies around, it is a special place. Mike and Kai Geldard have been running the Crask Inn for over 10 years now and in that time have made their mark, providing genuine hospitality, good food, and a convivial atmosphere over drinks and dinner. Combining their hostelry with hill farming provides a close link with the land, and advice on fishing the lochs and burns is freely given.

Ben Klibreck's great 6km ridge stretches north-eastwards: it starts at this end with A' Chioch and terminates with the Whip,

Crask Inn. Hostelries on the Watershed are scarce, but this one offers the best in home-grown conviviality.

and all of it a SSSI. The line of the Watershed climbs towards this mountainous bulk from Crask by Cnoc Sgriodain (544m) and Carn an Fheidh. Here there is a 90 degree turn to the right and the drainage changes from the River Vagastie to Loch a Bealach and Loch Choire, which becomes the Mallart River which joins the River Naver near the outflow from Loch Naver. Ben Klibreck is almost an island, surrounded on three sides, by water, both still and flowing.

A 400m descent beside the Forestry Commission boundary to the Bealach Easach offers increasingly good views along the lengths of the two lochs, Bealach and Choire. With steep northern slopes coming down from Ben Klibreck, the other side is less severe, and heavily wooded with native trees. When I reached this bealach, the strong westerly wind whistling through was raising white horses on the surface of the lochs below, and the dancing light had become a maelstrom.

The Forestry Commission boundary follows the Watershed for only another kilometre, just beyond Creag Sgoilteach (471m), but continues to mark a change in drainage to the Allt Gobhlach and the River Brora catchment. This finds its way to the North Sea at Brora, though some of its water is channelled via a weir at Dalnessie and thus into a burn that empties into Loch Shin. When the engineers were planning most of the major hydro-electric schemes of the 20th century, they always looked further afield than the natural confines of the river catchment they were working on. They sought ways to capture water that was bound for elsewhere, and then by weir, tunnel, channel or culvert, were able to raise the output of the scheme in hand.

The line of the Watershed then enters Ben Armine Forest, where it traverses a number of smaller flows at Meall an Fhuarain (503m), a few other unnamed spot heights and Monadh Stairneach. This area has a network of stalkers' paths crossing it and at their junction the former Ben Armine stalkers stables have recently been converted into a very fine open Bothy. It must be almost unique, as it is the only one that I know of that has a stock of peat piled against the gable waiting to fuel the stove. A well-worded request posted just inside the door asks that any peat used should be replaced. The pony stalls have been retained, and with the addition of some boards have been turned into rustic sleeping platforms. Ben Armine Bothy was an excellent find, only two kilometres south of the Watershed. It sits beside the burn in a wide amphitheatre of moor and flow almost surrounded by hills; a magical setting for such a shelter.

In the middle of this hollow in the hills at spot 521 the upper reaches of Strath na Seilge start and these in turn feed the Black Water which joins River Brora at Balnacoil. The long gradual climb out of the hollow onto Creag na h-Iolaire (694m) and Meall nan Aighean (695m), with only a metre in height between them, open out to magnificent views over an entirely new landscape to the north

Gorm-loch Beag in the Flow Country. Emerging from the hills after a night in the peat-warmed Ben Armine Stables bothy; this vista heralded a change in terrain, texture, and dancing light.

and east. Again, it is marked by the contrasts between the peat-marked moorland of the hollow that has just been left behind, to the rocky tops and eastern crags of these two hills, and then the vast expanses of open water and flow which lie ahead. Chief amongst these sheets of water is the loch with three names, or in three parts. Nothing separates Lochs Rimsdale, Nan Clar, and Badinloch and their combined irregular shape of just over 800 hectares represents a lot of fairly shallow water. To the east, the morning light catches the myriad of silver pools on another flow or two, and the reflection of clouds on the surface of Loch Truderscaig is in real contrast to the dark green forest beyond. But it is perhaps the apparently featureless emptiness of the wider vistas to the east which prevail, for a while at least. The Strath of Kildonan is almost 20km off and, beyond the features I have mentioned, there is little to break the gentle, oh so gentle, rise and fall of the meandering moorland for all that distance. It is most likely the preserve of the stalkers, shepherds and perhaps the odd ghillie on the River Skinsdale; few laymen will enter these wide acres.

A long and, in places, rapid descent over grass and heather towards the access track for Loch Choire Lodge focuses the attention on the task in hand (or at foot), rather than the bigger picture. This touches on the Skinsdale Peatlands SSSI, and just beyond the track, where the surface levels out, there are hardly any contours marked on the map; caution is needed for there are a number of wet areas in this crossing to Truderscaig Forest. Just before the deer fence and right on the Watershed, a couple of ancient hut circle sites show clearly as rings of ditch and low bank on the firmer ground. Many other such historic monuments are located in and around the forest, and this concentration does bring into question whether the forest should have been planted here in the first place; what other less visible remains were ploughed up and obliterated in the process? And, it has to be said, that finding a way through the forest is not easy; the rides are not in the right places. But, taking the longer term view, this is Forestry Commission land, and the process of extraction has started to the north. Hopefully the restocking plans will provide the opportunity to leave a way through, which will link the southern hut circle with the three Cnocs of Bad an Leathaid (284m), Bad an Fainne (261m) and then out of the forest at na Gaoithe (216m).

Whilst becoming slightly preoccupied with forest, deer fences and hut circles in Truderscaig, there has been another change to the eastwards river pattern. Loch Truderscaig and the linked lochs of Rimsdale, Nan Clar and Badanloch, combine to form the River Helmsdale, which in turn flows through the Strath of Kildonan, otherwise known as Strath Ullie, and concludes its journey to the sea at Helmsdale itself. Truderscaig SSSI starts on the open ground at the forest edge.

The lonely ruin of Badinloskin, about halfway between the northern edge of the Truderscaig forest and Beinn Rosail, touches on that sad and brutal episode in our history; the Clearances. For it was here and in the townships and cottages throughout Strathnaver that people were either evicted from their homes before they were dismantled, or had them burnt down over their heads. In the Rosal township just two kilometres to the west the memorial is a poignant reminder of the dreadful suffering that the Dukes of Sutherland inflicted on the people who once lived here. At Whitsunday 1814 the people of Rosal were ordered out. The factor, Patrick Sellar, was chief perpetrator of the emptying of the glens, and indeed he stood trial for some of this inhumanity. He was arrested and charged with murder for his actions at Badinloskin, where a woman of almost 100 years of age was left in the house whilst it was torched. As the cries of protest from the local people went up, Sellar was heard to say:

Damn the old witch, let her burn.

The poor woman was rescued with her bedding well alight, and was given shelter in a hovel close by, where she died two days later. One particular account of these deeds and the misery they wrought on the people has been handed down in Donald Macleod's work entitled *Gloomy Memories*. Patrick Sellar was acquitted of murder at his trial in Inverness two years later and, whilst it could be said that he got off with – it in a legal sense at least – history has been a more candid judge of his actions. He went on to run one of the biggest and most profitable sheep farms in the land, covering a vast area stretching northwards from Truderscaig for 15km, and running almost 14km from west to east – over 200 square kilometres of farm. The next 20km of the Watershed lies in Sellar's sheep farm, which was almost on an Australian scale.

The Strathnaver clearances extended throughout all of the upper reaches of the river valley, around Loch Naver, through Altnaharra, and beyond to Mudale and the very start of this side of this Northland March. And as we stand on Beinn Rosail (260m) on the lip of this Strath which witnessed so much sorrow, we can look west to Altnaharra and beyond, and north down the Strath in the direction of the seashore, where some of the dispossessed subsequently sought to scrape a living. In the very shadow of Beinn Rosail lies the Palm Loch; a touch of irony in the name, perhaps, in such a place.

After crossing the B871, and the start of the Lon a' Chuil SSSI, the terrain that the Watershed crosses is strangely reminiscent of Rhidorroch on the Moine march. There seems to be no pattern in it, with loch and small hill, moor and meandering burns all jumbled up. Tracing the line of the Watershed is less than straightforward here and, in at least one place, the features are so confused that a burn appears to cross the line and flow in either direction, or none. But this is untamed and quite random wildness at its best and the lack of any apparent structure simply adds to its interest and appeal. From Creag nan Laogh the Watershed meanders to Creagan Dubha Reidhe Bhig (337m), but such is the confusion in it that it may include Cnoc Bothan Uisge-beathan, which I suspect is a reference to a house for distilling illegal whisky! Meall Cean Loch Strathy (344m) is just included, and Meall Bad na Cruache (337m) is at the end of the ragged makings of a ridge, where a sharp swing south east is called for, in order to skirt the southern lip of Caol-loch Beag. The drainage northwards changes hereabouts from the River

Naver to River Strathy, which flows into the sea at Strathy – unusual to have a loch at the head of a river, river itself and a village at the mouth all sharing the same name. West Halladale SSSI is located in this area.

At Cnoc nan Tri chlach (345m) the earlier reference to tax breaks for the wealthy and the damage this inflicted upon this precious landscape is once more relevant (an unlikely issue for such an isolated and hopefully unspoiled location). But, for the next 20km or so the Watershed skirts or runs through the largest RSPB reserve in the UK. The Forsinard Flows National Nature Reserve is now a site of active conservation for this unique bird habitat. Nature trails round and among the many lochans and moors have opened the area for public appreciation, and large areas of commercial forest have been felled. The drains, which had dried out the habitat, have been blocked, so the water table is rising once again. From just west of Cnoc nan Tri-clach to Cnoc Maol-dhuin on the Knockfin Heights, and with another holding to the east of that, the RSPB is maintaining its active conservation role.

Just over the hill to the south lies what is billed in the *Guinness Book of Records* as the most remote hostelry in mainland UK. The Garvault Hotel caters largely for fishers and stalkers, but walkers, pony trekkers and those pursuing a largely off-road Lands End to John o' Groats may find its location suits their route. Ben Griam Mor looms over this lonely whitewashed cluster of buildings in an otherwise empty moor.

The Watershed reaches the rocky top of Ben Griam Beg (580m), with its ancient fort, from where the views are spectacular, and the Atlantic-bound drainage turns to the Halladale River, which will join salt water at Melvich. With its slightly larger namesake of Ben Griam Mor to the south, these twin tops stand out boldly in an otherwise gently rolling green and brown landscape, peppered with lochans and larger expanses of water.

Looking down on the RSPB reserve there is a patchwork of different textures and colours to appreciate, with the pools, moors and felled areas of earlier planting. A few areas of forest, which remain almost enclosed by the reserve or beyond its boundary, are in stark contrast; they are a grim reminder of that damaging regime. Cnoc Bad an Amair (233m) is almost marooned in this liquid landscape, with flows on three sides; its only escape would be to hoist sails and float away! Because of the active conservation in the reserve the bird species to be seen are many and varied, and they include kestrel, peregrine, curlew, oystercatcher, short-eared owl, greenshank, golden plover, common sandpiper, dunlin, merlin, skylark, golden-eye, red-necked phalarope, dipper and wood sandpiper. The protected habitat in the reserve supports a concentration of bird-life in this locality, but most of these species are to be found throughout the Flow Country; only the densely forested areas lack the diversity and numbers. Many of these species have been companions throughout much of the journey along the Watershed. From the clearer areas in the forests of the Border hills, to the Campsie Fells, to Rannoch Moor, and lochs Fannich or Droma, some of these have featured alongside species with a more localalised presence.

Crossing the flatlands between the upper reaches of the Kildonan and Halladale river systems, the burns wander in search of somewhere to go, and the railway loops to the west in order to find the lowest point on the crossing and a reasonably firm footing for the ballast. In the Forsinard Flows SSSI it is hare's tail cotton-grass that predominates. Ascent from the A897 onto Meall a Bhealaich at the forest edge is made easier with the track leading up to yet another mast. The glaciated crag and tail formation is just discernable here. As the ice-sheet moved in a south-easterly direction it scraped the steeper north-west side, and scoured the hollow round three sides of the hill beyond that. Loch Lucy is part of the evidence of this action.

About 2km north of the Watershed lies the scattered settlement of Forsinard, with its station, hotel, a few houses and lodge. Here the railway crosses the A897, and the redundant station buildings have been converted into an excellent visitor centre for the RSPB reserve. In the hollow before Cnoc nan Bo Rabat the strident line of pylons that had taken power from Dounreay nuclear power station to the markets in the south crosses the Watershed. Could it be used in the future when tidal power becomes a reality? For it has been estimated that there is enough energy in the Pentland Firth tides to power half of the United Kingdom's needs, if only it can be harnessed effectively. Whilst we are at the very cusp of the commercial installation of this capability, the other more environmentally convincing course would be to utilise some of the technology that has enabled us to get the oil and gas out of the North Sea, and install a sub sea cable right down the east coast. Forsinard would be the better without the pylons.

A short gap in the protected area comes to an end at Cnoc Riabhach (385m), and the designations continue without let-up all the way to the A9. Knockfin Heights, *heights of the fair hill,* and the SSSI of the same name are of interest for the contrast between the saturated acid flows on the top of the ridge, and the drier areas on the steeper slopes to the west. The lochans are a favourite hunting ground for the local raptor population. Another trig point is almost lost in the morass at spot 438 where, at the start of the headwaters of the River Thurso, the Glutt Water comes into play. This passes a very remote shooting lodge called simply The Glutt, *hollow place in the hills.* On the other side of the Watershed, it is the Langwell Water which drains to the sea at Berriedale that takes up the flow. Cnoc Maol-dhuin, Cnoc Sguabach Cadha, Leathad Leanain and Cnoc Loch Mhadaidh (318m) are the next sequence of low tops on a ridge that gently undulates its way eastwards, with the access track crossing on its way to The Glutt. Loch Mhadaidh, *loch of the dog,* Loch Braigh na h-Aibhne, *the loch of the hill of the river* and thus the source of the Berriedale Water, Allt a Chaorain, *the stream of the rowan,* Allt Synbaich, *rough stream of the broom,* and Cnoc na Saobhaidhe (290m), *hill of the fox's lair*; these and many, many, more names show that every feature was significant; the landscape was packed with meaning. Its apparent emptiness is deceptive. A full lexicon of all of the names on and along the entire Watershed would be a substantial tome, but would shed so much more light on this neglected feature.

Although it is not particularly easy to discern from the appearance of the surface, with its mantle of peat and moorland vegetation, the underlying rock changes hereabouts from the moine schist which has featured almost continuously all the way from the Highland boundary fault line, to the softer old red sandstone. The geological map shows that these rocks extend throughout Caithness and Orkney, giving the continuity referred to earlier.

The name Gobernuisgeach appears for a second time close to the Watershed at this point – the earlier version that had ended with 'gach' is some distance back to the north of Ben Hee.

The 6,000 hectare Rumsdale Peatlands sssi takes up the area's designations with deer sedge, cross-leaved heath and heather in profusion. A number of chalybeate springs are marked close to the Watershed along the stretch on either side of Ben Alisky. These are near to the source of particular streams, and would have been regarded as having healing qualities in the past, their waters being impregnated with iron. The name Dunbeath features strongly here around the start of Dunbeath Water, an area of yet another sssi, named the Dunbeath Peatlands. And, whilst most of the plant species to be found in it are very much the same as on its neighbours, this does serve to emphasise the continuity within the flow country. Neil Gunn, the author, was born in Dunbeath and we will return to his eloquent description of what he saw in his landscape.

There are a few areas in which the Watershed is shown on the first Ordnance Survey 6 inch series of the 1860s. These locations appear to be somewhat random, and include a number of minor watersheds between adjacent valleys. In this area the main Watershed is marked though, and corresponds with the parish boundaries. These are often shown as undefined, with nothing fixed on the ground for it to follow, and therefore tend to be a series of straight lines linking specific definable points. Such a depiction of the Watershed is misleading of course, because on the ground it can be plotted as a much more flowing line – nature would not constrain its fundamentally organic character in any such linear way – but it will be of interest in the future to examine the factors which the

Ordnance Survey used all those years ago to determine why and where it elected to show a watershed.

Just a kilometre apart the twin hills of Beinn Glas-choire and Ben Alisky rise almost 200m above the flatlands along the River Thurso to the north and, somewhat unusually, they are both exactly the same height at 348m. Their rocky northern profiles look down benignly on the derelict Dalnawhillan Lodge just across the river. Many other shooting lodges across the moors and straths of Caithness have somehow retained their function as centre-piece of a sporting estate, and most look well cared for. In the shooting and fishing seasons these lodges come into their own, with parties of 'guests' ready to do business with gun, dog and rod – at a price. Outwith the season most are available to rent for fairly exclusive out-of-the-way house parties. No longer the plaything of a single family or laird, they have been reinvented to meet a wider international market, and to pay their way. But Dalnawhillan will echo to these sounds of activity no more, as the mouldering rot and the wind take their toll on its fabric. Just east of the lodge though, at one of the cottages, a dog barks and a bright red post-van passes along the track nearby; the rhythm of life continues.

The life and work of those employed in deerstalking is a hard and often isolated calling, which requires a particular range of skills and demeanour. Though some may choose to live in a village or close to a settlement, others will find that their accommodation is remote, and may carry with it some responsibility for the lodge and its paying guests. This task is often shared with wife or partner.

The principle aim of the job is twofold: enabling shooting guests to 'get a bag' is the main focus, for they generate the income for the estate, while maintaining the herd and its habitat comes a close second in the priorities. An intimate working knowledge of the estate and its herd of deer are essential, with the lie of the land and seasonal movement of the deer playing a big part in this. Weather conditions, available vegetation, activity on neighbouring estates, the effects of walkers and cyclists, maintaining the right balance of hinds and stags, and the expectations of guests all contribute to the success of the sporting estate. The stalker will feel a pride in his ability to balance the effects of these variables, and work in the knowledge that he will be judged on their outcome.

The deer, of course, belong to no-one; it is merely the right to shoot them that the estate holds. For, although there is predictability in deer movement, the estate march may not hold them to any particular piece of ground. As a result, the stalker will find himself out in all weathers and right through much of the winter months, in pursuit of the shooting guests' expectations. But the acquisition of local knowledge, a wide range of skills and, as the years pass, a wealth of experience in a harsh environment, invariably come together and provide a successful day on the hill.

In many places on the Watershed, the deer population is too high, and both the herd and the habitats suffer. So, with targets for the cull being agreed, the stalker will often find himself on a mission to reduce numbers. The challenge is to do this whilst somehow maintaining a herd size that is viable for commercial stalking too.

This is inevitably just a brief glimpse into a way of life that predominates in these wide moors, and in so many other places on the Watershed. It can be harsh, and rarely entirely free of controversy, but I found that the wider environmental awareness of these people is prodigious. They have a part to play in the care for our landscapes and, with careful planning, the diversity of local habitats.

Scottish Natural Heritage coordinates a useful and very practical system for providing information for hillwalkers about deer stalking activities in the main Deer Management Group areas. A website and network of more local phone numbers provide up-to-date advice on where stalking is taking place and which areas should be avoided on a particular day. This service has the full support of the Mountaineering Council of Scotland, and is invaluable in ensuring that the Outdoor Access Code is followed effectively.

Back onto the Watershed, where our journey continues, Sithean na Gearra (209m) and Caplaich Hill (246m) gently dominate the Strathmore Peatlands SSSI, and Loch a Chearacher appears to drain nowhere, though north towards Loch Ruard and the Blar nam

Facileag flow is the most likely. This is one of those areas where the exact route of the Watershed can be deceptive; where it is unclear as to its precise direction, but it could be that it runs about 1km further north at Cnocan Ruar (214m). An outpost of the RSPB's NNR lies just a further 1km to the north and extends for almost 9km to the edge of Blar Geal forest and the strangely named Dirlot Castle site. The RSPB's presence in the area is considerable and represents a bold statement for proactive habitat conservation. It is a positive influence which in time will no doubt have further welcome impact.

A landscape with such a high proportion of protected areas is most unusual, and a final SSSI before the A9 is reached centres on the mires around Lochan Coire na Beinne. Here the peat is deep, especially in the hollows, and the oval pools and lochans give an added vibrancy to the scene; the ever-changing contrast between the deeper hues of the moorland and the reflected light on the water.

Another line of pylons rather dominates the skyline above the A9, and there are wind-farms on either side of the Watershed at Houstry and Bad a Cheo; contrasting sources of power, with the pylons marching from the nuclear Dounreay, and the wind-farms tapping that almost endless source of energy – especially in these northern climes.

Meeting the tarmac of the A9 at a point where it has climbed just 6km from the east coast at Latheron is a dramatic change. This, the main transport artery for Thurso and Orkney beyond, is busy with traffic either hurrying for the ferry in one direction, or set on the prospect of a long journey south on the other. And the A9, or the 'causewaymire' as it was know in an earlier existence, comes after the Watershed has traversed over 40km of some of the finest of the Flow Country; a lot of moor and mire. So, climbing easily up to the trunk-road, and then further onto the ridge that will take the Watershed due north, invites a quick look back in pleasure. At the spot height 198m the minor road to Sheppardstown crosses and Stemster Hill (248m) becomes the next goal. To the left the loch of the same name catches the eye, and may merit a brief diversion, for on its banks lies a most unusual ancient monument. A unique horseshoe configuration of 40 upright stones standing sideways to the centre suggests that this location was of major significance some 4,000 years ago. Its purpose is unknown, and gives rise to all manner of speculation, but the discovery during excavation of some human remains does suggest a religious or ceremonial role. A few yards away the remains of a chambered cairn can be seen, and the broch sitting by the shore of Loch Rangag tells of yet more human activity in this area in the past. This is just the start of a succession of other ancient remains that this part of Caithness is so well-endowed with, adds interest to all that the Watershed has to offer. During the 19th century the level of Loch Stemster was lowered to enable farmers to extract a kind of clay called marle, and they then spread this on their fields to improve the soil.

But halt a while – look south and to the left of the shoulder of Ben-a-chielt (287m) (avoiding the clutter of masts), and the open waters of North Sea can be seen. This must be the first full view of open water on the eastern side of the Watershed; a special moment. And there is more, because beyond that the horizon is a long low strip of distant land – the Buchan coast. The jigsaw of Scotland is almost complete.

Just beyond the hill a track crosses which leads to Munsary, a former shooting lodge turned shepherd's cottage. The 1,200 hectare Munsary Peatlands Nature Reserve, which is a Plantlife International site, lies alongside the Watershed at this point. As the 'wild-plant conservation charity', it has a number of reserves elsewhere in the UK, and this is its one Scottish site, where the peatland habitat is its prime interest and focus of activity. The reserve, which is a SSSI, and part of the wider Ramsar and SPA sites is also a candidate for SAC status. The commonest plant species on the site include sphagnum, cotton and deer grasses, heather, bog asphodel, deer slender sedge and bog sedge. Although wild-plants and their conservation are its *raison d'etre*, Plantlife International has an interest in all of the fauna which follows from that and, in the case of Munsary, the more notable species are golden plover, curlew and greenshank; a rich biodiversity. The reserve includes areas of flow habitat, and it is recorded that in places the peat is up to six metres deep.

Munsary can be seen as an excellent foil to the larger RSPB reserve to the west. There are many similarities, in that both include significant areas of flow habitat, and both enjoy considerable protection because of their rare and valuable wildlife status. Whilst the protection and conservation activity at Forsinard is focused on birdlife, and the biodiversity that this requires, at Munsary it is the plant life which is the prime interest, but birds and other fauna follow naturally from that.

As the motorist speeds past on the A9 on the other side of Stemster Hill, there will be little thought given to the rich diversity and colour which was so close. But that is the way with motor transportation; the Watershed experience can only be done and fully appreciated on foot. Many of the lochans on this, the final area of flow, are called 'dubh loch'; their colour being black because of the peat that they lie in and are surrounded by. But therein lies the paradox for, if the light catches them as it so often does, they are anything but dark; the light dances and flashes in the breeze and the sunshine. All the light that caresses their surface is tossed about and given back to be enjoyed. To the right is the Wick River and Loch Watten catchment, which finds its way to the sea in Wick and to the left, the quaintly named Little River, which later joins the River Thurso, as it heads for the Atlantic.

The author Neil Gunn (1891–1973) wrote evocatively of the coastal life and landscapes in the north-east. He was born in the village of Dunbeath not far to the south of here, with its fishing harbour and cluster of houses at the mouth of the Dunbeath Water, which rises on the southern slopes of Ben Alisky. He was in touch with the sea and the land and all that they could bring to the human experience. In *Highland River* he gives a passionate word-picture of his affinity with the hinterland; the Watershed as seen and experienced from his beloved coastal village.

He describes the contrasting character of the area thus:

This is the northland, the land of exquisite light. Lochs and earth and sea pass away to a remote horizon where a suave line of pastel foothills cannot be anything but cloud.

Or in more severe mood:

This bare, grim, austere Caithness, treeless, windswept, rockbound, hammered by the sea, hammered too by successive races of men.

He casts his eye northwards, where he sees:

... the Orkneys anchored in the blue seas, with the watermark white on their bows. Brave islands...

A very different view of this landscape is given in *Wainwright in Scotland*. He starts his journey at Duncansby Head, and quickly warms to what he finds there – the cliffs and sea stacks in particular. Then he pours scorn on John o' Groats, but continues in negative mode by dismissing the whole of Caithness in one sweeping gesture that:

There is nothing for the lover of countryside here.

To me, however, the Neil Gunn evocation of the Caithness landscape is a delight, and strikes a much happier and more perceptive chord.

We keep company with the A9 for some distance, where the wildness is marred by the Halsary and Moss of Toftingall Forests – it would have been much better had these areas been left as a moss. The uncompromising line of pylons seems to march boldly towards the electricity substation where some judicious planting would have been much more desirable. Just beyond Knockglass Farm and the B870 a quarry with its hole in the ground and spoil heaps straddles the Watershed, and great care is needed to pass through. Interestingly, though, this whole site has been designated as the Spittal Quarry SSSI, where 13 hectares are protected for their geological interest. Some 380 million years ago these rocks formed in the sediments that were washed into the shallow Lake Orcadie. This covered much of what we now know as Caithness, and it was in these conditions that the stones known as Caithness flag formed. Stone quarried from this area has provided floors in cottages and castles throughout the length of the land, and pavements in towns and cities beyond. The designation though is all about fossils, the plate-skinned fish called *Dickosteus threiplandi*, and a jawless fish, the *Trewinia magnifica*.

A short ascent of Spittal Hill (176m) follows – these heights may seem modest, but good views are to be had nonetheless. Banniskirk Mains is the next target and the very unfamiliar sight of arable fields is encountered for perhaps half a kilometre. This does erode the continuity of the wildness, but the strange patchwork of fields includes arable, permanent pasture, and rough grazing side-by-side. Banniskirk Quarry is another fossil find sssi, with a mere 3.8 hectares providing a variety of very rare fish remains, and will be a source for considerable research in the future. Hillhead may be aptly named for a farm on the Watershed, but the rise is very modest indeed. A culvert under the railway at Claycock offers safe crossing, but the bridge on the A882 will do just as well. Moving across a mix of arable and rough grazing towards Sordale Hill (109m) and a veritable clutter of simple cairns and chambered cairns are passed. On Sordale the first good view of Thurso and its bay with Holborn Head beyond can be seen. In fact this is also the first good view from the Watershed of the Atlantic Ocean off the north coast. The ferry to Orkney can be seen leaving Scrabster Harbour, as it plies its way north close to the cliffs of Hoy, and the Old Man himself.

With a right turn on Sordale, via a horseshoe round Knockdee and Stemster, two long cairns add to the ancient monument catalogue along the way, and the few arable fields have again been left behind, with rough grazing and areas of moor surrounding the small blocks of forest. The landscape may lack sudden or dramatic discoveries, but the very gently rolling hills, or low humps, present an evolving mix of terrain underfoot. It is mostly rough grassland of one sort or another and the only hazard is the occasional electric fence. Within the horseshoe lies Loch Scarmaclate, another SSSI and marl loch, where pondweeds and stoneworts abound alongside reed canary-grass and rich tall-herb fen. Unsurprisingly, the birdlife is even more varied, with widgeon, mallard and tufted duck, goldeneye, teal, greylag and greenland white-fronted goose, as well as both mute and whooper swans.

I have had many conversations with people about different sections or features on the Watershed and find that most add to my appreciation of it, especially if the person shares a passion for wild places. Many of those I have had these discussions with are sadly with Wainwright when it comes to Caithness, especially its hinterland, where the Watershed is to be found. To them I would say that the outstanding character of the Watershed is its sheer variety, and you can't have high if you don't also have low; the savage and the tender. Caithness is wide in a way that contrasts perfectly with much that has gone before, and the appeal is in the detail. The rich variety and tapestry of wild flowers can be enjoyed at almost every turn, the movement that light dancing on the surface of a pool gives back, or a low clump of willow crouching against a windy environment, or a bird gliding effortlessly on that same wind. These, and so many more little wild gestures, have endeared me to this, the final section of the journey.

In bidding farewell to the River Thurso catchment, we leave the last river which is Atlantic bound and, for the last few kilometres, all of the drainage is by short burns which empty directly into the ocean at places like Castletown, Ham and Gills. With the mention of these little settlements it will seem like a very long journey is nearing its conclusion; this may be an emotional time, as the enormity of the Watershed and the quintessential experience it has turned out to be becomes fully evident.

Loch of Durran is a seasonal expanse of water which only fills in the rainy season, having been substantially drained in 19th century to expand farming activity. But this was only a partial success, as it has created a wet marshy area which, in summer, is a mass of colourful and lively vegetation, including meadowsweet and reed grass. It is now protected as a SSSI.

At Red Moss the Burn of Lythe catchment is reached next; and we can say of this ' here endeth the rivers' – no more river systems from the Watershed. It steers a path between Tain and Bowermaddden, Greenland and Reaster, with Loch Heilen catching the eye. In winter it is a lively stretch of water with great numbers of wintering wildfowl coming and going in the shorter daylight. Houses and farms, some new and some just a rickle of stones, are dotted about the countryside, and much of the terrain is rough pasture or moor. Bog cotton, yellow iris, orchids, the vivid purple bell heather, and modest tormentil abound in a landscape that is alive with colour and aroma. And, if the forest above Slickly and Brabstermire calls for a small diversion or two, it merely prolongs the time spent in an environment that is, in season, simply filled with delight. In reality though, there are many rides and old fence lines to be picked up, so the diversions are not tedious. Hill of Slickly, at 73m, is a whole 7m higher than the trig point beside the minor road to the right, and to the left Schoolary Cottage is a ruin with a fine view.

Stroupster Peatlands SSSI, just across the road to the right, is a site in two halves; the north and south are set apart by a large L-shaped block of forest. This must surely be a classic example of land that should never have been planted; a casualty of that tax-break disaster. The northern part of the SSSI has an area with the delightful name of the Battans of Brabster right in the middle of it. Just beyond Brabstermire a ruined stone tower, which may have been a drying kiln, is all that is left of what must have been a substantial farm complex. The humps and hollows in front of it give some indication of the layout. At the mast, some 2km from Upper Gills, a vista opens out which demands a pause for a brew-up, and time to get the binoculars out. For, just beyond the few farms and houses of Gills and Canisbay, is a view that has been almost 1,200 kilometres in the coming.

To the left is Dunnet Head, the northern most point on the UK

Ruin at Brabstermire. Or perhaps it should be called 'The Stack of Brabstermire', as a portent of things to come.

mainland, which juts out assertively into the Pentland Firth and is one of the most recently established RSPB reserves. Moving closer along the coast, St John's Point with its Men of Mey sea-stacks lead on to the island of Stroma just 2km offshore. Drawing a veil over the disappointment which is John o' Groats, Ness of Duncansby sets the scene very fittingly for our ultimate goal. The waters of the Pentland Firth with their wild currents, where the North Sea and the Atlantic Ocean meet and do battle twice in every 24hrs, fill the middle distance, and a tanker or container ship ploughs its way round the northern UK mainland, en route for some distant port. This vantage point is fine, and offers a tantalising prospect of the last few kilometres of the journey.

Before packing up the stove though, there must also be time to take in the cliffs of Hoy which Neil Gunn described so well. The flare-stack from the Flotta oil terminal within Scapa Flow adds a very different dimension to the picture, but one which brings Orcadian activity into focus. The lower lying and closer South Ronaldsay is the destination of that ferry that has just left Gills Bay, and the boat leaves a wake that is like a white ribbon seeking to bind this coast to that island. The tide flowing over the Boars of Duncansby soon erases the attempt. It was with a note of regret that I shouldered my rucksack and passed the foundations of a new house that is being built here right on the Watershed, and will increase the number of dwellings on the line by about 4 per cent, excluding Cumbernauld of course.

Warth Hill (124m), the last hill on the Watershed, or the first were you travelling north to south, is reached by a right turn at the mast, and crossing the northern section of Stroupster Peatlands to Giar Hill where the vista is, if anything, even more impressive; Orkney seems to be oh so close. Passing over some peat workings, and the gentle rise onto Warth Hill is invigorating. The ancients built a cairn here, but it has either been quarried or plundered, for there's a hollow in the middle. And, with that last descent towards the A99 crossing and the Lint Lochs, the spirits soar at the imminent prospect of Duncansby Head. Journey's end is at hand.

And, for one final fling with the flows, this last couple of kilometres before the clifftop is a fine example of a bog, with all of the colour, pools, and springy surface. Loch of Lomashion is one of those which isn't quite sure if it has an outlet; where is there for the water to go? And then the clifftop, yes the final 3km of the Watershed is along the clifftop with the ground sloping gently to the left towards John o' Groats, and dropping vertically into the North Sea to the right. Here the dramatic coastline is dominated by a number of stunning sea-stacks and arches. A ghostly sound rises up from the tidal slabs below, as seal calls echo off cliff and stack; it is a spooky call, but provides a vivid link with the seascape. Muckle, Peedie and Tom Thumb are the Stacks of Duncansby, and the arch of Thirle Door will, with the passage of time, stand separate and proud beside whatever is left of its near neighbours.

A sea of bog cotton on the moor is matched by a tumbling torrent of pink and red thrift on the cliff-top; and the aroma is a mix of guano from the thousands of birds which inhabit the cliffs. This is a noisy place, with wind, wave and wing making the symphony of the sea. These old red sandstone cliffs are indeed the home to many sea birds, with razorbill, gull, puffin, shag, kittiwake, fulmar, and cormorant in abundance, whilst the cliff tops and steep slopes are salt-sprayed, and provide a fine, if narrow, habitat for maritime heath and grassland. After a final sssi, and passing a final geo which slices clear and deep into the cliffs, the trig-point and surface debris of a Cold War bunker are reached, and the lighthouse appears; a yellow and white marker to the journey's end above the Pentland Firth – *strait of the land of the Picts.*

The Northland March has far exceeded all expectation, it has formed the final, and in some ways most magnificent, link in the ribbon through the wilds. Colour, light, immense variety, and the many rewards of the conclusion of a long journey, all combine to create a true sense of occasion here on the clifftop.

CHAPTER SEVEN

Conclusion

THIS, THE FIRST COMPREHENSIVE introduction to the Watershed, has outlined a journey over Scotland that is like no other; in its entirety, it is relatively unexplored, and hopefully has some appeal for that reason alone. The route which is described in these pages no doubt touches upon many readers' own memories, and will help to prompt their own mental journeys. These individual experiences can now be melded into the bigger picture, and form a very personal part of the *ribbon*. For those who are unfamiliar with any of the route, and find that it is all entirely novel, this will surely have opened a fascinating and significant vista on Scotland's unfolding landscapes, and the many points of interest to be found along the way. For me, the Watershed has become a major new interest, and one which I am delighted to share with a wider public; for it is now so much more than just an abstract geographical line.

Looking back and reflecting on those 64 days of walking is a source of immense pleasure to me. Given the health problems which came along subsequently, and needed a triple heart by-pass to sort out, I am so very glad that I did the walk when I did. Now fully recovered, I can once again enjoy days out on the Watershed, and both recapture something of the experience of 2005, and continue to make new discoveries too. If I was able to undertake such a journey, whilst in my late 50s, and with the early onset of what I have just described, then it is well within the capability of a great many other people who enjoy walking, love the hills, and appreciate Scotland's magnificent and varied landscapes; it comes highly recommended.

At no time during the trek did I wonder if it was wise, nor nurture any doubts about why I was doing it. There were a few dull days of course, but that might just have had more to do with the weather than the landscapes I was passing, but could only imagine.

There were a few alarming moments on very steep descents, or a grim stormy night on Conival, but I was focused on completing what I had set out to do. With only a few minor adjustments to the order of play, I was finally greeted by my wonderful and tolerant family on Duncansby Head, at my journey's end. A short but quite strenuous section had been kept back for the *finale*, so that more friends and family could join in, and we could celebrate this particular 'completion' in appropriate style. Early October found about 10 of us doing the round of the Black Mount tops; a demanding day by most standards, and in the evening we were joined by more valued supporters for a meal and ceilidh; a truly magical finish.

Having set out to complete my journey, I naturally feel pleased that I succeeded with what was undoubtedly a big venture; I have gained much from both the accomplishment and the experience. Not everyone would get the chance to do such a thing, whether it is because they would never choose to do so, or circumstances would prevent it. I am greatly privileged to have had the opportunity, and to have taken it. In a sense though, I created the opportunity, and then made something of it. A metaphor, perhaps, for so many other things in life.

The appearance of that brocken spectre back at the start was indeed a good omen, and clearly signalled something that was even more ambitious than I could ever have envisaged at the time. This book is a major part of that much bigger and expanding horizon; it offers more than just a hint, at some of the things I would now like to see happen. I hope that the new *ribbonofwildness* website, my continuing passion for all that I have written about and a growing body of public interest in the Watershed might all combine to promote something immensely positive.

The whole experience, my subsequent research, and the book itself all call for a bit of summing up; adding the final tints and hues to the picture, giving it an appropriate mount, and framing it to bring out the best. The assertion that the Watershed is substantially wild or wilder throughout should come in for scrutiny (this alone will be central to the case for designation or protection of some sort), and there are a number of additional factors which serve to put the Watershed into the wider context.

The centenary of the death of John Muir will occur in 2014; a noteworthy anniversary. How will this event be marked, and his great influence celebrated as a lasting legacy? What would capture the wider public' imagination and passion in a fitting way? Bold vision is called for, which will encompass something both real and relevant over the length of Scotland.

The knowledge that public opinion supports the care and protection of wild places and landscapes in Scotland is reassuring. Research by SNH has identified the extent to which public perceptions of wild places and landscapes can be quantified and understood. In summary, it shows that these areas are indeed highly valued, and that there is strong popular support for their conservation. Many people appreciate the variety of ways in which they contribute to the quality of life for those living in, or visiting, them. The popular understanding of the concept of wild places focuses on what many describe as the *naturalness of the land*, covering a number of different types; including woodland and forest, mountain and hill, loch and moorland. The geographic areas which best demonstrate these characteristics are to be found throughout the Highlands, but were deemed to be least evident in the Clyde, Forth and Tay valleys. Although the survey could only report on what the respondents said, it is worth adding that the areas between these valleys do demonstrate the very landscape types which were identified in *the naturalness of the land*; the watersheds – our Watershed.

Returning to the SNH policy document of 2002 concerning *Wildness in the Scottish Countryside*, a distinction is drawn between wildness and wild land, with:

> Wildness being the quality experienced by people (through such values as feeling close to nature and enjoying a sense of solitude), and wild-land being those extensive areas where wildness (the quality) is best expressed.

Almost the entire length of the Watershed most certainly offers people the chance to feel close to nature and enjoy a sense of solitude; a relatively high proportion of it is in parts of the country where the *quality of wildness* is expressed to perfection.

In its *Declaration for the Wild* of 2004, the John Muir Trust commits to:

> Encourage and support people of all ages and of all backgrounds to experience and understand the value of wild places, for the benefit of their health and spiritual well being.

The business of enabling people to simply experience the benefits which wild land can bring is borne out of optimism, and confidence in its value for health and spiritual well-being. It is not an abstract exercise, but rather it is a prompt for practical action. The Watershed provides an accessible avenue for pursuing this goal, as it naturally leads out from close proximity to many of the most populous areas of the country to some of the wildest and most remote. As an artery of nature it is special, precious, and brimming with potential for the public good.

In the Concordat between the John Muir Trust and Scottish Natural Heritage of 2005, both organisations affirm that:

> We want to work with others to develop recognition of the need to care for wild places and their natural heritage. The management of our wild places and natural heritage affects many people and organisations, with a broad range of interests.

The many different wilder landscapes which are woven into the Watershed of Scotland provide a unique continuity, and an opportunity which fully merits some form of recognition; its designation *for what it is* would be amply justified.

Avoiding the use of the word wilderness in these documents is prudent; our hand may have been gentle and our footfall light in the remote areas, but it is rarely entirely absent.

The idea of the 'Great Wood of Caledon' as an ancient forest covering most of the Highland landscape, was in all probability something first put about by Ptolemy in the second century, and the image has endured ever since. This poses the question of Scotland as 'paradise lost'; having suffered a kind of ecological falling from grace, for which we were largely responsible. But was there ever a single golden age for Scotland's environment? Was there ever a time in which the woodland cover thrived in equilibrium, in which nature and early Man co-existed satisfactorily? Today we find new energy and commitment to biodiversity, in particular to native forest regeneration or re-establishment, but do we understand fully all of the factors and timescales through which our landscapes evolved? There is a growing and prolific environmental research industry which seeks to inform our legislation and practice. And, with a target of 25 per cent woodland cover by 2050, it is important to ensure that the regeneration and replacement are well planned and appropriately sited.

The implications of all of this for the Watershed merit some consideration. The natural tree-line is about 500m, and the average elevation of the Watershed is just over 450m. Above the tree-line, there would have been only limited scrub, with the tops and higher ground devoid of trees altogether; very much as we see these areas today. There is evidence to support the theory that the loss of woodland occurred slowly over considerable time, and that it was a largely natural process; that it would have happened anyway. So the extent to which we contributed to it is perhaps more limited. Some of the key factors involved in this long, slow decline include climate change and the formation of peat, which in its turn became a thick mat; a hostile medium for the regeneration of trees. This new but evolving habitat then experienced further change as some larger native animal species became extinct, and the deer population no longer had any predators – other than man. The effects of cattle and sheep came to bear on this either and, certainly with the latter, this continues to the present day, with overgrazing in some areas. There is of course a subtlety in grazing pressures, in which sustaining a healthy flock of either species will almost certainly be at the expense of native vegetation. Managing the deer population and muir-burn for grouse shooting have had a significant effect on this balance too.

The woodland cover was also affected from time to time by other natural events, such as fire, flood, wind-blow and volcanic ash fallout and in the wet and windy west, these would have had a disproportionate and cyclical impact on regeneration; the evolving peatland habitat would have added to the regressive trends.

It has been worth dipping into the growing body of research material in order to gain an understanding of where woodland and its regeneration fits into the wider picture of Scotland's upland landscapes. I have found work by James Fenton particularly helpful in this, as he draws on a wide range of sources in order to build the evidence. It has a bearing on appreciating the Watershed landscape, on how it may have appeared in the past, and its character and appearance today. It will surely inform what action should be taken in the future.

The extent to which the Watershed has been affected by these influences will have been more muted, with much of it beyond the montane or natural tree-line. Some of the more recent changes and improvements along the way have been described briefly, and some of those that are projected have been noted too.

I am conscious that this book provides only a passing reference to wildlife species on the Watershed; this was due to a number of factors. Firstly, I confess that I am no great expert in these matters, and there are probably others who are much better qualified to do so. Whilst the material could have been gleaned from a number of sources, space did not permit a more detailed account. Finally, and more significantly, I set out to give a flavour for what can be seen and experienced, but in a way that would satisfy the average walker. So this is not an apology, but puts it all into perspective.

In the contact that I have had with people living or working close to the Watershed, it has been evident that there is an awareness of its significance locally; a consciousness that there is a divide from which water flows from that, to either ocean or sea. In some cases the knowledge was quite detailed, but still confined to the locality. When the bigger picture was offered though, most were able to grasp it without much difficulty, but some were easily sidetracked with thoughts of the West Highland Way and rather vaguely by other long-distance routes. The mist clears with a reminder that the Watershed is always on the higher ground, and not down on the valley floor.

There are around a hundred settlements which back onto the Watershed, and it is an invisible, but tangible thread that links all of these communities. One of the prime objectives in this book is simply to raise awareness of the distinctive qualities of the Watershed in each locality, and then to establish its unique character throughout. I found evidence that people in these settlements do value their hinterland and its wilder character, and that some see it as a valuable asset, in offering sustainable local development by catering for visitors that come to experience the area *for what it is*; for its beauty and wildness and all that this has to offer them.

The Watershed of Scotland has the potential to become a singular focus for wildness and its many benefits in a *community of interest* running the entire length of country. This will not eclipse in any way the many extensive areas of wild land which sit astride the Watershed, but will offer a new unifying theme that touches gently on the majestic and more modest, the long established and the regenerated, the widely acclaimed and the more obscure, alike. And there is the potential to invite or inspire the many communities associated with its landscape to work together to waken the sleeping giant; to have a real stake in all that it has to offer.

I am a great believer in involving people wherever possible, and much of the future success of the Watershed as a popular asset will surely rest with the variety of ways in which the energy and imagination of the wider public can be engaged. Voluntary effort is a potent and sustainable force, and I have already stressed the enormous potential and value of involving young people. Local knowledge is fundamental to the care and monitoring of the Watershed, and there are a great number of individuals and local organisations which can play an active part in this. It is therefore proposed to nominate one March Warden for each of the five marches. Their role will be to walk their section of the Watershed, and become familiar with its route, terrain, access, wildlife, land ownership and use, conservation interests, development proposals and threats, Biodiversity Action Plans, historical events, legends and lore, and to foster local interest in all of these factors. Sensitively building positive relationships with relevant interests will be an important part of this process, and there will be scope for organising events in partnership with established local organisations.

There is now no ambiguity whatever about whether and where we can roam in the Scottish countryside; our rights are enshrined in law. This legislation has in turn been translated into the Scottish Outdoor Access Code, which is simple to understand and follow, by both walker and landowner. Everyone has the right to be on most land provided they act responsibly, and this is expanded with just three key principles:

Take responsibility for your own actions.
Respect the interests of other people.
Care for the environment.

Most guides to Scottish mountain landscape offer a perspective that is road-based; they describe what the traveller will see from a car, by inference at least. There is something very practical in this, because every journey, whether physical or mental has to start somewhere. This book has, however, given a very different starting point and rather novel linear vantage throughout; a rolling access and vista.

The approach that I have described to many of the hills has often not been the guidebook version, for the Watershed has its own distinctive locus in the landscape which is not in any way constrained by any logical point of access. The geo-glacial timescale that put the Watershed where it is, certainly avoided any future human convenience, and it placed a few natural but challenging obstacles in the way. Popular hill-walking convention, which evolved over the last century or so, has led to the publication of many useful guides, in which relative ease of access and ascent, safety and fine views all play an understandable part. There is something strangely liberating though, in following a route that is where it is, simply because Nature put it there; it offers a refreshing connectedness with nature, because Nature alone is the inspiration.

If, like the Grand Old Duke of York, simply getting to the top of the hill and back down again (and ticking the box) is what it's all about, and then the Watershed will either disappoint, or be a diversion too far. For those with a bit of passion for wild places, on the other hand, it will be a delight. With Nature as guide, solitude almost guaranteed, all of the vagaries of the weather, and the grand terrain being experienced in what may be a new way, the Watershed offers magnificence.

I have undoubtedly underplayed the hill-walking experience which the Watershed provides though, and this is deliberate, because it is about so much more than that. As a Guide to a major geographic feature, it was important to touch on so many other things too. Although the landscapes appear to be largely empty of people, there has been much of both incident and interest to discover. With conservation and regeneration schemes having a growing impact, it was important to consider why this is so, and the Watershed's central place in the much wider physical geography of Scotland needed to be explored further. The concept of wildness, its meaning, its continuity and the evidence for it, required examination too. Many hill-walkers will take these and other factors into their personal experiences of the hills; the Watershed will provide an additional and enriching opportunity to be amongst it all.

But of course the Watershed is not purely a mountain experience, as both the Laich and Northland Marches have shown. There may still be the odd mountain aficionado who would pour scorn on these parts, but to them I would say that the Watershed in its entirety is the complete picture of Scotland; Scotland's landscapes – *the experience*.

That the most populated areas of Scotland sit relatively closely on either side of the Watershed puts it in prime position for much wider public enjoyment and appreciation. I can honestly say that it provides an excellent walking experience which runs close to familiar landmarks, but gives a novel approach. Many sailors round our coastal waters have commented that travelling by boat gives an entirely new image of the coastline, and the settlements and features dotted along it; it is a fascinating vantage for those who are generally land-bound. So too with the Watershed, we normally see its environs from the motorway or railway, and then pass by. I found that walking over the central belt was a revelation which, along with my subsequent research, provided me with a new understanding of the area; one which I now value greatly.

The notion that there is a spiritual experience to be had in a state of being at one with Nature has in recent years been much more widely appreciated and expressed. Whether this is in any way due to our otherwise more secular culture, or simply a deeper understanding of our dependence upon the natural world, could form a much wider discussion. Certainly, neither religion nor science has all of the answers; the confidence and certainties which both in their time seemed to represent are now somehow inadequate. Humankind has an undoubted spiritual need though, and many are finding that this can be met and celebrated through sensitivity to all things natural; for many, that is where there is purpose and one-ness.

John Muir succinctly advised:

> Keep close to Nature's heart... and break clear away, once in a while, and climb a mountain or spend a week in the woods. Wash your spirit clean.

And Mandy Craig asks:

> What triggers a spiritual experience is unknown but we do know that a wilderness environment can alleviate stresses and give time for self-reflection. The setting can provide beauty and aesthetics, time can become stretched and pressures of

everyday life can fade away. Could this environment be enough to trigger a spiritual experience?'

It will therefore come as no surprise that I am suggesting that the Watershed has a particular quality and dimension that can give some form of spiritual uplift, at the very least. I am not in the least awkward in making such an association; the Watershed has been created by all of the forces of Nature, and is closer to its naturally evolved state than almost any other large-scale feature in Scotland. Most lovers of the outdoors will have their own micro-spot where Nature touches their inner self; it is suggested that the Watershed can provide the macro-dimension to the same process. All of the sights and sounds, smells and textures, colour, chaos and order of things natural are present, and lift the human spirit to where it can soar in harmony and fulfilment.

Although it may sound like an old familiar cliché, it has to be said: this book is not an end in itself, but is a means to an end. That was the intention from the outset, and there are a number of things which I hope will spring from it. I confidently anticipate that there will be wider and growing public awareness of the Watershed, its splendour, landscape and evolving character. And I hope this book will inspire those who are willing to put their boots on to venture out, and tread lightly. The immense variety of challenge and experience that the Watershed has to offer will perhaps become the focus of some discussion over coffee or beer; there might be energy and passion in the chat. The matter of wildness will be caught up in the banter, and those who have sampled it will add their own anecdotes to the rough sketch which *Ribbon of Wildness* has provided.

For those who have either done all the Munros, or didn't want to do them in the first place, the Watershed of Scotland is presented as *the* magnum challenge of the early 21st century. For sheer variety and personal enjoyment, it comes with a 5 star rating.

The realisation and evidence that there is a continuous strip of wild and wilder land, a *Ribbon of Wildness* which almost magically meanders for the entire length of the country, has truly been an eye-opener. In the quest for new ways to describe wildness, to enhance popular awareness and appreciation, and to create the means for the public to obtain the health and well-being which it brings, the Watershed can be seen as being the giver of a unique opportunity – promising an unrivalled experience.

APPENDIX ONE

Munros and Corbetts on the Watershed

Munros – mountains over 3,000ft (914.4m) in height

	Top	Height (m)	Place list	Meaning
1	Ben Lomond	974	183	*Beacon mountain*
2	Beinn Chabhar	933	247	*Mountain of the antler, or hawk*
3	An Caisteal	995	147	*The castle*
4	Beinn a Chroin	942	233	*Mountain of harm, or danger*
5	Cruach Ardrain	1,046	85	*The high heap, or stack of the high part*
6	Beinn Dubhchraig	978	176	*Mountain of the black rock*
7	Ben Oss	1,029	103	*Mountain of the elk or stag*
8	Ben Lui	1,130	28	*Mountain of the calf*
9	Beinn Achaladair	1,038	94	*Mountain of the soaking field*
10	Beinn a Chreachain	1,081	61	*Mountain of the plunderers*

	Top	Height (m)	Place list	Meaning
11	Stob a Choire Odhar	945	224	Peak of the dun corrie
12	Stob Ghabhar	1,090	54	Peak of the goats
13	Meall a Bhuird	1,108	45	Hill of the roaring
14	Carn Dearg	941	231	Red hill
15	Ben Alder	1,148	25	Mountain of the rock, or water
16	Beinn Bheoil	1,019	114	Mountain of the mouth
17	Carn Liath	1,006	128	Grey hill
18	Stob Poite Coire Ardair	1,051	77	Peak of the pot of the high corrie
19	Sgurr nan Coireachan	953	205	Peak of the corries
20	Garbh Chioch Mhor	1,013	116	Big rough breast
21	Sgurr na Ciche	1,040	92	Peak of the breast
22	Sgurr a Mhaoraich	1,027	105	Peak of the shellfish
23	Creag nan Damh	918	276	Rock of the stags
24	Sgurr an Lochain	1,004	130	Peak of the little loch
25	Sgurr a Doire Leathain	1,010	122	Peak of the broad thicket
26	Sgurr a Bheallaich Dheirg	1,036	96	Peak of the red pass
27	Beinn Fhada	1,032	99	Long peak
28	Sgurr nan Ceathremhnan	1,151	22	Peak of the quarters
29	Bidein a Choire Sheasgaich	945	226	Little peak of the reedy corrie of the barren cattle
30	Sgurr Choinich	999	139	Mossy peak

APPENDIX ONE

	Top	Height (m)	Place list	Meaning
31	Sgurr a Chaorachan	1,053	78	*Peak of the field of the berries*
32	Sgurr a Ceannaichean	915	282	*Peak of the merchants or peddlers*
33	Moruisg	928	252	*Big water*
34	A Chailleach	997	145	*The old woman*
35	Fionn Bhein	933	246	*White mountain*
36	Sgurr Breac	1,000	140	*Speckled peak*
37	Sgurr nan Clach Geala	1,093	53	*Peak of the white stones*
38	Sgurr Mhor	1,110	42	*The great peak*
39	Beinn Liath Mhor Fannich	954	210	*The big grey mountain of Fannich*
40	Beinn Dearg	1,084	57	*Red mountain*
41	Meall nan Ceapraichean	977	178	*Hill of the lumps, or little tops*
42	Eilidh nan Clach Geala	928	256	*Covering, or web of white stones*
43	Seana Braigh	927	258	*The old mountain, old upper part*
44	Conival	987	161	*The enchanted mountain*

Corbetts – mountains between 2,500ft (762m) and 3,000ft (914.4m) in height

	Top	Height (m)	Meaning
1	Hart Fell	808	*Hill of the deer*
2	Beinn a' Choin	770	*Hill of the dog*
3	Beinn Chuirn	880	*Cairn hill*
4	Beinn Odhar	901	*Dun coloured hill*
5	Beinn Chaorach	818	*Sheep hill*
6	Cam Chreag	884	*Crooked crag*
7	Beinn a' Chaisteil	886	*Castle hill*
8	Beinn nam Fuaran	802	*Hill of the springs*
9	Carn Dearg	834	*Red hill*
10	Meall na h-Eilde	838	*Hill of the hinds*
11	Ben Tee	901	*Cone shaped hill or fairy hill*
12	Geal Charn	804	*White cairn*
13	Sgurr Mhurlagain	880	*Rough topped peaks*
14	Fraoch Bheinn	858	*Heather hill*
15	Sgurr Cos na Breachd-laoigh	835	*Peak of the hollow of the speckled calf*
16	Sgurr a' Choire-bheithe	913	*Peak of the birch corrie*
17	Sgurr a' Bhac Chaolais	885	*Peak of the hollow of the narrows*
18	Sgurr Gaorsaic	839	*Peak of the horror*
19	Beinn Dronaig	797	*Hill of the knoll, or ragged hill*
20	Beinn Tharsuinn	863	*Transverse hill*
21	Beinn Enaiglair	890	*Hill of the timid birds*
22	Breabag	815	*Hill of the cleft or little kick*
23	Beinn Leoid	792	*Hill of the slope or breadth*
24	Ben Hee	873	*Fairy hill*

APPENDIX TWO

Key Areas with Conservation and Biodiversity Objectives

SSSI From the 1981 Wildlife and Countryside Act.
SPA   From the EC Directive on the Conservation of Wild Birds.
SAC   From the EC Habitats Directive relating to non-bird habitats.
NNR   From the National Parks and Access to the Countryside Act of 1949.
NSA   Local Authority designation based on advice from SNH.
Ramsar From the Convention on Wetlands of International Importance, ratified by the UK Government in 1996.

	Site or Property Ref:	SSSI	SPA	SAC	NNR	NSA	Ramsar	Proximity
1	Kielderhead Moors	840		*				on
2	Wauchope Forest							on
3	River Tweed – source mosses	1336						beside
4	Moffat Hills	1172		*				on
5	Grey Mare's Tail – NTS							on
6	Carrefran – Borders Forest Trust							on
7	Corehead – Borders Forest Trust							on
8	Dolphinton Fens	523						1km
9	Westwater Reservoir	1621	*				*	1km
10	Craigengar	430	*					on

	Site or Property Ref:	SSSI	SPA	SAC	NNR	NSA	Ramsar	Proximity
11	Cobbinshaw Moss	373						on
12	Cobbinshaw Reservoir	374						on
13	Hassockrigg & N Shotts Mosses	1690		*				on
14	Central Scotland Forest							on
15	Black Loch Moss	1661		*				beside
16	Longriggend Moss	1099						on
17	Slamannan Plateau	9171	*					on
18	West Fannyside Moss	8178	*	*				on
19	Palacerigg Country Park							on
20	Cumbernauld Woodland							on
21	Cumbernauld Community Park							on
22	Dullatur Marsh	548						on
23	Denny Muir	508						1km
24	Carron Valley Forest							on
25	Endrick Water	1693						1km
26	Wester Balgair Meadow	1614						1km
27	Loch Lomond & Trossachs National Park							on
28	Loch Ard Forest							on
29	Beinn Bhreac – Cashel Farm							on
30	Ben Lomond – NTS					*		on
31	Rowardennan Woodlands	186		*		*		500m
32	Craigrostan Woodlands	444		*		*		1km
33	Pollochro Woodlands	1301		*		*		1km
34	Loch Katrine – Scottish Forest Alliance							on
35	Ben More – Stob Binnean	190						on
36	Glen Falloch Pinewood	706						1km

APPENDIX TWO

	Site or Property Ref:	SSSI	SPA	SAC	NNR	NSA	Ramsar	Proximity
37	Ben Lui (Beinn Laoigh)	188	*		*			on
38	Allt Coire Chailein	39						1km
39	Crannach Wood	451			*			500m
40	Rannoch Moor	1331	*		*	*		on
41	Kingshouse	854						1km
42	Rannoch Lochs	8111			*			1km
43	Ben Alder and Aonach Beag	176	*	*				on
44	Laggan Woods – Laggan Forest Trust							on
45	Kinlochlaggan Boulder Beds	858						500m
46	Creag Meagaidh	457	*	*	*			on
47	Parallel Roads of Lochaber	1272						beside
48	River Spey	1699		*				beside
49	Glen Tarff	725		*				1km
50	South Laggan Forest							on
51	South Laggan Fen	1454						500m
52	W Inverness-shire Lochs – Loch Blar	9189	*					beside
53	Glen Barrisdale	699				*		on
54	Affric – Cannich Hills	18		*				on
55	Monar Forest	1181						on
56	Achnasheen Terraces	16						1.5km
57	Coulin Pinewood	411				*		1km
58	Fannich Hills	627		*				on
59	Beinn Dearg	165	*	*				on
60	Rhidorroch Woods	1347		*				on

	Site or Property Ref:	SSSI	SPA	SAC	NNR	NSA	Ramsar	Proximity
61	Loch Urigill	1668	*					1km
62	Loch Awe and Loch Ailsh	1710	*	*				1km
63	Ben More Assynt	191		*	*	*		1km
64	Loch Glencoul	986				*		500m
65	Fionaven	647		*		*		500m
66	Druim na Bad	534	*	*			*	on
67	Cnoc an Alaskie	369	*	*			*	on
68	Ben Klibreck	184						on
69	Skinsdale Peatlands	1439	*	*			*	on
70	Truderscaig	1569	*	*			*	on
71	Naver Forest							on
72	Lon A' Chuil	1091	*	*			*	on
73	West Halladale	1607	*	*			*	on
74	Ben Griams	179	*	*			*	on
75	Forsinard Flows – RSPB							on
76	Forsinard Bogs	651	*	*	*		*	on
77	Knockfin Heights	878	*	*			*	on
78	Rumsdale Peatlands	1397	*	*			*	on
79	Dunbeath Peatlands	560	*	*			*	on
80	Strathmore Peatlands	1492	*	*			*	on
81	Coire na Beine Mires	387	*	*			*	on
82	Shielton Peatlands	1426	*	*			*	on
83	Spittal Quarry	1463						on
84	Banniskirk Quarry	147						beside
85	Loch Scarmaclate	1049	*				*	500m
86	Loch Heilen	989	*				*	500m
87	Loch of Durran	1029	*				*	500m
88	Stroupster Peatlands	1503	*	*			*	on
89	Duncansby Head	564	*					on

APPENDIX THREE

Agencies and Organisations with an Active Conservation or Biodiversity Role

	Organisation	Relevant Function	Evidence
1	Borders Forest Trust	The aim of the Trust is to conserve, restore and manage native woodlands and other natural habitats for the benefit of people and wildlife. The John Muir Trust is a partner in this work.	2 native forest regeneration sites. 10km on Watershed
2	British Waterways Board	In maintaining and operating the canal network, the Board is committed to the effective protection of the natural environment and heritage.	2 canal crossings with related wild habitats.
3	Cairngorms National Park Authority	The Authority is charged with the conservation and enhancement of the natural and cultural heritage of the area, the promotion of sustainability in relation to both the use of natural resources, and its economic and social development. It has a responsibility to develop public understanding and enjoyment of the Park.	12km of the Watershed is within the National Park
4	Central Scotland Forest Trust	The Trust and its partners are committed to the long term development of a forest as a scattered mosaic of woodland	

	Organisation	Relevant Function	Evidence
		throughout some 620 square kilometres of the Central Belt, and to maximising benefits and life chances this will bring to the people who live within it.	91km of the Watershed is within the CSF area.
5	Friends of Cumbernauld Community Park	The trust is working with other partners for development of a range of outdoor recreational facilities within the context of an extensive native woodland setting.	2km of Watershed in park area, and links directly with other woodland areas.
6	Deer Commission For Scotland	The task of the Commission is to further the conservation, control and sustainable management of wild deer in Scotland.	Culling deer population is critical to much habitat regeneration
7	Forestry Commission – Scotland	The mission of the Commission is to protect and expand Scotland's forests and woodlands and to increase their value to society and the environment.	Forests, restocking plans, woodland grants, etc. Large distance
8	John Muir Trust	The sensitive management of key wild areas is at the heart of the Trust's work, by combining the needs and interests of the local community with safeguarding the natural environment.	Active partnership with a number of local organisations along the Watershed.
9	Laggan Forest Trust	Working in partnership with Forest Enterprise in the use and development of parts of Strathmashie Forest, the Trust aims to promote its environmental quality, and to enhance the job creation, recreation and tourism potential for the benefit of the local community.	Access and woodland habitat development. 3km on Watershed

APPENDIX THREE

Organisation	Relevant Function	Evidence
10 Loch Lomond and Trossachs National Park Authority	The aims for this Authority are the same as those for the Cairngorms National Park, however, the challenges and opportunities are distinctive, not least with the close presence of a large urban population.	68km of the Watershed is in the National Park area.
11 National Trust for Scotland	The Trust protects and promotes Scotland's natural and cultural heritage for present and future generations to enjoy.	3 large properties with a total of 27km on the Watershed.
12 North Lanarkshire Council	The Council maintains Palacerigg Country Park for the benefit of local residents with a focus on conservation, environmental education and countryside recreation.	The Park sits astride the Watershed. 3km on Watershed
13 Plantlife International	This organisation is dedicated to conserving all forms of plant life in their Natural habitats.	1 property – 3km is on the Watershed.
14 Royal Scottish Forestry Society		1 property – Cashel Farm – 4km on the Watershed
15 Scottish Natural Heritage	The Government agency with responsibility for our natural heritage and people's enjoyment of it, with a number of goals which it has set. These include that people will care effectively for their natural heritage that it will enrich their lives thereby, and that sustainable use will be central to this.	71 SSSI 5 NNR 37 SAC 20 Ramsar 28 SPA 37 SAC 27% designated
16 Royal Society for the Protection of Birds	This is one of the largest membership organisations in the UK, and its prime work is the conservation of wild birds, other	1 site – the largest in the UK, plus 1 adjacent.

261

	Organisation	Relevant Function	Evidence
		wildlife and the places in which they live.	8km on the Watershed.
17	Scottish Environmental Protection Agency	SEPA aims to provide an efficient and integrated system that will improve the environment, in particular in relation to monitoring and regulation of pollution and waste.	General control of habitats for water quality.
18	Scottish Forest Alliance	This is a dynamic partnership involving BP, the Forestry Commission, The Woodland Trust for Scotland, and the RSPB. Its aim at Loch Katrine is to create a new forest of native woodland which will be of lasting benefit to the people of Scotland and to biodiversity in the area.	9,500ha site with 20km on the Watershed.
19	Scottish Water	This company is charged with bringing clearer and fresher water to the people of Scotland. This involves dealing effectively with waste water, and advising on management of areas that are used for public water supply.	2 reservoirs and a number of other areas where land-use is controlled to support water quality.
20	Scottish Wildlife Trust	SWT's work is focused on the enhancement and preservation of habitats and wildlife. A key to this is through encouraging access, and involving people in understanding, conserving and shaping our landscapes.	2 areas of ancient woods 1 area of established woods 1km on Watershed
21	Woodlands Trust for Scotland		

APPENDIX THREE

	Organisation	Relevant Function	Evidence
22	Local Authority – Biodiversity Action Plans	The following Local Authorities have current Plans which will have some bearing on the Watershed terrain: • Scottish Borders Council • Dumfries and Galloway Council • South Lanarkshire Council • West Lothian Council • North Lanarkshire Council • Falkirk Council • East Dumbartonshire Council • Stirling Council • Argyll and Bute Council • Perth and Kinross Council • Highland Council	

APPENDIX FOUR

Land Classification and Capability for Agriculture on the Watershed

Classes 1, 2 and 3/1 – There is no land on the Watershed within these classifications.

3/2   17km   1.6%   Capable of average production of some crops and low in others.

Land which is marginal for economic crop production.

4/1   11km   1%   Long ley grassland and rotation with forage and stock feed.

4/2   18km   1.6%   Primarily grassland with limited potential for other crops.

Land which is suited to use as grassland and to mechanised improvement.

5/1   5km   0.5%   Well suited to reclamation and use as improved grassland.

5/2   21km   2%   Moderately suited to reclamation as improved grassland.

5/3   66km   6.3%   Only marginally suited to reclamation.

Land which is unsuited to improvement by mechanised means but has some sustained grazing value.

6/1   4.5km   0.4%   Plant communities contain high proportion of palatable herbage.

6/2   55.7km   5.3%   Moderate quality herbage.

6/3   790km   75%   Low grazing value.

7   125km   12%   Very limited or no agricultural value.

Note: This data has been obtained from mapping produced by the Macaulay Institute.

Bibliography

Bleau, Joan; *Atlas Maior of 1665*; Taschen; Cologne Germany; 2000.
Boswell, James; *A Journey to the Hebrides* (with Johnson); Canongate; Edinburgh 1996.
Cawthorne, Mike; *Hell of a Journey*; Mercat; Edinburgh; 2005.
Cameron, AD; *The Caledonian Canal*; Birlinn; Edinburgh; 2005.
Craig, Mandy; *A Journey from Wilderness to Home*; Centre for Human Ecology; Edinburgh; 2003.
Crane, Nicholas; *Clear Waters Rising*; Penguin; London; 1996.
Crofts, Roger; *Land of Mountain and Flood* (with McKirdy and Gordon); Birlinn; Edinburgh; 2007.
Dorward, David; *Scottish Place Names*; Mercat; Edinburgh; 1998.
Drummond, Peter; *Scottish Hill and Mountain Names*; Scottish Mountaineering Trust; Glasgow; 1991.
Drummond, Andrew; *The Abridged History*; Polygon Birlinn; Edinburgh; 2004.
Edwards, Kevin J; *Scotland After the Ice Age* (with Ralston); Edinburgh University Press; Edinburgh; 1997.
Fenton, James FC; *A Postulated Natural Origin of Open Landscape of Upland Scotland*; Plant Ecology and Diversity; Scottish Natural Heritage; 2008.
Gittings, Bruce: *Scotland an Encyclopaedia of Places and Landscape* (with Munro); HarperCollins; Glasgow; 2006.
Gordon, J; *Land of Mountain and Flood* (with Crofts and McKirdy); Birlinn; Edinburgh; 2007.
Groome, Francis H; *Ordnance Gazetteer of Scotland*; TC and EC Jack; Edinburgh; 1895 and 1901.
Gunn, Neil M; *Highland River*; Canongate; Edinburgh; 1991.
Haldane, ARB; *The Drove Roads of Scotland*; Birlinn; Edinburgh; 1997.
Johnson, Samuel; *A Journey to the Hebrides* (with Boswell); Canongate; Edinburgh; 1996.
Kempe, Nick; *Hostile Habitats* (with Wrightman); Scottish Mountaineering Trust; Glasgow; 2006.

MacKenzie, Alexander; *Stories of the Highland Clearances*; Lang Syne; Glasgow; 2003.

McKirdy, A; *Land of Mountain and Flood* (with Crofts and Gordon); Birlinn; Edinburgh; 2007.

MacQueen, Hector; *Atlas of Scottish History* (with McNeill); Edinburgh University Press; Edinburgh; 1996.

McNeill, Peter; *Atlas of Scottish History* (with MacQueen); Edinburgh University Press; Edinburgh; 1996.

Martin, Daniel; *Upper Clydesdale*; Tuckwell Press; East Linton; 1999.

Mitchell, Ian R; *Mountain Outlaw*; Luath; Edinburgh; 2003.

Mitchell, Ian R; *Walking Through Scotland's History*; Luath; Edinburgh; 2110.

Moffat, Alistair; *Before Scotland*; Thames and Hudson; London; 2005.

Muir, John; *Wilderness Journeys*; Canongate; Edinburgh; 1996. Fontana Paperbacks; London; 1985.

Muir, Edwin; *Scottish Journey*; Fontana: London; 1985.

Munro, David; *Scotland an Encyclopaedia of Places and Landscape* (with Gittings); HarperCollins; Glasgow; 2006.

Omand, Donald; *The Borders Book*; Birlinn; Edinburgh; 1995.

Ralston, Ian; *Scotland after the Ice Age* (with Edwards); Edinburgh University Press; Edinburgh; 1997.

Richards, Eric; *Patrick Sellar and the Highland Clearances*; Polygon; Edinburgh; 1999.

Rixon, Denis; *Knoydart – a History*; Birlinn, Edinburgh; 1999.

Robertson, Kenneth; *The Wilderness*; Private publication; 1998.

Scott, Sir Walter; *Lay of the Last Minstrel, Redgauntlet, and The Lady of the Lake*; Penguin; London; 1994.

Stevenson, Robert Louis; *Kidnapped*; Ward Lock; West Sussex; 1960.

Thomson, Ian R; *Isolation Shepherd*; Birlinn; Edinburgh; 2002.

Wainwright, A; *Wainwright in Scotland*; Michael Joseph, London 1988.

Wightman, Andy; *Who Own Scotland*; Canongate; Edinburgh; 2000.

Wilson, John; *Tales of the Borders*; William MacKenzie; London; 1901.

Wrightman, Mark; *Hostile Habitats* (with Kempe); Scottish Mountaineering Trust; Glasgow; 2006.

Index

A
A Chruach 42
A Chuil Bothy 167
Alltbeithe Hostel 176

B
Badinloskin 220
Balgair 120, 256
Bat a Charchel 119, 122
Bealach Bhearnais 182, 186
Bealach Easach 215, 217
Bearneas Bothy 186
Beinn a Choin 134
Beinn Achaladair 42, 139, 251
Beinn Bheag 136
Beinn Dearg 43, 178, 192, 194–196, 198, 253, 257
Beinn Dronaig 181, 184, 254
Beinn Fhadda 43, 176–178, 252, 269
Beinn Leoid 43, 204
Beinn Tharsuin 37, 184–186
Beinn Uird 126
Ben Alder 42, 125, 147–150, 178, 252, 257
Ben Alder Cottage Bothy 148
Ben Alisky 44, 225–226, 230
Ben Armine Stables Bothy 218
Ben Griam Beg 37, 44, 222
Ben Hee 37, 43, 206, 208–210, 225, 254
Ben Lomond 42, 103, 119, 125–126, 128, 130, 251, 256
Ben Lui 37, 42, 125, 135–136, 251, 257
Ben Tee 43, 160, 164, 205, 254
Bidein Clann Raonaild 188
Biggar Common 25, 41, 89
Birkhill 74
Black Law 25, 41, 92, 98, 113
Black Loch 41, 105, 256
Black Mount 41, 42, 90–91, 142, 239
Blaeu, Joan 21, 70
Blind Harry 117
Bodesbeck Law 71, 72
Borders Forest Trust 75, 78, 259
Boswell, James 174
Breabag 43, 148–149, 200–202, 254

C
Cairngorms National Park 127, 261

Caledonian Canal 162, 265
Callants Club 61
Cam Chreag 137, 254
Camban Bothy 176
Camoqhuill 121
Cant Hills 103
Carleatheran 118–119, 128
Carn Dearg 43, 147, 157, 160, 206, 254
Carn Liath 42, 153, 202, 252
Carn na Breabaig 180
Carrifran 71, 75, 79
Carron Reservoir 25, 112, 116–117, 119
Cashel Farm 126, 128–129, 256, 261
Cauldcleuch Head 37, 56
Cawthorne, Mike 186, 204
Central Scotland Forest 93, 101–102, 256
Centre of Scotland 150–151
Clyde Law 41, 75, 79, 135
Cnoc an Alaskie 211, 214, 258
Cobbinshaw Reservoir 95, 256
Coire na Beinne 228
Concordat 30, 241
Conival 43, 202–204, 239
Coomb Dod 81
Craig, Mandy 247
Craigengar 41, 86, 92–93, 101, 134, 255
Craik Cross 62–63
Craik forest 41
Crask Inn 208, 214–216
Creag an Sgamhlainn 205
Creag na h-Iolaire 218
Cromalt Hills 43, 200–201
Cruach Ardrain 134, 251
Culra Bothy 149–151
Culter Fell 41, 81, 114
Cumbernauld 25, 34–35, 37, 41, 85, 107–109, 112–113, 236, 256, 260

D
Declaration for the Wild 241
Devils Beef Tub 78–79
Droma, Loch 43, 192–194
Drummond, Andrew 194
Duncansby Head 17–19, 32, 40, 44, 209–210, 231, 236, 239

E
Ettrick Pen 70–71

F

Fannich, Loch 189–190, 192
Fannichs, The 43, 190–191
Fannyside Lochs 106
Feagour 42, 152
Fionn Bheinn 188–190
Flow Country 43–44, 208, 212–213, 218, 223, 225, 228
Forestry Commission 48, 51, 53, 60, 62, 102, 114, 131, 162, 201, 217, 219
Forsinard 209, 222–224, 230, 258
Forth and Clyde Canal 111, 122
Fraoch Bheinn 166, 254

G

Gameshope Bothy 75
Gawky Hill 41, 81–82, 84–85, 122
Geikie, Sir Archibald 88
Glen Affric 175–179
Glen Shiel 172, 173, 175, 177
Glenbeg Bothy 197
Glencoe 55, 125, 204
Goldsworthy, Andy 38
Gorton Bothy 141
Great Glen 20, 25–26, 42, 157, 160–163, 165, 201, 208
Green Team, The 1
Greengairs 106–107
Groban 191
Groome, Francis H 19
Guilann 122, 126
Gunn, Neil M 31, 43, 225, 230–231, 236

H

Half-way point 151, 157
Hart Fell 41, 77, 254
Heartland March 42, 125–126, 132, 136
Heilen, Loch 234, 258
Hewitt, Dave 18, 205
Highland Boundary Fault 41, 72, 84, 122, 126, 131, 225
Hill of Slickly 234
Hill, David 63
Hillhouseridge Farm 101
Hogg, James 71
Holehead 101, 115

I

Inchnadamph 43, 203
Iorguill 195
John Muir Trust (JMT) 30, 36, 75, 155, 241
Johnson, Samuel 174

K

Killilan 181, 183
Kinbreack Bothy 166
Kinloch Hourn 32, 172, 173
Kintail 26, 175, 177–179
Knockfin Heights 222, 224, 258

L

Laggan (Great Glen) 26, 161
Laich March 41, 84, 89, 93, 99, 111, 119, 122, 125
Land classification for agriculture 264
Lapworth, Charles 74
Leven Seat 41, 97
Loch Lomond and Trossachs National Park 122, 127–128
Lochcraig Head 73, 75–76
Luib-Chonnal Bothy 154

M

Macaulay Institute 264
MacIntyre, Duncan Ban 138
Meall a Bhuird 37, 143, 252
Meall Buidhe 139
Meall Cean Loch Strathy 221
Meall Coire nan Saobhaidh 165
Meall Leac na Sguabaich 151
Mendick Hill 92
Merkland, Loch 205
Moine March 42, 160, 201, 205, 221
Moine Thrust 32, 42, 148, 200
Moruisg 43, 187, 253
Muir, Edwin 193
Muir, John 9, 13, 38
Munsary 229, 230
Murray, WH 143

N

National Nature Reserves (NNR) 73, 136, 152–153
National Scenic Areas (NSA) 175
National Trust For Scotland (NTS) 35, 75
Northland March 43, 89, 208, 210, 221, 237, 246
Note o' the Gate 51

O

Orkney 9, 17, 18, 20, 40, 210, 225, 228, 231–232, 236
Ossian, Loch 139, 147
Over Phawhope Bothy 71

INDEX

P
Pattack, Loch 151
Peel Fell 17, 23, 26, 40, 47–49, 52, 65, 79, 185
Pentland Firth 17, 26, 43, 210, 224, 236, 237
Pentland Hills 86, 91–92
Plantlife International 229
Poll-gormack Hill 157

R
Ramsar Sites 211
Rannoch Moor 42, 139–143, 223, 257
Reiver March 40–41, 47, 49, 65, 79, 81–82, 114, 135
Rhidorroch 25, 43, 148, 197–200, 221, 257
Robertson, Kenneth 145, 177
Rough Bounds 32, 43, 148, 165, 167, 170–172
Royal Scottish Forestry Society 127
Royal Society for the Protection of Birds (RSPB) 35, 44, 128, 131, 222–223, 228, 230, 236

S
Scott, Sir Walter 40, 61, 78, 132, 134
Scottish Forest Alliance 131
Scottish Natural Heritage (SNH) 29
Scottish Outdoor Access Code 245
Scottish Wildlife Trust (SWT) 108
Seana Braigh 178, 198, 200, 253
Sgor Gaibhre 147
Sgurr a Choire-bheithe 254
Sgurr a Mhaoraich Beag 173
Sgurr Breac 192, 253
Sgurr Mhurlagain 37, 165–166, 254
Sgurr Mor 43, 192
Sgurr na Ciche 32, 37, 43, 167, 252
Shaw Hill 41, 86
Shetland 18, 210
Sites of Special Scientific Interest (SSSI) 33, 48, 60, 73, 75, 77, 79, 92–95, 101, 103, 105–106, 111–112, 117, 120, 129, 134, 139, 142–143, 147, 154, 162–166, 172, 180, 186–188, 191–192, 194, 198, 201, 204, 206, 209–211, 217, 219–225, 227–229, 231–234, 237, 255, 257–258, 261
Sordale Hill 232
Sourlies Bothy 167
South Glenshiel ridge 43, 175

Southern Upland Way 71
Southern Uplands Fault 82
Special Areas of Conservation (SAC) 48, 75, 209
Special Protection Areas (SPA) 92, 209
Spittal Hill 232
Stacks of Duncansby 237
Stane Bents 101, 103
Stemster Hill 228, 230
Stephen, Walter M 25
Stevenson, JW 86, 272
Stevenson, Robert Louis 147
Stob Ghabhar 143, 252
Stronachlachar 130, 133–134
Stronend 37, 42, 112, 119

T
Tomtain 37, 112–113
Truderscaig 219–221, 258

W
Wainwright, A 267
Warth Hill 236
Wauchope Forest 50, 54–55, 57, 255
Weir, Tom 112
West Highland Way 38, 123, 125, 135–136, 142–143, 244
Wildness in the Scottish Countryside 30, 240
Wisp Hill 59
Woodlands Trust 131, 262

Some other books published by **LUATH** PRESS

The Ultimate Guide to the Munros
Ralph Storer
PBK £14.99
Volume 1: Southern Highlands ISBN 1 906307 57 1
Volume 2: Central Highlands South ISBN 1 906817 20 0
Volume 3: Central Highlands North ISBN 1 906817 56 1

From the pen of a dedicated Munro bagger comes *The Ultimate Guide* to everything you've wished the other books had told you before you set off. The lowdown on the state of the path, advice on avoiding bogs and tricky situations, tips on how to determine which bump is actually the summit in misty weather… this is the only guide to the Munros you'll ever need.

This comprehensive rucksack guide features: detailed descriptions of all practicable ascent routes up all Munros and Tops in the area; easy to follow quality and difficulty ratings, enabling you to choose a Munro for any level of experience; annotated colour photographs and OS maps; the history of each Munro and Top from the development of Munro's Tables from 1891 onwards; notes on technical difficulties, foul-weather concerns, winter conditions and scenery.

A brilliant book for any hillwalker – as indispensable as your boots!

His books are exceptional… Storer subverts the guide-book genre completely… Storer's effort would be the bedtime reading, the one where I might laugh out loud, and it contains the passages to quote to the fearful Mrs Warbeck – who would of course be memorising every pronouncement by Baffies.
THE ANGRY CORRIE

While most climbing authors appear to have had their funny bones surgically removed, Storer is happy to share numerous irreverent insights into the hills, and this acts as a timely reminder that walking should, after all, be primarily about enjoyment of the great outdoors. A further advantage is that the book will easily fit in a rucksack and does not require SAS training to lug it up the slopes.
SCOTTISH FIELD

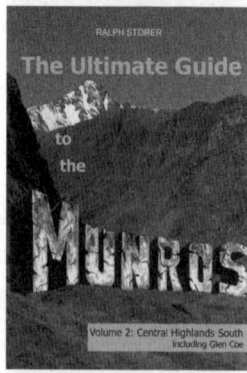

Skye 360: walking the coastline of Skye
Andrew Dempster
ISBN 0 946487 PBK £8.99

Skye's plethora of peninsulas and sea-lochs contain awesome cliffs, remote beaches, storm tossed sea-stacks, natural arches, ancient duns, romantic castles, poignant Clearance settlements, tidal islands and idyllic secluded corners.

Andrew Dempster took one month to walk the whole coastline; he describes not just a geographical journey along the intricacies of Skye's coastline but also a historical journey from pre-historic fortified duns to legendary castles, from the distressing remains of black-houses to the stark geometry of the Skye Bridge.

- 8 detailed maps and travel information
- Long-distance walks to day-trips
- Black and white sketches
- Colour photographs

Whether you want to follow the author on his month-long trek around the coast, or whether you have a week, a weekend or just want to spend a day exploring a smaller part of the island, *Skye 360* is the perfect guidebook.

Mountain Days & Bothy Nights
Dave Brown & Ian R Mitchell
ISBN 1 906307 83 0 PBK £7.50

'*One thing we'll pit intae it is that there's mair tae it than trudging up and doon daft wet hills.*'

This classic 'bothy book' celebrates everything there is to hill-walking; the people who do it, the stories they tell and the places they sleep. Where bothies came from, the legendary walkers, the mountain craftsmen and the Goretex and gaiters brigade – and the best and the worst of the dosses, howffs and bothies of the Scottish hills.

On its 21st anniversary, the book that tried to show the camaraderie and buccaneering spirit of Scottish hill-walking in the early days has now become part of the legends of the hills. Still likely to inspire you to get out there with a sleeping bag and a hipflask, this new edition brings a bit of mountaineering history to the modern Munro bagger. The climbers dossing down under the corries of Lochnagar may have changed in dress, politics and equipment, but the mountains and the stories are timeless.

Dave Brown and Ian R Mitchell won the Boardman Tasker Prize for Mountain Literature in 1991 for *A View from the Ridge*, the sequel to *Mountain Days & Bothy Nights*.

Details of these and other books published by Luath Press can be found at:
www.luath.co.uk

Luath Press Limited
committed to publishing well written books worth reading

LUATH PRESS takes its name from Robert Burns, whose little collie Luath (*Gael.*, swift or nimble) tripped up Jean Armour at a wedding and gave him the chance to speak to the woman who was to be his wife and the abiding love of his life. Burns called one of 'The Twa Dogs' Luath after Cuchullin's hunting dog in Ossian's *Fingal*. Luath Press was established in 1981 in the heart of Burns country, and is now based a few steps up the road from Burns' first lodgings on Edinburgh's Royal Mile.

Luath offers you distinctive writing with a hint of unexpected pleasures.

Most bookshops in the UK, the US, Canada, Australia, New Zealand and parts of Europe either carry our books in stock or can order them for you. To order direct from us, please send a £sterling cheque, postal order, international money order or your credit card details (number, address of cardholder and expiry date) to us at the address below. Please add post and packing as follows: UK – £1.00 per delivery address; overseas surface mail – £2.50 per delivery address; overseas airmail – £3.50 for the first book to each delivery address, plus £1.00 for each additional book by airmail to the same address. If your order is a gift, we will happily enclose your card or message at no extra charge.

Luath Press Limited
543/2 Castlehill
The Royal Mile
Edinburgh EH1 2ND
Scotland
Telephone: 0131 225 4326 (24 hours)
Fax: 0131 225 4324
email: sales@luath.co.uk
Website: www.luath.co.uk